Ethics
of
Information
Management

�ొ Sage Series in Business Ethics

Series Editor: Robert A. Giacalone
The E. Claiborne Robins School of Business
University of Richmond

◱ Editorial Board

Richard O. Mason
Florence M. Mason
Mary J. Culnan

Ethics
of
Information
Management

SSBE
Sage Series in Business Ethics

SAGE Publications
International Educational and Professional Publisher
Thousand Oaks   London   New Delhi

Copyright © 1995 by Sage Publications, Inc.

All rights reserved. No part of this book may be reproduced or utilized in any form or by any means, electronic or mechanical, including photocopying, recording, or by any information storage and retrieval system, without permission in writing from the publisher.

For information address:

SAGE Publications, Inc.
2455 Teller Road
Thousand Oaks, California 91320
E-mail: order@sagepub.com

SAGE Publications Ltd.
6 Bonhill Street
London EC2A 4PU
United Kingdom

SAGE Publications India Pvt. Ltd.
M-32 Market
Greater Kailash I
New Delhi 110 048 India

Printed in the United States of America

Library of Congress Cataloging-in-Publication Data

Mason, Richard O.
    Ethics of information management / Richard O. Mason, Florence M. Mason, Mary J. Culnan.
        p.   cm.—(Sage series in business ethics; 2)
    Includes bibliographical references and indexes.
    ISBN 0-8039-5755-6 (c: alk. paper).—ISBN 0-8039-5756-4 (p: alk. paper)
    1. Information society—Moral and ethical aspects.   2. Business ethics.   I. Mason, Florence M.   II. Culnan, Mary J.   III. Title.
    IV. Series.
    HM221.M297   1995
    303.48'33—dc20   95-15770

This book is printed on acid-free paper.

95 96 97 98 99 10 9 8 7 6 5 4 3 2 1

Production Editor: Tricia K. Bennett
Typesetter: Andrea D. Swanson
Copy Editor: Linda Gray

To C. West Churchman and William F. May
for their guidance in the past and present
and to Nicholas,
who must make sense of this for the future.

An individual without information cannot take responsibility; an individual who is given information cannot help but take responsibility.
—Jan Carlzon

Contents

Preface

This book is written for those who handle information in their work and for citizens who are concerned about what those who handle information do and how it affects them. Actions taken with information and its related technologies affect the lives of other people and therefore have an ethical and moral component. The ethical issues that spring up from acquiring, processing, storing, disseminating, and using information have some special characteristics, due primarily to the unique nature of information. Responsible managers, workers, and citizens in this information age must be aware of these issues and be equipped to cope effectively with them.

Later in the book, in Chapter 7, those who handle information will be described as "information professionals," and the ethical considerations of professionalization will be applied to them and their work. In a very real way, however, the entire book is devoted to helping us all become information professionals in the most positive sense of the term. Our abilities to (a) identify and frame ethical issues surrounding information and its use, (b) examine those issues using ethical theories and principles, and (c) apply the theories and principles to situations that develop at the individual, organizational, and societal levels—all of these abilities being hallmarks of a professional—will materially shape the world in which we live. The book is intended to provide guidance in acquiring these abilities.

A simple logic underlies this work:

- In every new age, a society must develop afresh its own set of moral and ethical values and renegotiate its social contract.
- Modern society is now deeply immersed in an information age and is in the process of creating an information society. It is estimated, as just one indicator,

that by the year 2,000 over 95% of all jobs will require that at least some time be devoted to generating, processing, retrieving, or distributing information. All jobs will require using it.

- Therefore, modern society must develop a new social contract and an appropriate moral and ethical stance for the information age.

Throughout our careers, in a small way, we have been contributing to the creation of an information society by means of our teaching, writing, and consulting. We have been part of a massive, historical process we call the "ascent of information." Indeed, we believe that the entire history of civilization can be described in terms of innovations and the ever-increasing use of concepts and technologies for handling information. These innovations started as ideas and artifacts on the periphery, important but not essential to the conduct of everyday affairs. As humankind evolved, however, innovations in information moved closer to the center until, sometime about the middle of the 20th century, they began to form the very core of our society, especially in the developed world.

We believe that as information has become a fundament of modern society, those of us who work with information, or who teach, write, or consult about it, have a concomitant obligation to ensure that the new society we are creating is, as the ancient Greeks put it, "good," and this means that it must be ethical. Undertaking this obligation is the motivation for this book.

The book is written primarily for those who are or will soon become information professionals. It contains a set of concepts, methods, arguments, and illustrations that we hope will sharpen your ethical focus. In this complex, changing world, many new challenges face those of us who toil and play with information. We provide you with some ways of thinking about information and the new responsibilities engendered by acquiring, processing, storing, disseminating, and using information. Whenever you make decisions or take actions that affect the flow of information or influence the use of information technology, some of the ideas in this book should apply.

We also intend for this book to provide guidance for the writing of a new social contract for the information age. We believe that all of your actions, and ours, reverberate within a broader societal framework. Members of all societies implicitly—and, occasionally, explicitly—enter into agreements, called "social contracts," that they use to form their social structure and to regulate their relations with each other. We believe that it is time, once again, to reach such an agreement and that we all need to be a part of the process.

The book is organized into three parts. Part I provides motivation and conceptual background for the book as a whole. In Part II, we shift gears and focus on some fundamental concepts about ethics. The two chapters in this part describe the process of ethical thinking and a range of theories and principles that can be used in ethical situations. In Part III, the concepts of information, and the need for ethics and ethical thinking, are applied to the various levels of the social system to which they pertain: individual and professional, organizational, and societal or systemic.

The theme of the first chapter is an elaboration of the argument presented above. Humankind, we argue, has been engaged in a long-term historical process called the ascent of information (or expansion of mind) to secure more wealth, security, recreation, and control. This has culminated in the creation of an information society in which most people spend most of their time dealing with information and information technologies. The ascent of information has also created a new set of responsibilities. These responsibilities emerge during a process we call the "information life cycle"—the acquisition, processing, storage, dissemination, and use of information. Three key socioeconomic roles carry out these activities: information givers, information takers, and information orchestrators or gatekeepers. The people who have these roles must assume these responsibilities. The imputation of responsibility occurs at a crucial point in time we call a "moment of truth."

A primary mission of this book is to prepare the reader to identify moments of truth concerning information, to be able to think clearly about them, and to act ethically when they occur.

Chapter 2 covers some very basic notions about the nature of information. In particular, information is quite different in its attributes and in its being from other kinds of resources. It is more malleable, movable, and shareable than other entities we use to achieve human goals. We define information very broadly, and accordingly, the book covers many different information activities, including computer programming, systems analysis, communications, libraries, journalism, and entertainment. This sweeping view, we believe, is absolutely essential as our society enters into the "ubiquitous, networked, multimedia," technological era in which all information technologies are being merged and laced together and in which all forms of information are being fused together into a common form. As a result, what were once diverse, information-based occupations are merging together and creating a more unified set of responsibilities. We return to this theme in Chapter 7.

Chapter 3 discusses the important relationship between information and decision making. The idea of a "decision," of course, is an abstract notion, one used to capture the moment of truth at which relevant information is congealed, possible states of the world identified, alternative courses of action specified, and a choice of behavior made and taken. Because information is essential to all phases of this process, a tightly coupled link exists between information and decision making. An information society is essentially a decision-making society and vice versa.

We stress the idea that the new society needs a new model of human being. "Information person," we argue, must replace "economic man" in our thinking. Economic man is a conceptual artifact of the industrial revolution, whereas information person is an archetype for the information age. Information person is covenantal rather than purely rational. Fundamental is the establishment of a trust or fiduciary relationship between givers and takers of information. This also generally requires that takers obtain the informed consent of information givers. The principles of fair information practices serve as a beginning for developing the covenant.

Chapter 4 rounds out our discussion of the relationship between information and ethics by exploring the implications of the seemingly trite, but deeply profound, maxim "information is power." Power is the ability to achieve one's goals, and in an information society information replaces weaponry and monetary wealth as the principal source of power. The exercise of power always raises ethical issues. It either helps or harms people. For the Athenians of Thucydides's time (about 400 B.C.), morality was irrelevant. The strong could do whatever they wanted and were able to. Since that time, however, civilizations have attempted to curtail the wanton use of power and guide its application in more socially acceptable directions. A new source of power—information—calls for a new set of guidelines.

Chapter 5 begins Part II and introduces the notion of ethics as "corrective vision," an idea that pervades the rest of the book. Ethical thinking requires seeing what is, envisioning what ought to be, and designing a plan to correct reality accordingly. This chapter describes the thinking processes necessary for applying the concept of corrective vision and summarizes a six-step method for arriving at ethical judgments and evaluations.

Understanding what ought to be is the topic of Chapter 6. The possibilities are enormous. The chapter summarizes in a few pages some of the key theories and principles that have emerged from the great historical conversation about ethics. It provides access to a rich trail of ethical ideas and thinking. All ethical principles, the chapter maintains, may be classified according to four main centers of focus: (a) the agent(s) who took (or who are contemplating taking) the actions under question, (b) the act itself, (c) the results of the act and its effects on stakeholders, and (d) justice, the idea that all implicated parties should be treated fairly and evenly. Most philosophers' theories and ethical points of view fall, for the most part, into one of these four cornerstone categories.

Sometimes, applying different theories to a situation results in different advice. For this reason, the concept of trumping or *supersession,* is introduced. Essential to ethical thinking, the principle of supersession holds that an ethical principle can be ignored or violated only if it is supplanted by another principle, one presumed to be of a higher order. This calls for careful reasoning and judgment on the part of a moral agent at any moment of truth.

Chapter 7 begins Part III and develops a model of an information professional. Whereas the archetype *information person* refers to the role that members of the general public assume in an information society, the archetype *information professional* refers to the special, frequently credentialed, roles in a society that are responsible for producing and distributing information. These people must agree to a stronger covenant, we believe. They must manage and execute the activities in information cycles to improve their client's intellectual state and hence to effectively influence their client's behavior or state of mind. They possess special knowledge and skills for achieving this social purpose, which can be summarized as follows: an ability to get the right information from the right source to the right client(s) at the right time in a form most suitable for the use to which it is to be put at a cost justified by its use. Practically, this takes the form of systems design skills, computer programming skills, writing skills, media and presentation skills, cataloging and indexing skills, economic interpretation skills, and the like.

These special skills and the functional knowledge base that underlie them convey a unique source of power to these professionals, giving them a power advantage in exchange relationships with their clients and others. Because they enjoy this power advantage, information professionals must accept additional responsibilities. In this chapter, we identify 17 specific kinds of responsibilities that information professionals should adhere to in their day-to-day interactions with their clients and others. We also discuss, briefly, 5 broader responsibilities that the information professions as a collective body assume with respect to the society as a whole.

Chapter 8 describes the distinctive ethical issues that arise within organizations. It can be said that the age of information is also the age of organization.

In today's society, most people spend much of their time and energy either working in organizations of some type or interacting with them. These organizations have amassed enormous social and economic power; and in an information age, much of this power derives from acquiring, processing, storing, disseminating, and using information. First, we describe some of the unique features that distinguish organizations from other social phenomena and that become the basis of their power. Then we explain why neither the marketplace nor the law adequately constrains the exercise of organizational power. Case studies demonstrate that, with respect to information, these tools of social control have not been very effective, at least in a sample of information-intensive organizations. Finally, an agenda is set for recasting organizations to make them more responsive to the ethical needs of information handling and use.

In Chapter 9, we pose the question of what makes for a "good" information society. This question is formulated as a problem in resolving the tensions created by two dialectically opposed forces, each of which represents competing goods in forming a social contract. One axis describes the position accorded individuals in a society. Here, one innate force, called *liberty,* pulls toward a social agreement that lets all members of a society act as freely and in as unconstrained a way as possible. Running counter to this force is another compelling force that reaches out for *equality.* It stresses the rights of all people to be treated equally in a society.

Orthogonal to the individual axis is what might be called the collective axis because it deals with the forces that serve as the constitutive glue of a society. On the one hand, there is a strong and primal force for people to form communities in which collective demands and interpersonal relations dominate individual goals and choices. Communities bring people together to honor their diversity; they have scant concern for efficiency. Running counter to this force for *community,* however, is a force that seeks to bring people together to achieve just a few, prespecified goals. The major impetus of this force came from the industrial revolution and the establishment of the nation state. Philosophers refer to it as *corporatism;* James O'Toole called it *efficiency;* we call it *control* because this force pulls toward achieving goals as efficiently as possible, using information as an essential input in the process. Bureaucracies, organizations, and management information systems are among the major tools used to achieve social efficiency and control. These four poles— liberty, equality, community, and control—are used to create a "societal moral compass map" and to evaluate various legislative initiatives and policies of the information age.

Finally, in Chapter 10, "Beacon Toward the Future," we identify and discuss six major tensions that must be resolved in the future as the information society progresses. These are timeless issues and concern property; privacy; accuracy and quality of information; access, burden, and other issues of information justice; social gatekeeping; and the effect of technology on society. In an important way, Chapter 10 is as much a reprise as it is a forecast. These latent tensions, which spring into action with every new innovation in information handling, are also eternal. They are relics of the past as well as harbingers of the future. Consequently, they infuse every chapter of this book. This chapter of summation merely crystallizes them and extends them into the future.

Two people have guided our thinking in these matters. One is C. West Churchman, who has devoted most of his life to philosophical inquiry into knowledge, information, and ethics. Now in his 80s, West is still actively pursuing the notion that science, knowledge, and information can be used to secure improvement in the human condition. He has provided us with spiritual as well as intellectual guidance, not just for this book, but for a lifetime.

Our second guide has been William F. May, a renowned medical ethicist, coteacher, and friend. His notion of ethics as corrective vision, his application of drama to ethics, and his distinction between ethical theories that emphasize agents, actions, or results—among many other of his ideas—permeate the view of ethics presented in this book. Bill, too, has provided us with spiritual guidance.

Much of what we have learned from both of these guides has come from personal exchange and is not fully contained in the literature. Our limited citations of their work do not do them justice. Moreover, we should hasten to add, it is unlikely that either of them would have written this kind of book in this way. We hope, nevertheless, that they will appreciate it.

We have also drawn heavily on the work of several other scholars, especially in the chapters on information, power, organizational ethics, and societal ethics. Christopher D. Stone has provided new insights into the ethics of organizations, especially as to the limitations of market forces and legal proceedings for ensuring ethical behavior. H. Jeff Smith has provided some very useful empirical evidence that describes the shortfalls some organizations experience in establishing and enforcing ethical information policies. James O'Toole has provided us with a distillation of a broad sweep of the history of social values. His years of discussing ethics and philosophy with executives at the Aspen Institute and at the University of Southern California have honed within him a deep sense of the Western philosophical tradition. In the last two chapters, we reinterpret his executive's compass—the four dialectically opposed poles of liberty, equality, community, and efficiency (which we have changed to *control*). This forms the basis of our societal moral compass map used to plot and explain information policies.

Harlan Cleveland's writings on the nature of information, Alvin Toffler's on the shift in social power that the information age brought about, and James Beniger's on the key role that information plays in modern society in establishing control over social and economic events also pervade the book. In addition, conversations with Warren Bennis, Ian Mitroff, George Widmeyer, and Bob Rasberry have added greatly to our understanding. Early work on this book was begun while Richard and Florence Mason were in Umeä, Sweden, on a Fulbright grant. Olov Forsgren and Kristo Ivanoff have been provocative discussants on these issues and helped us learn from examining the Swedish information landscape. Sue Conger, Martha Hale, and Ernest Kallman provided very thoughtful reviews of an earlier draft. We are much indebted to them for their suggestions as we are to Chris Dobson and Bruce Miller for their insights. Lucy Toton managed the manuscript producing and correcting process with her usual cheerfulness and care with the help of Nida Pattranupravat and Mary Cathryn Pullin.

Although our indebtedness to those who have helped us in the past is enormous, our primary concern is with the future and future generations. We hope this includes you.

Use this book as a guide, as Buckminster Fuller once put it, for "the perplexed." There is great opportunity and joy to be had in the information society. You are very likely to play a major role in shaping its character. But be aware. Many ethical pitfalls lie in the road ahead. This book should help you avoid them. You can enjoy the manifold benefits of information and partake of the many advantages provided by the exciting new information society yet at the same time be true to your responsibilities.

Richard O. Mason
Southern Methodist University

Florence M. Mason
F. Mason and Associates

Mary J. Culnan
Georgetown University

PART I

Why Information and Ethics?

It has been said that every new age ushers in a new set of ethical challenges and problems for people to solve. These challenges can arise any time a decision is made or an action is taken. These crucial points in time are important "moments of truth" that shape the future. The new age in which we are all now immersed can fairly be called an information age. Around 1950, about 50% of the jobs involved generating, processing, retrieving, or distributing information. By 1980, it had reached 77%. In the year 2000, the figure is expected to be 95%. Most of this information handling will involve computers and advanced communications devices. Much of it will be done in the home as well as in the office or wherever a person travels.

The chapters in Part I respond to several pressing questions: What is the relationship between ethics and information? That is, why is ethics needed in an information age? What is the nature of information that makes it so different? Because all decisions have an ethical component, what is the role of information in decision making? And how can information and information systems be used to gain power and, thereby, create additional ethical issues?

Information and Responsibility:
New Ethical Challenges

◪ INFORMATION AND ETHICAL CHALLENGES

Sometime during the last decade of the 20th century, the developed world irreversibly entered the information age. A bundle of "infotainment" services, such as telephones, television, publishing, films, radio, spectator sports, and the like, surpassed $1 trillion annually in sales as customers clamored for news and entertainment and information services of all types. As many as 30 million people throughout the globe communicate and search for information by means of a computer-based network facility called "Internet," and their numbers are growing exponentially. Other information services such as Prodigy, CompuServe, and America Online are also expanding rapidly.

By 1994, nearly 50,000 U.S. firms exchanged data electronically as thousands more made plans to join the electronic data interchange (EDI) parade. Flows of electrons and photons replaced flows of money as some 130,000 automated teller machines processed more than 100 million customer transactions per month. Flows of electrons also substituted for thousands of hours of library searching as customers turned to commercially available text and statistical databases to complete more than 60 million search transactions per year.

Corporate executives are also caught up in the change. In 1993, corporate capital spending for computers and communications approached $150 billion annually, well above the approximately $100 billion they spent for construction, agriculture, petroleum, mining, and other industrial-era plant and equipment investments. These are among the many indications that a new society is being created and that new social and economic values are emerging. All this, too, is rooted in information.

Information is the fuel of social change. All human beings use information to make decisions in their daily lives, and they also rely on it to take flights of fancy away from their day-to-day affairs. The people who handle information—managers, reporters, entertainers, systems designers, analysts, technologists, white-collar workers of all types and, increasingly, blue-collar workers— are both the sources and users of this all-important fuel that is now necessary to power the engines of change. In the process, they have become vital partners in the processes by which individuals and societies are transformed. All of this, of course, is helped along by the use of information technologies—tools for capturing, storing, processing, moving, and disseminating information. Indeed, the entire history of civilization can be outlined as a story of the ever-increasing use of information enabled by innovations in information-handling technologies, a story we call "the ascent of information."

The ascent of information opens up dramatically the possibilities of change in our society. Innovations emerge that make more information available to more people cheaper, faster, more accurately, and more captivatingly; and they induce social change in the course of their use. All of the benefits of innovations in information, however, come at a cost. They carry with them a concomitant responsibility. Because information and the people who use it are causes of change, they also deserve both the praise and blame for the social outcomes it produces.

This puts information use squarely in the field of ethics. Ethical evaluations are necessary, most philosophers agree, whenever one human being's actions materially affect another human being's ability to achieve his or her own goals. The issues raised by this conflict are resolved by evaluating human conduct through the lens of moral principles. As the ascent of information accelerates and as we become more fully entrenched in an information society, our ability to become "good" citizens and contribute to a "good" society changes. It becomes increasingly dependent on our ability to make the right judgments when issues concerning information confront us. And this challenge faces us all. In an information society, everyone is affected by information and must learn to cope effectively with these issues. That is to say, we must all become effective managers of information; and this means that we must understand ethics.

◩ CALL FOR A NEW SOCIAL CONTRACT

The challenges posed by the information society call for a new social contract. A *social contract* is the agreement (often implicit) that members of a society make among themselves to bring a new society into being and to regulate relations among themselves, including their plans for governance. Such a contract must reflect the primary social and economic activities of the society. As information and information technology move to the core of our social system, our mutual contract must incorporate provisions for dealing with their effects on individuals, organizations, and the functioning of the society as a whole.

A social contract for the information age must deal with several key social tensions that are peculiar to the use of information. These tensions are discussed in detail in Chapter 10 and summarized in what follows.

One of these tensions focuses on the issue of who owns and controls the information produced by members of the society. This tension revolves around *intellectual property rights* and pits demands from people to share knowledge, ideas, and information against the claims of those who produce it to reap the benefits for themselves.

A second tension focuses on gathering and sharing information about people. One side makes a case for very broad sharing of such information so that all members of the society can build more trusting relationships and make more reliable decisions. The other side honors the dignity and autonomy of individuals to share just that information about themselves that they choose and in a manner of their own choosing. *Privacy* is the name given to this issue.

Concerns for the quality of the information produced and provided underlie the third tension. One point of view claims that all information should be as accurate, valid, reliable, and clear as is conceivably possible, whereas the counterview holds that the resources and competencies necessary to avoid error are very scarce and must be conserved. Inaccuracies, and their effects, must be tolerated. We call this issue *accuracy*.

Yet another fundamental tension centers on securing justice and fairness among those who produce information and those who want to use it. One aspect of this issue involves members' access to society's corpus of information. Some argue that, in effect, all members of society should have universal access to all of its information. Membership amounts to entitlement; "share and share alike," they say. The counterposition argues that access should be dictated exclusively by one's economic ability to pay for it or by one's legitimate need to know. The other aspect of *information justice* concerns the allocation of the burden of producing information. That is, who carries the load? Bears the costs? Expends the effort? One extreme pole of this tension holds that all members should be willing to contribute their information and information-producing capability to the society whenever they are required to. The other holds that those who provide information must be fully compensated for it and should have the right to withhold their efforts if they desire.

Gatekeeping is the subject of the fifth tension. One position holds that information should be allowed to flow freely and expeditiously throughout the society—"let it seek its own level"—no information should be withheld or blocked. This can be thought of as the "First Amendment" position. The antithetical point of view stresses the need for censorship, secrecy, confidentiality, and other control devices to prohibit the flow of information that is perceived to be dangerous or in bad taste.

Finally, a central tension revolves around introducing technology into the social system itself. It is the tension created by *technological implementation.* One side of this tension believes that new technologies are part of an inevitable march of progress. New technology must be employed no matter how it affects people's jobs or their lives. Counter to this protechnology view is a point of view that seeks to avoid the social disruption, dislocation, and human misery that accompanies technological innovation. Quality of life must dominate technological progress, it holds.

The new social contract for the information age must contain provisions for resolving these six basic tensions—intellectual property rights, privacy, the quality and accuracy of information, information justice, gatekeeping, and technological implementation. Consequently, these tensions are discussed in various places where they are appropriate throughout the book. Chapter 10, "Beacon Toward the Future," summarizes the discussion and recasts these tensions as challenges for the future.

These tensions form the social and economic milieu within which information is gathered and distributed. They spring into play whenever an information-handling activity is performed. These activities tend to follow in a sequence we call "the information life cycle."

▧ THE INFORMATION LIFE CYCLE

To understand the ethical issues surrounding the use of information, we must first understand information and the processes used to create and use it.

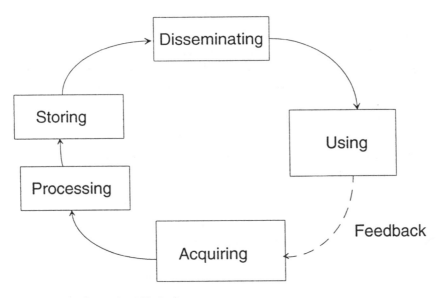

Figure 1.1. Information Life Cycle

The information life cycle is a sequence of functions through which information is handled. The key stages in this life cycle are acquiring, processing,
storing, disseminating, and using information (see Figure 1.1). Managers and
workers can be brought to an ethical crossroads at any one of these stages. The
using stage, perhaps, creates the most obvious issues because we all understand
that information can be used in ways that either help or harm people. Disseminating false or misleading information or withholding vital information from
someone who needs it may, of course, have severe effects on people. So can
retaining it or destroying it. In fact, the act of processing information in ways
that change its character or interpretation may also eventually lead to miscom-
munication and wrongdoing. Even the process of acquiring can have its ethical
pitfalls. Information can be acquired by means that are legitimate, or it can be
acquired by means of deception, intervention, or coercion. Thus, at every stage
in the information life cycle, managers must make crucial decisions about
information and its handling, and these decisions can have considerable ethical
implications. The rapid adoption of new technology has required great numbers of people to be involved in a staggering number of information life cycles
every day, all of which have potential ethical implications.

E-mail, or electronic mail, which many firms have installed to allow their employees to send electronic messages to each other via computers, is just one among many new innovations that have changed the nature of the information life cycle in organizations. In the process it has created several new ethical issues. Using computers, it is much easier to intercept and read a flow of electrons than it is to read a person's regular mail (p-mail, or paper mail, some call it). One can readily invade another's privacy. To date, there is no external legal restriction to capturing and reading intraorganizational e-mail; but many individuals consider it to be unethical, and some companies have corporate policies against it. In fact, reading another person's e-mail may result in dismissal. Despite these rules and cautions, the temptation to eavesdrop electronically is just too much for some people to resist. Apparently, it was too much for correspondent Michael Hiltzik of the *Los Angeles Times* Moscow bureau, who, allegedly, was caught reading the electronic mail of another Moscow correspondent in a sting operation set up by the paper after several of Hiltzik's colleagues became suspicious. The paper's action was swift. "In a stunning example of growing concern over technology and privacy in the workplace," the *New York Times* reported, "the *Los Angeles Times* has recalled a foreign correspondent from its Moscow bureau for snooping into the electronic mail of his colleagues" (Sims, 1993, p. A3).[1]

This is not an isolated story. Consider the case of the Big Six accounting firm that installed an electronic mail system geared to improve employee communications and coordination within the firm. In the beginning, its employees generally agreed that using the e-mail system had made them much more productive. As they became more familiar with it, junior accountants began to use the system frequently to pass messages about their audit engagements and to exchange private communications of the "watercooler" or "coffee room" type. A few senior audit managers soon discovered, however, that they could break into their junior accountants' private files and monitor their messages. This snooping gave them a little edge in power over the people who reported to them. In one case, a manager uncovered personal correspondence in the electronic files and used that information to reprimand the young accountant and to justify withholding his bonus. Indignant, the junior accountant complained that his rights had been violated, claiming that these kinds of discussions took place in the office all the time and that, furthermore, he had never been forewarned that his communications were being monitored. In contrast to the *Los Angeles Times,* this firm had no policies or safeguards in place. The firm's managers had never considered the possibility that breach of privacy in regard to personal communications and files could take place. As a result, the e-mail system that started out as a benefit for all created enormous morale and ethical problems that threatened the firm's ability to get its work done. The firm's managers had not asked the right questions early enough in the implementation process. They were not sensitive to the new issues of the information society.

▧ ETHICS INVOLVES ASKING THE RIGHT QUESTIONS

What questions should the executives at the Big Six firm have asked? What types of ethical questions should managers and citizens in general ask when they contemplate the use of information and information technologies? What questions should people ask when they are designing, operating, or using information systems? What questions should they ask when they are in the process of providing information to others?

This book was written to help you ask the right questions about the ethical issues you will face in the information society, and it provides some guidelines for answering them. The book is predicated on the fact that those of us who work with or use information carry a distinct moral responsibility. We are responsible, in whole or in part, for the social consequences of the information systems in which we participate. To satisfactorily discharge this responsibility, we must be able to make good ethical decisions. We should be able to detach ourselves momentarily from the maelstrom of day-to-day activities and pause to reflect on the ethical consequences of our actions. This requires two fundamental abilities: (a) an ability to frame good questions concerning the ethics of our proposed activities and (b) an ability to reason through situations to arrive at good answers. In short, as the ancient Greeks implored us, we must be able to live an "examined" life. We can gain some insight as to what this means by exploring the case of the Lotus MarketPlace: Households (see Culnan & Smith, 1992).

▧ LOTUS MARKETPLACE: INFORMATION AT AN ETHICAL CROSSROADS

In June 1988, executives at Lotus Development Corporation and at Equifax, Inc., began discussions about the possibility of developing a desktop product for small businesses wanting to use direct marketing to target new customers. That same year, Equifax, one of the three largest credit bureaus in the United States, began marketing mailing lists compiled from its consumer-credit-reporting database, public record information, and licensed data acquired from other direct marketers. This Equifax Consumer Marketing Database would provide the data for the new product, and Lotus would develop the software. The two firms refined the technical and conceptual aspects of the project during 1989 and 1990, and on April 10, 1990, the companies jointly announced Lotus MarketPlace: Households. The product, which would be marketed by Lotus, consisted of a CD-ROM database containing actual and "inferred" data, such as name and address, age, gender, marital status, household income, "lifestyle," and "purchasing propensity," on about 120 million individuals residing in approximately 80 million households. Although the original source for the name and address was an individual's credit report, the remaining information contained on the CD-ROM was either inferred or estimated.

Almost immediately, Lotus MarketPlace: Households stirred controversy. Articles decrying the product's potential threat to personal privacy appeared in the local and national press. Testimony against the product was given in two hearings held before the U.S. House of Representatives. Moreover, in an unprecedented series of events, hundreds of members of public conferencing networks formed an electronic grassroots campaign to protest release of the product. The Lotus chief executive officer's (CEO) electronic mail address was broadcast across the Internet with a call for those who shared a concern about the ethics of the product to express it to him directly.

On January 23, 1991, Lotus MarketPlace: Households was withdrawn before ever reaching the market. A spokesman said that this action was taken due to "the substantial, unexpected additional costs required to fully address consumer privacy issues" (Culnan & Smith, 1992, p. 11). Jim Manzi, CEO of Lotus, C. B. (Jack) Rogers, CEO and President of Equifax, and their employees had unknowingly reached an ethical crossroads in 1988 and had been following a precarious path until they decided to cancel the product. Of special interest, in August 1991, Equifax also announced that it would discontinue the sales of direct marketing lists derived from its credit-reporting database (see Culnan & Smith, 1992).

This case has a familiar pattern, one that executives and information professionals must understand if they are to deal effectively with many of the ethical issues raised by the information age. Modern information technology has greatly expanded the possibilities of providing large quantities of information of all types, including very personal information, to almost anybody located almost anywhere in the world to be used for an infinite variety of purposes. Information "any place, any time, any how," is the way some explain it.

In the Lotus MarketPlace: Households case, executives and systems developers at the two companies understood well the enormous market potential of information they possessed. They knew the "upside" of the information assets they possessed, and they knew how to unleash its power. At the time, there were thousands of mailing lists already on the market, and the three largest credit bureaus were also selling lists. Perhaps assuming that selling the lists amounted to a precedent, these well-meaning people seriously underestimated the ethical implications of their actions. They failed to understand fully the deep concerns many people had about how information about them is collected and disseminated. They had not adequately addressed questions about who owns the information and what their obligations for privacy and accuracy might be. Consequently, they were taken by surprise by the countervailing forces of popular dissension that reached them by way of electronic networks and the media.

There is a second lesson in this story: Ethical issues must be addressed well beyond finding initial or surface solutions. The people at Lotus and Equifax were aware early on that they were treading on squishy ethical ground and had asked noted privacy expert, Dr. Alan Westin of Columbia University, to join the project development team. Westin was given the task of examining the privacy implications of the product and developing safeguards. His "privacy audit" resulted in a number of privacy controls being incorporated into the software and procedures for the product's use. Focus groups were also held in several U.S. cities. The result of these activities was a set of privacy principles and protection mechanisms that were used as guidelines for designing and using the product. These were unusual (and prophetic) precautions for companies to take; but unfortunately, they were not enough. They were inadequate to assuage the fears of those who felt that either they or someone they cared about would be harmed by the general use of Lotus MarketPlace: Households. Some of the right questions were asked but the answers were not pursued vigorously enough. As a result, the ethical concerns became overwhelming and led to the product's withdrawal.

▨ ETHICAL DECISION MAKING IN ACTION: A FRAMEWORK

Hardly a day goes by that we are not faced with an ethical issue of some kind. Every day presents us with moments—we call them *moments of truth*—at which we must decide what to do. For the most part, these decisions present few problems for us because, as a rule, we generally know which behaviors are normal or expected of us. Furthermore, we know which behaviors should result in either accolades of praiseworthiness or condemnations for unethical actions. Figure 1.2 summarizes the domain of ethics and can be used for classifying behavior into three key categories. Most people's behavior most of the time raises no ethical issues; that is, it is behavior that falls within acceptable norms and is unobtrusive or expected. Occasionally, however, people perform acts of exceptional merit, well beyond the norm or the typical "call of duty." These acts the schematic labels as "praiseworthy" behavior. Finally, people act in ways that harm other people or keep them from achieving their legitimate goals. This "wrong," "bad," or "unjust" behavior is called "unethical." The domain of ethics encompasses all three kinds of behavior, and the major task of ethical thinking is to evaluate moral agents' decisions and behavior, classify them into one of these three categories, and determine the reasons for their classification. This evaluation is made increasingly difficult as new technologies or social innovations are used by a society. As illustrated by Figure 1.3, the introduction of a new technology or innovation into a society expands the range of behaviors possible by its members and thereby increases the size of the domain of ethics. More unethical behaviors as well as praiseworthy or normal behaviors are now possible.

Sometimes, as was the case with the people at the *Los Angeles Times*, the Big Six Accounting firm, and Lotus and Equifax, crucial moments of truth come and go without being adequately subjected to ethical analysis. In a society like ours, one that is undergoing substantial change, it is rather easy to overlook some very important decisions that are being made and directions that are being taken, especially if they involve unfamiliar processes of acquiring, processing, storing, disseminating, and using information. These ethically potent moments can best be understood by placing them within a broader framework, one that describes how events in general unfold. The framework described here originates in drama called moments of truth. It can be used to pinpoint where you are currently in an ethical situation or to review other cases long after the fact, as the Lotus MarketPlace: Households case illustrates. There are four key phases in the moment-of-truth framework (see Figure 1.4).

First, there is a "business as usual" phase during which one or more *moral agents* are pursuing their own self-interests in a normal way. These agents, at the outset, are often described as being in a rather steady state or one of raising fortunes. They face no crucial challenges. Manzi, Rogers, and their employees

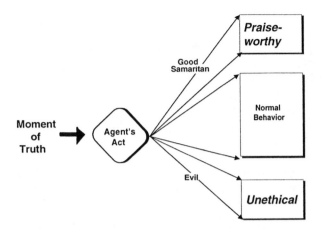

Figure 1.2. Domain of Ethics

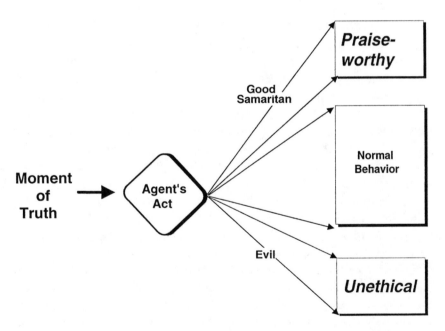

Figure 1.3. Technology and Innovation Expand the Size of the Domain of Ethics

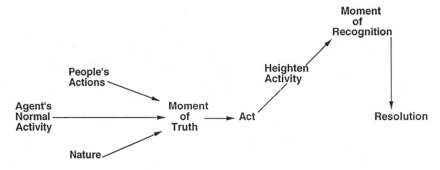

Figure 1.4. Moment-of-Truth Model

were the agents in the Lotus-Equifax case. They were actively engaged in their normal activity of running their businesses and trying to conceive of new products and strategies.

Second, an opportunity or threat arises in an agent's field of action to which he or she must respond. The decision situation may be generated by the agent's own creative efforts, as happened in the Lotus-Equifax case, or it may have been foisted on the agent by external forces. Chance, "acts of God," or the activities of some other party may place a barrier, problem, or temptation in the agent's way and force the agent to respond to it. Whatever its source, the new decision situation encompasses a set of *stakeholders,* parties who are affected by the decision or who have an interest in its outcome. The point in time at which this challenge occurs is the moment of truth. It is the trigger point for change. The choice an agent makes will ultimately determine the final outcome and will have important implications for the stakeholders. Consequently, this is the point at which key ethical decisions are consciously or unconsciously made.

The moment of truth is an appropriate time for deep ethical reflection. At this point, an agent can respond in one of three ways: (a) Act on impulse and let one's emotions control, (b) act out of habit and respond as one always has in the past ("business as usual"), or (c) act on the basis of a reasoned consideration of the situation and options for action the agent has available. In the face of new or challenging situations, good ethical thinking, as will be covered thoroughly in Chapters 5 and 6, requires the third approach. It requires a pause to reflect on the ethical implications of one's behavior. In many situations, unfortunately, the time available to think is very short. Consequently, ethical reflection must take place rapidly. Every moment of truth contains a kind of "call to action," which may be either quite subtle or very dramatic. Importantly, each moment of truth also tests one's mettle. It reveals an agent's virtues or uncovers fundamental flaws in his or her character.

The spirit underlying the idea of a moment of truth is found in its etymological roots. Anglicized by Ernest Hemingway (1932) in *Death in the Afternoon,* the term derives originally from a Spanish phrase describing the pivotal moment in a bullfight when the matador faces the bull head-on and begins the final thrust of his sword. The idea is now used more generally. "As the excruciatingly painful moment of truth nears on voting a half-billion dollars of new taxes," a *New York Times* article observes, "a rash of substitute proposals can be expected from lawmakers" (quoted in *Thorndike Barnhart World Book Dictionary,* 1987, p. 1340).[2] More recently, business writers Igor Ansoff (1965) and Jan Carlzon (1987) have brought the idea into management use. In all cases, the term is used to denote a point in time at which a challenge with crucial consequences occurs and a response is required.

There are several moments of truth in the Lotus MarketPlace: Households case. The first occurred late in 1988 when Lotus and Equifax began their discussions. The crucial moment occurred just before April 10, 1990, when the product was announced. The announcement decision unleashed a series of subsequent events. Prior to these dates, the agents had many options available to them. Had they fully anticipated the public's outcry, they might have scuttled the project or drastically reconfigured it. It is apparent, however, that at the first moment of truth they were generally aware of some of the ethical implications of their plans and, appropriately, began inquiry into the ethical dimensions of the potential product offering. In fact, the Lotus-Equifax case is in some ways exemplary because the parties took the unusual step of including ethical considerations at the outset in their systems design and business plan. It is unfortunate, however, that these considerations did not run broadly or deeply enough to protect them from the backlash they received. The product was subsequently altered to reflect what they learned from their first ethical review.

Soon after the April 10 announcement, executives at Lotus and Equifax discovered that their earlier ethical examination had not been complete enough. As news of the product hit the market, citizens from all walks of life lodged complaints. This feedback carried the Lotus and Equifax executives on to the next phase.

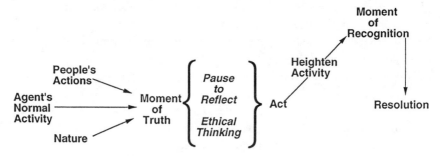

Figure 1.5. Ethical Thinking: "Think Before You Act!"

Third, generally, a period of more intense activity follows during which stakeholders and nature react. This feedback, in turn, redounds to the agent. As the events unfold, the ethical significance of the choices made are revealed. The process culminates in a *moment of recognition*. At this point, the agent understands more fully the ethical impact of his or her behavior. Often, the agent is a victim of a "reversal of fortune" as the results prove to be the very opposite of what was originally intended. Lotus and Equifax reached their moment of recognition sometime before January 23, 1991, when the accumulation of newspaper articles, congressional scrutiny, and e-mail messages convinced them to withdraw the product.

Finally, there is a time of *resolution*—a period following January 23 in the Lotus-Equifax case—during which the ethical issues raised have been dealt with, the situation corrected to the extent possible, reparations and atonements made, guilty parties punished if necessary, lessons learned, and insight and wisdom gained.

Figure 1.4 illustrates the moment-of-truth model. An agent makes a choice at the moment of truth. He or she can either act on impulse, act out of habit, or reflect on the matter before acting. A consistently moral person pauses to reflect at crucial moments of truth and draws on the process of ethical thinking as illustrated in Figure 1.5. Chapters 5 and 6 describe this process in more depth.

These four components—agents and stakeholders, moment of truth, moment of recognition, and resolution—form a broad dramatic framework in which all ethical issues can be examined—both in prospect and retrospect. The moment-of-truth framework has several practical uses as discussed next.

First, because each of us acts in the capacity of moral agent at some time (i.e., we are able to make ethical choices and to take responsibility for those choices) the framework alerts us to the fact that we will face important moments of truth in our careers at which the decisions we make and the course of action we follow will have significant ethical implications. An ability to think through the implications of our situation and of our actions is essential if we want to be ethical people. An ethical person is able to (a) recognize a moment of truth when confronted with it, (b) to reflect on the situation, (c) anticipate the ethical consequences of his or her actions, and (d) arrive at an ethically defensible judgment. Meeting these four demands requires an agent to pause in the midst of hectic activity, as illustrated in Figure 1.5, to reflect and to engage in ethical thinking. This is the framework's prospective role.

The second use of the framework involves the reexamination of actions taken in the past. Even the most ethical and well-intended person is fallible. We all make mistakes. Sometimes stakeholders are unintentionally harmed. Frequently, we lack important items of information and a wrong turn is taken. Consequently, the framework suggests that following a moment of truth, an agent should also monitor subsequent events carefully. It is possible to recover from some ethical slips, at least in part, if one corrects his or her actions quickly enough. Put differently, generally, it is useful to reduce the time between the moment of truth and the moment of recognition to as short a period as possible. When a flawless, omniscient, and perfect ethical decision is made, the two occur at the same time along with a complete resolution.

Ethicist William May (personal communication, fall 1994) points out, however, that a study of history generally reveals that this ideal is extremely difficult to achieve. "The awareness of an ethical problem and the willingness to do something about it rarely surface before the solution is out of reach, usually because the resources necessary to solve the problem have long since been depleted." May observes, for example, that in the 1940s, when the first proposals to redesign the U.S. health care system emerged during the Truman administration, health care accounted for only about 4% of the gross domestic product (GDP). This was a moment of truth at which it was possible to have a major effect. Fifty years later, however, as the Clinton administration addresses the same issue, health care accounts for more than 14% of the U.S. GDP, and about 11 million people are employed by the system. It will require many more resources and be far more difficult to effect a change in the 1990s than it would have been in the 1940s. One of the interesting aspects of the Lotus-Equifax case is that the parties did eventually recognize the ethical issues their actions had created and responded quickly enough to save their companies and their reputations.

A third way the framework can be used is to examine actual cases and evaluate the actors' behavior. As we have seen with the Lotus-Equifax case, an ethical situation can be analyzed in terms of the agents, moments of truth, moments of recognition, and resolutions involved.

▧ PENTIUM: INTEL'S "CHIPWRECK"

A flaw discovered in the Intel Corporation's popular Pentium microprocessor created a problem for the company. Unfortunately, the way it reacted to the problem not only led to a public relations nightmare but also threatened its $6.8 billion business and an $80 million advertising campaign boasting "Intel Inside." Intel's crucial moment of truth occurred during the summer of 1994 when a test revealed that due to a few missing circuits, the Pentium chip would occasionally make errors in mathematical division operations involving numbers with long strings of digits. In one case, the number 4,195,835 was divided by 3,145,727 and then multiplied by 3,145,727. This should have yielded the original number (4,195,835), but instead, the chip returned an answer of 4,195,579, an error of 256 on a straightforward problem. Estimating that the frequency of encountering the error was 1 in 9 billion—one error about every 27,000 years—executives at the company decided to make the necessary corrections on all new chips to be shipped subsequently, but as for the existing installed base of users, to ignore the problem. This meant that thousands of customers would not be informed of the flaw. But as so often happens in cases of rationalization and cover-up, the problem only festered and didn't go away.

On October 30, 1994, Dr. Thomas R. Nicely, a mathematics professor at Lynchburg College, Virginia, published a note about the flaw on the Internet. Internet users started exchanging information about Pentium fast and furiously. These interchanges worried Intel personnel, but they made no move or announcement. In fact, Intel's first public acknowledgment of the flaw came on November 7 when in response to an *Electrical Engineering Times* article, Intel admitted that it had known about the flaw since the summer and offered to replace faulty chips but only if it could be demonstrated that the user really needed an unflawed chip. Intel executives still maintained that the average customer's exposure to processing errors was very low.

Toward the latter part of November, the media broke the story on TV and in the popular press, and the company's stock began to fall, losing about 2% of its value. Meanwhile, Intel executives held steadfast to their position that the flaw was substantially insignificant while at the same time, on the Internet and in the corridors of universities, government agencies, and businesses, the company was being lambasted for not having disclosed Pentium's problems earlier.

A major blow came on December 12, when IBM, one of Intel's largest customers, announced that it was halting all shipments of its computers containing the flawed Pentium microprocessors. IBM experts calculated that an error might occur as frequently as once every 24 days of typical computer use. Although some computer manufacturers who were major customers of Intel held ranks, thousands of end-user customers did not. Especially distressed were consultants and other information workers who had to guarantee the quality and accuracy of their information-based products and who used Pentium-based computers to produce analyses and reports. They demanded replacements before they would issue their standard guarantee to their customers.

Not only was the popular media reporting on the Pentium disaster on a daily basis, but the Internet and the World Wide Web also became an active forum for sharing information and, primarily, for lodging complaints. Paul Otellini, Intel's senior vice president for worldwide sales, and Andrew S. Grove, a self-assured Hungarian immigrant who became an engineer and helped found Intel and then became its president and CEO, were inundated with messages of outrage. One that hit particularly close to home came from a professor of engineering who concluded that he would have to tell all of his young students that the "Intel Inside" machines they were using were not perfect.

So in a moment of recognition complete with apology, on December 20, 1994, Intel announced that it would recall and replace all flawed Pentium chips, and it suspended its stringent qualification requirements. What took so long?

The answer seems to be that executives at the company, being for the most part engineers, focused on the chip and not on the customer, on circuitry rather than people. Certainly, the cost of replacing the flawed chips figured high in their evaluation; but many observers claimed, *too* high. As a result, at several pivotal moments of truth, Intel executives failed to envision the full consequences of their acts. People use computers to get reliable information, and they must be able to trust their machines; but somehow this fundamental notion escaped the executives' attention. Any known flaw, no matter how insignificant, tarnishes the trust relationship that is absolutely essential between a manufacturer and a customer. All future business dealings are colored by this lack of trust. Executives at Johnson & Johnson recognized this problem immediately when in Chicago several bottles of Tylenol were discovered to contain poison. Although due to Johnson & Johnson's computerized control system, they knew their real exposure was quite limited, Johnson & Johnson's executives withdrew all of their product from the retail shelves as quickly as possible. The customer came first in their credo. Intel apparently had no such moral guidance. It took a great deal of external pressure to bring them to a full moment of recognition. (The role of external pressure on an organization will be discussed more thoroughly in Chapter 8.)

▨ WHY INFORMATION AND INFORMATION TECHNOLOGY CREATE MOMENTS OF TRUTH

The moment-of-truth framework is a valuable tool for analyzing issues raised by the information age. The ascent of information with its high incidence of new technology and new uses of information naturally triggers a multitude of moments of truth. Two fundamental forces are at work to cause this (see Figure 1.6).

First, in an information society, people tend to covet information. They covet it because the value of information in decision making continues to increase and becomes, as former Citibank CEO Walter Wriston (1988, p. 71) has observed, the new coin of the realm. People, consequently, are motivated to acquire and use information because they believe that it will make them more profitable, improve their business, or bring them enjoyment. This explanation is called the "demand pull hypothesis." Ethical issues are created, it maintains, because so many people are actively acquiring, processing, storing, disseminating, and using information.

The "technological imperative" is the second point of view. It is based on a "supply push hypotheses." Progress, according to this explanation, requires that new technologies be implemented. Ethical issues are created due to the increased use of computers, telephones, radios, televisions, videos, satellites, and numerous other technological devices. The use of new technology is inevitable, its proponents argue; therefore, society will always have new ethical issues with which to cope.

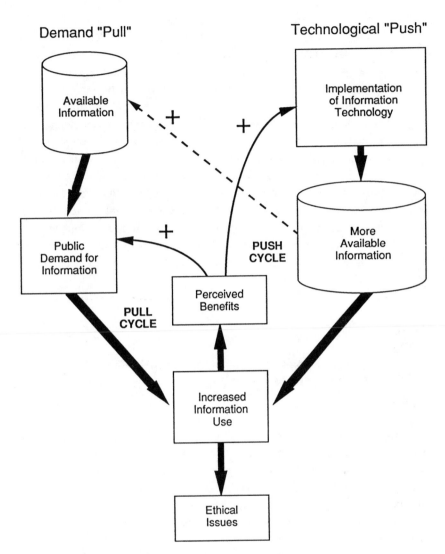

Figure 1.6. Sources of Ethical Issues

It is likely that both explanations are largely true. A third, synthetic point of view argues that both forces are working together today, simultaneously, feeding on each other and escalating in intensity like a family feud. The installation of new technological systems does indeed create new issues to be resolved and, in turn, spawns additional uses of information. Perceived advantages from the use of information certainly motivates people to implement new technological systems. And so it goes. The desire to use information encourages the installation of new technology; the installation of new technology stimulates ideas about new uses. Both forces form a positive feedback spiral.

Fortunately, to appreciate the ethics of information we need not break into this circle and track down its quintessential cause. We need only recognize that such a circle exists and that, moreover, its global swath is expanding steadily.

The interplay between the demand for information and the supply of information technology has a long history. It began in ancient times and has continued to spiral outward and to encompass more and more of society within its sphere of influence. Today, more people are facing more moments of truth concerning the use of information and information technology than ever before. We have inherited a tradition that can be traced back to the beginnings of civilization.

▧ THE ASCENT OF INFORMATION: THE EXPANSION OF MIND

Human beings have been in the process of creating an information society since the beginning of human development. It started about 370 million years ago when amphibia first emerged out of the sea. Humans took their present form about 2 million years ago when *Homo habilis* first appeared. Homo habilis had evolved a larger brain than his predecessors. It was a brain sufficiently nimble, for example, to conceive of shaping stone. Using that brain, Homo habilis learned to craft stone tools, thereby creating the first true technology. By combining brain with tools, Homo habilis was able to became a hunter rather than remain a scavenger and to begin to develop a civilization.

This was a uniquely human undertaking. The ability to think and to reason coupled with the capability to make tools are distinctively human characteristics. Many philosophers, beginning with Aristotle, propose that these two abilities—thinking and toolmaking—are the fundamental criteria for determining whether living things are human beings or not. In fact, Aristotle was so impressed with the centrality of these abilities that he made them the basis of a moral law. Human beings, he argued, are obligated to expand their minds and to develop their skills.

For the past several million years, humankind has pursued Aristotle's quest. We have developed new modes of thinking, and we have developed a dazzling array of technologies—cave painting, hieroglyphics, the abacus, printing, telegraph, telephone, radio, motion pictures, television, and computers, just to name a few—which we use as aids to our thinking processes. An especially potent type of technology is that which we use directly to aid and extend our intellectual capabilities. Today, we call these "information technologies," and they are playing a fundamental role in our society and economy.

In *Megatrends,* John Naisbitt (1982) summarized succinctly the key stages in the ascent of information: "farmer, laborer, clerk." By 1979, more people were employed in the United States as "clerks," broadly defined, than held occupations as laborers or as farmers. This signified a dramatic change in our social structure.

The magnitude of this change was revealed in Marc Porat's classic study *The Information Economy* (Porat & Rubin, 1977). Using U.S. Bureau of Labor Statistics data and a method pioneered by economist Fritz Maclup, Porat demonstrated that sometime around 1950, the United States reached a position in which a larger portion of people were employed in information-based occupations than were employed in services, industry, and agriculture. These informational occupations included entertainers, computer programmers, operators, teachers, accountants, lawyers, managers, and communication workers.

By 1980, about 50% of the U.S. workforce was employed in these occupations. Today—and this is a central theme of the ascent of information—the vast majority of peoples' work fundamentally involves the gathering, processing, storing, disseminating, and using of information. These jobs are based on information ideas and information technology. The work performed by the people holding these jobs materially affects all of us in our roles as individuals, members of organizations, participants in the economy, and citizens of society as a whole. In today's information society, the almost universal prevalence of information and the immense power it represents has become a source of new moral and ethical demands.

The transition to a society in which information and service occupations dominate was first noted by Daniel Bell (1973). The "axial principle" in Bell's "post-industrial society" is "the centrality of theoretical knowledge as a source of innovation and of policy formation for the society" (p. 2). He argues that a new professional and technical class of service and information workers is being created and furthermore that decision making will increasingly be accomplished by means of "intellectual technology."

Writing nearly two decades later, Robert Reich (1991) augments this theme and points out that a new and increasingly powerful class of information professionals is emerging in our society. He calls them "symbolic analysts." These information workers—in contrast to routine laborers and in-person service personnel—spend most of their time manipulating symbols to identify problems, solve them, or broker the activities necessary to solve them. "Worldwide demand for their insights is growing as the care and speed of communicating them increases" (p. 219). In Bell's and in Reich's postindustrial society, information becomes a strategic resource, just as in an industrial society, physical and financial capital emerged as the most important resource.

This informational revolution—Alvin Toffler's (1980) "third wave"—is also spawning a new set of social values. Sociologist Pitirim Sorokin (1937-1941) called them "ideational" values and contrasted them with the materialist, "sensate" values that characterized the industrial revolution. The driving force in an industrial society, according to Sorokin, is the pursuit of pleasurable physical sensations. Beginning with Adam Smith (1776/1986), economists of the classical school formulated a new conception of humankind called *economic man* and used it to formulate their theories. Economic man is a hypothetical person who is moved only by economic and sensate motives and whose decisions are perfectly logical and objective. He is a product of the industrial revolution.

Today's new social values, however, deal more with the mind than with the body. They focus primarily on units of thought and of meaning. Materialist values, of a former era, are being replaced by values associated with the acquisition, possession, and expression of information. These values are more psychological and inner directed in nature. As Erich Fromm (1978) argued in *To Have or to Be*, modern values are shifting from "having something" physically to "being someone" both psychologically and spiritually.

In an information society, a new conceptualization of humankind is needed. We call this new archetype *information person*. Information persons are primarily givers, takers, and orchestrators of information. They live and work in a period in which most people have close contact with information technology and in which all of us are affected by it. Many different metaphors are used to describe information persons' environment. They inhabit "cyberspace"—that vast, global airway and fiberway through which people communicate by means of electronic pulses; they travel an information "superhighway"; and they must deal constantly with "ubiquitous, networked, multimedia" information technologies that run the gamut from personal-data assistants and cellular phones to large-scale supercomputers and include faxes, telephones, and stereos. Information persons must learn to function effectively during a time in which the emerging values and concepts of human beings center on the mind, or mental processes, and on the role that information plays in the human experience.

Information persons must also deal competently with the many new social institutions being created around the production and use of information. For economic man, the crucial moments of truth occurred when decisions were made about the allocation of scarce material resources. In contrast, information person's moments of truth are more psychological in nature. They involve making decisions about acquiring, processing, storing, disseminating, and using strings of symbols and selecting technologies for handling them. Every one of these decisions carries a potential ethical burden. As a result, the courses of action taken by information persons at moments of truth that arise during the information life cycles in which they participate shape the character of an information society.

All of this emphasis on information and information technology leads to some basic questions. What has motivated the development of the information society? What are the goals of the ascent of information? Why has information person evolved? Why has humanity embarked on this particular journey? The answer is that the human mind has sought to reach several basic human ends and has set out to achieve them by means of information. Central among these are wealth, security, recreation, and control.

▨ WEALTH, SECURITY, RECREATION, AND CONTROL: FOUR PRINCIPAL MOTIVATIONS

Wealth is one crucial goal of humankind. It is pursued as an end in its own right and as a means to be used to acquire other things. Human beings acquire resources and try to manage them in a way that better satisfies their needs. Information and toolmaking are essential aids in this process. Organizations and people use information to manage their affairs better and improve the delivery of their products and services. In short, they use it to make profits and money. The pursuit of wealth was a major motivation behind the Lotus and Equifax executives' decision to develop the Lotus MarketPlace: Households. It was also the main reason for which small businesses would purchase the product.

Security, the second end, ultimately means survival in a hostile and unknown world. Information is used to cope with uncertainties and to deal with the unknown. It is an antidote for fear and anxiety. To early civilizations, the ravages of nature and threats to basic survival surely generated a deep sense of fear. Strangers approaching from outside a community's bounds often made its inhabitants fearful. Information, knowledge, and tools help to overcome this fear. In business situations, information is used to ascertain risk in decision making. Banks use credit reports, for example, for the legitimate purpose of making lending decisions. The credit extended as a consequence provides considerable liquidity to the economy and stimulates economic growth. Most important, mortgage and consumer credit loans help people achieve their dreams. All of this is possible because information satisfies the banks' need for security as well as its needs for profit making.

Security motivates many other applications. The threat of hurricanes, such as the one that devastated Galveston, Texas, in 1900, for example, instills fear in the minds of residents who are potentially in their path. To respond to this human need for security, the U.S. National Oceanic and Atmospheric Administration (NOAA) operates satellites and systems designed to track changes in the weather. Their system is designed to alert people in a storm's path so that they can prepare for it. Not only has it saved many lives; it has also allowed people to live more comfortably in storm-threatened areas.

Life would be pretty dull, however, if it revolved only around pursuing security and wealth. So human beings developed ideas and technologies to entertain themselves. A broad set of information services, such as music, plays, shows, books, and games, are used to relieve tedium, to broaden insights, and to replenish faltering spirits and energies. The arts and entertainment were created so that people could be amused, satisfy their curiosity, and express their artistic impulses. We call this *recreation* or entertainment, and today, the so-called "infotainment" industry has become a significant factor in our economy. It is a major user of information and information technology and a key driving force in the creation of cyberspace.

"Space" has also been a focus of very interesting uses of modern information technology for entertainment. One of the earliest, and most successful, applications of microelectronic technology came in 1978 when Japanese manufacturers released *Space Invaders,* a fast-moving, colorful video game in which the player fires brightly colored lasers at swiftly descending alien invaders. Soon thereafter, video arcade games became a multibillion dollar business and the infotainment industry was born. With the advent of global information super-highways more people will play these games with partners across national boundaries and will form friendships and working relationships with electronic "buddies," some of whom they have never met in person.

Underlying security, wealth, and recreation is a fourth and, in a sense, a more fundamental human need: *control*. The alternative is chaos. Consequently, human beings seek the power of domination over the worldly activities that affect us. As philosopher John Dewey (1929/1960) argued eloquently in *The Quest for Certainty,* we want control. This is a fundamental reason why we create new ideas and technologies and generate information.

Something is "controlled," management scientist Russell L. Ackoff (1984) explains, "to the extent that it is efficiently directed toward the attainment of desired objectives" (p. 3). Knowledge and information play key roles in this process. Our ability to control is a function of the information we have or can generate. Just a few tools and a small body of knowledge are adequate for us to control a very small part of our environment. Unfortunately, control is ephemeral; even very small degrees of control have a way of forsaking us. Situations always change. Nature evolves, new competitors emerge, additional opportunities present themselves, or with a twist of irony, our very success in one arena often generates a whole new set of problems in other arenas.

Sociologist James Beniger (1986) notes that when a society is unable to cope with rapid change, it confronts a "crisis of control." He recounts how the widespread use of steam power and other technologies in the United States brought a dramatic rise in the speed, volume, and complexity of social and industrial processes. Railroads, for example, advanced faster than the systems used to control them, as evidenced by several fatal train wrecks, missing freight cars, lost shipments, and a rapid buildup of industrial inventories. The answer was better and improved information. This need was met during the period between the 1830s and the 1920s with the introduction of a wide range of new information technologies, including the telegraph, lightening press, transatlantic cable, telephone, radio, adding machine, cash register, and Herman Hollerith's famous punch card data processing system.

The effective use of these technologies permitted the processes of mass production, mass distribution, and mass consumption to be developed and, for the first time, allowed governments to respond to a substantial growth in population and economic activity. Essentially, information is the handmaiden of economic growth and of social progress. The gathering, processing, storing, disseminating, and using of information is essential to establish order in an ever-changing and expanding society. Buried in each of these processes, however, are crucial moments of truth. Ethical decisions are constantly being made as information is handled and used.

◪ INFORMATION AND RESPONSIBILITY

Information is productive; but it is also seductive. It has its shadow side. Not only can it be used to achieve desirable human ends, but it can equally well be used to thwart them, as the conflict of interests in the Lotus-Equifax case reveals. Information's very availability creates the temptation to use it, and this use may very well do harm to some people while at the same time, it is helping others. Herein lies the origins of our new responsibilities.

The moral responsibilities associated with the use of information flow from an implied covenant that exists between the key parties that participate in all information relationships. Four principal parties can be identified (see also Figure 1.7):

1. Information *givers* provide information, especially information about themselves.
2. Information *orchestrators* gather, process, store, and disseminate information and serve as information gatekeepers. (The term *gatekeeper* comes from Austrian psychologist Kurt Lewin, 1947, who defined it as "a person or group of persons governing the travels of news items in the communications channel" [p. 143] and includes the people, institutions, and technology through which information must pass before it reaches its takers.)
3. Information *takers* receive and use information.
4. *Stakeholders* are affected by the information-based actions in which the takers engage.

Simply put, the covenant between these parties requires that (a) takers should use information only for the legitimate purposes for which it was collected and in ways that are just and beneficial to givers and to other stakeholders; (b) takers and orchestrators should obtain consent from givers to use the information for the purposes for which it was collected; (c) givers

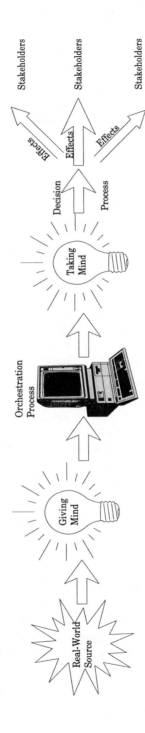

Figure 1.7. The Fundamental Information Process

should provide information that is necessary for takers to take actions that will benefit all stakeholders; and (d) orchestrators or gatekeepers should handle information with fidelity to its source while shaping, limiting, or expanding it so it best fits the takers' needs. Executives, managers, and all of us who work with information have a responsibility to honor the provisions of this basic covenant. As will be discussed in later chapters, this covenant underlies such important ethical notions as fair information practices and informed consent.

This covenant outlines our basic responsibilities as citizens of an information society. The concept of responsibility rests on two key assumptions. One, it is assumed that information givers, orchestrators, and takers at their moments of truth are normally free to make their own decisions and to do as they choose. That is, they have "free will." Second, it is assumed that the choices and actions taken by these parties normally have motives and reasons behind them and are therefore reasonably predictable. That is, their actions are not chosen at random. These assumptions underlie three senses in which the term *responsible* is normally used in ethical discussions.

First, we say that an agent is responsible for an action taken at a moment of truth if we want to assign praise, blame, or punish the agent or otherwise hold the agent accountable for his behavior. This involves tracing the causes of decisions, actions, and events and of finding out who is answerable in a given situation.

Second, we also say an agent is responsible when there is something to be done in the future and we expect that agent to do it. That is, there are rules and norms associated with the social role that the agent plays. Takers and orchestrators of information, for example, all have a *fiduciary* responsibility to be effective stewards of the information entrusted to them. In an information society, many givers provide information about themselves, about others, and about activities that is intended for limited use and placed in the stewardship of takers. Subsequent chapters elaborate on this point and discuss some of the responsibilities information workers carry in their roles as givers, takers, and orchestrators of information.

Finally, when someone has a morally favorable character—they have, for example, successfully coped with many difficult moments of truth in the past—we tend to call that party a "responsible" person. Individuals are responsible if they are trustworthy and reliable, display accepted virtues, and consider appropriate factors when making a judgment.

A simple, though extreme, example can be used to illustrate these concepts. An audience is enjoying a movie in a crowded theater when a member cries out "Fire!" The crowd then panics, and as people run hysterically to the exits, several people are trampled. The members of the audience—the information takers—acted in a predictable manner in responding to a message they should generally believe is true. So the information giver who yelled "Fire!" bears a special responsibility for the harm that was done. We would examine the conditions at the time the warning was issued. If there was no real threat and it was a silly prank, we would blame the yeller, whereas if smoke from an incipient fire was billowing up from under the screen, we might exonerate him. Likely, we would even praise that individual.

The situation at Lotus and Equifax is much more complicated and more typical. Equifax, in its role as information orchestrator and taker, held in trust substantial amounts of information about some 150 million people. As a credit reporting agency, each month the company received information about the payment histories of these people from the firms that grant consumers credit. This is the origin of Equifax's fiduciary responsibility. Thus, Equifax and their partner in the joint venture, Lotus, were responsible for their decision to sell this information in conjunction with their new product offering. Executives at the two companies were aware of this responsibility and assumed it fully when they withdrew the product from the market.

As an information orchestrator, Equifax could allow third parties access to the credit reports in its database only for the permissible purposes defined by the Fair Credit Reporting Act of 1970. The names and addresses in the Lotus MarketPlace: Households product had been gathered by Equifax for one specific purpose—credit reporting; but it would have been used by the small-business owner for another quite unrelated purpose, direct marketing, without the consent of the givers. Lotus MarketPlace: Households was an early attempt to distribute a consumer marketing database by means of CD-ROM. The critics were also concerned that this new distributed medium would make it impossible for either Lotus or Equifax to ensure that its customers would behave responsibly with the information they purchased.

SUMMARY

We live today in an information society, one in which most people live and work in the context of information and information technology. This is the culmination of an evolution of humankind that began in antiquity and has continued to the present time. The development of knowledge and information has been a critical factor in the growth and development of an information-based society over time and has created an "informational era." That is why this evolution can be described as the ascent of information.

The motivations for humanity to embark on the ascent of information have been fourfold: (a) the pursuit of wealth and the avoidance of destitution, (b) the pursuit of security and the avoidance of fear and uncertainty, (c) the pursuit of recreation and entertainment and the avoidance of boredom and depression, and (d) the pursuit of control and order and the avoidance of chaos. These are all worthy human ends. Achieving them requires more people to spend more time and effort engaging in the activities of the information life cycles—acquiring, processing, storing, disseminating, and using information.

Information also confers power on those who possess it or can control its flow in a way that enables them to achieve their own goals. This power, which can be enormous, unfortunately, can be abused as well as it can be used toward achieving good ends. Consequently, it must be used judiciously.

The ascent of information is also a journey filled with pitfalls and problems. It is a kind of "pilgrim's progress" in which society is confronted with challenges to which it must respond. These challenges can best be understood by means of a dramatic framework called moments of truth. The framework consists of four time-sequenced components. First, there are moral agents who are pursuing their own goals in a manner best described as business as usual. Second, the agents are confronted by a moment of truth created by their own inner need to do something or imposed on them by outside forces. The agents must deal with temptations and quandaries at this time. Following this focal point, events unfold and the agents receive feedback. Third, a moment of recognition is reached. This is the point at which the agents fully understand the ethical implications of the decisions made at the moment of truth. Fourth, this sets in motion a set of activities intended to resolve the ethical conflict and to move on to the next phase of life.

A special language is useful for discussing the rights and responsibilities of the parties involved in the ethics of information. Information givers provide the raw information that is used by the information society, including personal information about themselves. Information takers are the ultimate receivers and users of this information. By acting on and using information, takers are thus in a position to realize the potential power encapsulated in it. Information orchestrators handle information and move it from givers to takers. Orchestrators execute the four fundamental functions of all information systems.

They gather information from givers and other sources; they process the information by manipulating and combining it in various ways; they store the information in the systems' memories to be retrieved at later dates; and they disseminate information by moving it from point to point and making it available to takers. These functions are captured by the terms *acquiring, processing, storing, disseminating,* and when acted on by the takers, *using.* Finally, there are stakeholders who are affected by the activities of givers, takers, and orchestrators. Many ethical issues revolve around the effects of these parties' activities on stakeholders.

An implied covenant exists between the givers, takers, orchestrators, and stakeholders in an information society. Givers should provide valid information, orchestrators should handle it with fidelity, and takers should use it only for the purposes agreed on for its collection. All should conduct their activities in a way that helps rather than harms stakeholders. The covenant forms the basis for the unwritten agreement between the members of a society that specifies all members' mutual responsibilities to one another. This is called a "social contract." The social contract of the information society has not been fully articulated as yet. The ideas discussed in this book, however, are intended to be fuel for the debate that will eventually result in such a contract.

The new social contract must reflect and accommodate society's new values. In agrarian and earlier societies, the principal values were aimed at survival and security. This was the era of "traditional man," and this vision was supplemented as the industrial era emerged. Sorokin (1937-1941) called the values of the industrial society sensate because they are the values of materialism. These are the values of economic man, who uses logic and objectivity to pursue the acquisition of jobs, money, productivity, radios, television sets, automobiles, vacation homes, and, in general, a higher standard of material living.

The informational era layers another set of values on top of these. They are ideational values. Pursuing them requires richer reasoning skills than those of economic man. More than helping people "have something" these reasoning skills must help humanity also be someone psychologically and spiritually. The new moral vision that is evolving is called information person. Information persons inhabit a world abuzz with flows of information from telephones, radios, televisions, newspapers, personal computers, and computing and communication devices of all sorts. Consequently, information persons must successfully negotiate many difficult information-centered moments of truth. In addition, they are responsible for the actions taken around the use and abuse of information. The concepts and ideas discussed in this book are part of the agenda for developing ethically responsible information persons.

The ascent of information has brought us to the information society. As we have seen, the key resource in this new society is information. But what is information? This question is addressed in the next chapter.

▨ NOTES

1. Copyright © 1993 by The New York Times Company. Reprinted by permission.
2. Copyright © 1966 by The New York Times Company. Reprinted by permission of the *New York Times* and *Thorndike Barnhart World Book Dictionary*.

2

Information: *Its Special Nature*

◩ UNDERSTANDING INFORMATION AND INFORMATION PROCESSES

Information is the symbolic means by which one mind influences another mind. According to Davis and Olson (1985), "Information is data that has been processed into a form that is meaningful to the recipient [the information taker] and is of real or perceived value in current or prospective actions or decisions" (p. 200). In common parlance, information is simply the "message," and it is a familiar phenomenon. Managers and workers alike use information every day in their work just as students use it in their studies. Normally, most of us do not think about information in this rather abstract way; but just reflect for a moment on what you do when you, say, write a report. First, you collect your notes and other materials from which you intend to draw facts and ideas. These materials, when you examine them closely and objectively, are really nothing more than a batch of symbols. You next think about what these symbols mean and what sense you might make of them. As your ideas become clear, you put another string of symbols down on paper or into the keyboard of your computer. When you are finished, you give the report to someone else—your information taker—to read and, perhaps, to make use of in some way. In the process of reading and thinking about your report, his or her psychological state is altered—sometimes only slightly; sometimes, however, quite profoundly. Your information taker is now changed. This describes, in outline, a process that is fundamental to all information work. As described in Chapter 1, symbols are acquired, processed, stored, disseminated, and used in an information life cycle. All of this takes place so that one mind can influence another.

We all engage in some kind of information work from time to time. Some of it, of course, is relatively inconsequential. Take for example the act of jotting down an appointment in your date book. This is an information activity, albeit a common one. Your mind at one time formulates the message that you are, say, to meet Barbara for lunch at 11:45 on January 11. Subsequently, your mind at a later time (and it is a "new" mind at this time) reads the message and acts on it. The minds are different; but the giver, taker, and orchestrator are the same person—you—and you are responsible for the whole process.

▨ THE INFORMATION LIFE CYCLE REVISITED

Thinking about the ethics of information leads you beyond just understanding the importance of information. We want you also to focus on what information means and how it affects people's lives. For this, it is essential to grasp the essence of the phenomenon called *information*. As described in Chapter 1, information evolves through five fundamental processes. First, there is the intellectual process of observing or imaging something, expressing it in symbols, and gathering the symbols together. This acquisition task is assumed by the giving mind. Second, there is processing phase in which technology is used to capture the symbols in a medium, manipulate them, and perhaps alter their form. Third, the medium that holds the symbols is retained so that it can be retrieved later—the storing phase. Fourth, the symbols are moved through time and space by means of a dissemination process. Finally, there is a second intellectual process—a second mind—that receives those symbols and converts them to ideas and actions. This using phase also involves a productive process during which decisions and actions are taken by the taking mind that have consequences for stakeholders.

▨ CREDIT REPORTING:
A CASE OF INFORMATION TEMPTATION

Some information cycles are rather trivial in importance; but a considerable amount of information work is highly significant and quite pervasive.

Entire industries are based on it. Credit reports, for example, are typical pieces of information that are derived from processes like those described earlier. A credit report contains data about an individual's record of payment on bills in addition to information about the individual that has been collected from public documents and other sources. Initially, the information on a report derives from the minds of the many people who observed an individual's purchasing, credit, and paying behavior; that is, it comes from information givers. After a long, complex chain of processing and transmission, this information is finally delivered to another mind in the form of a summary document. The receiving mind—an information taker—accepts the information on the report, interprets it, and uses it to make decisions—decisions that may materially affect that individual and perhaps many others. One crucial interpretation that is derived from a credit report is a "credit rating."

A credit rating depicts the financial solvency and integrity of an individual. A "good" rating means that one can borrow money and participate with others in activities that require trust and dependability. In contrast, a "bad" rating means that one's opportunities can be severely limited. Consequently, without credit, many people are precluded from participating fully in our society.

The credit reporting industry was founded in about 1860 by a group of merchants in Brooklyn who formed an association for exchanging information about their customers. Their objective was to help prospective grantors of credit identify individuals who might be bad credit risks. From these humble beginnings, a massive industry has emerged. It is estimated today that the three largest credit bureaus—TRW, Trans Union, and Equifax—collectively have more than 400 million files on individuals from which they produce credit reports on a daily basis. This huge business—its annual revenues reach nearly $1 billion—is based almost entirely on information and information systems. Data extracted from these files, for example, has been used to grant hundreds of billions of dollars of outstanding debt. By 1990, private consumer and mortgage debt in the United States had reached in excess of 3.3 trillion dollars. This, of course, is the productive purpose for which the information was collected and for which the credit reports were prepared.

Once amassed, however, the data in these files can be put to many additional uses. The data includes presumed facts about individuals' credit accounts held, levels of credit granted, outstanding debts, and a record of payment of bills. Explanatory remarks are frequently appended to each account record to help the reader arrive at a clearer picture of the consumer's paying habits. Supplementing this information is additional data describing things such as federal tax liens, civil judgments involving money, chattel mortgages, divorce actions, marriage licenses, civil lawsuits, and other information usually obtained from public sources. All of this reveals a great deal about the givers—that is, those people about whom these records are kept. This knowledge, which has so many possible uses, can be very seductive to the information takers who have access to it.

Today, credit reports are sometimes used for purposes not explicitly authorized by the givers, such as preemployment screening, insurance underwriting, and credit prescreening. Credit card companies, for example, purchase lists of potential new customers who satisfy certain criteria from credit bureaus. These uses, too, influence many important decisions that affect people's lives. Some of these uses result in the invasion of individuals' privacy, often without their knowledge, usually without their consent.

◩ UNAUTHORIZED USE: A GROWING TEMPTATION

Before the Congress and the Federal Trade Commission (FTC) addressed the problem, credit bureaus routinely sold their lists to marketers who wanted to identify potential customers for their products. Robert Ellis Smith, the editor of *Privacy Journal* at the time, observed that targeted marketing was

> an example of credit information being used for secondary purposes—purposes different from the one for which the information was initially gathered. The credit bureaus are supposed to be in business solely to collect data that enables credit grantors to assess a person's creditworthiness, not to constantly broadcast little tidbits about each of us. (quoted in Rothfeder, 1992, p. 98)

Attorney Janlori Goldman of the American Civil Liberties Union added that "there's barely a piece of information about people that isn't used for far different purposes than it was initially gathered for, and always without approval" (quoted in Rothfeder, 1992, p. 25). These protestations, and others like them, eventually lead the U.S. government to examine the issue in more depth.

Why are people tempted to use information in unauthorized ways? Because information has productive power. It can be used to get many different kinds of things done. Its takers use it effectively to achieve a wide variety of personal and organizational goals and objectives. This anoints information with a kind of aphrodisiac quality, one that entices people to use it to satisfy their own personal desires. The former information management editor of *Business Week,* Jeffrey Rothfeder (1992), laments that "people can't be trusted with information about each other; they'll do harm with it" (p. 23).[1]

▧ INFORMATION ABOUNDS

Credit reporting is only a small piece of the world's total information activity. We are all familiar with other common examples as well. Take, for example, the text of an article in the *New York Times.* It is also information in the sense defined earlier. The mind of a journalist worked to observe events, organize them, and compose a message, and if she was successful, the mind of the reader was subsequently affected. Linking these two minds together required a fairly elaborate system that included the reporter's workstation, an editor's workstation, composing and page-setting technology, satellite communications (especially if you receive your copy of the *Times* in Dallas), printing technology, and, finally, a delivery person driving a car who tosses the blue-cellophane-wrapped paper toward the reader's lawn at about 6:00 a.m. All of this sociotechnological system is orchestrated so that the initiating or giving minds can influence the receiving or taking minds.

Some of us get our newspapers, books, journals, and other materials from libraries—electronic or traditional. The authors of these materials are the original information givers. Librarians, however, play a crucial orchestrating role when they select, categorize, organize, and deliver the authors' work to information takers. Their activities affect the lives of the information takers they serve, by the information they make available and how quickly it is delivered.

Likewise, sending a report of inventory stock levels to a supermarket executive involves linking several different giving and taking minds. In the simplest instance, a clerk walks down the aisles and counts the number of items on the shelves. This message is then formulated and reported to an executive who uses it to make decisions such as whether or not to place an order for additional items. In a more complex—and more typical—situation, some of the front end and tail end of this process may be automated. The mind of a systems analyst may have been used to program a bar code scanner that counts the items and feeds the count to a computer that develops the report. On the other end of this information chain, the thought processes of the executive may have been captured in a decision support program that analyzes the reported stock levels and automatically places a new order whenever a "reorder" condition is reached.

There is an important observation to be made from these examples: The separate giving and taking minds that form an information relationship are not always directly connected. In fact, they usually are not. An orchestration or gatekeeping process almost always intercedes. Your mind today, for example, can reach back over 2,000 years and access the mind of Plato simply because his thoughts were written down and because many people, including some dedicated Florentine merchants during the 15th century, preserved his writings and they have been made available. Nevertheless, in any information relationship, the giving and taking minds are always present, even if they are hidden far away behind the scenes and lie in a distant past.

In today's information society, activities such as those just described are omnipresent. This represents a great challenge to you because you are undoubtedly, from time to time, a member in the orchestrating chain of events as well as a giver and taker. Because you are a participant in the process, you bear some of the responsibility for what takes place as it unfolds. Our goal in this book is to help you discharge this responsibility ethically.

▨ INFORMATION, POWER, AND ETHICS

What, then, is the relationship between the roles of information giving, orchestrating, taking, the information life cycle, and ethics? Why is ethics important? The answer to these questions is fundamental to our information society and can be summed up as follows: The giving, orchestrating, and taking of information is a basic source of *power*. Power is capability, the ability to get things done that one wants done. We will have more to say about power in Chapter 4. Suffice it to say now that, like weapons and money, information can be used by agents to exercise their will over stakeholders and to achieve their own goals. In the process, however, information can also be used in a way that deprives some stakeholders of their ability to achieve their own goals. Herein lies the rub. As the credit reporting industry discussion illustrates, people who acquire, process, store, disseminate, or use information to achieve their own goals can either harm or significantly benefit other people in the process. Consequently, the way in which activities in information life cycles are carried out is the cause of many ethical issues. But as we will see, it is a very special kind of causal factor.

▧ KEY FEATURES OF INFORMATION

Unlike weapons, money, and many other sources of power, however, information is *not* a thing. It is not materialistic. Information obeys different laws. It is, as the eminent political scientist Harlan Cleveland observes, "unique among resources" (see Cleveland, 1982a, 1982b).

As is clear from its definition, information is essentially human in its origin and is inherently intangible. Most resources, most other bases of power, are, in contrast, basically tangible. Guns, tanks, ships, and bombers are clearly tangible. Buildings, machines, industrial plants, and other sources of wealth are tangible. For most of its historical existence, money has also been tangible: stones, jewels, cows, grain, gold. All have served as a medium of exchange. Paper money and coins, of course, are also tangible. This distinction, however, becomes murky in an information-based economy in which money takes the form of credit or "bits" of binary data traversing in the form of electronic pulses through an electronic funds transfer system. Management theorist Peter Drucker (1989) refers to this as the "symbol economy" and notes that the evolution to this unique economic realm is a crucial aspect of the new reality of doing business in the modern world. When money and information become one, a powerful force is at work—a circumstance that will be discussed more fully later.

Because it originates in the mind and is intangible, information has some surprisingly different characteristics that clearly distinguish it from other kinds of resources and from other sources of wealth. Cleveland (1982a, 1982b) has identified seven special characteristics of information: Information, he asserts, is human, expandable, compressible, substitutable, transportable, diffusive, and shareable. Collectively, these make information a unique resource, the use of which creates some rather unique ethical issues.

Information Is Human. Information itself exists only in the human mind—what it observes, remembers, and can retrieve—and what it then analyzes, intuits, and integrates. It is the input and output of human perception and imagination and is given and taken by human minds. Rocks and trees, guns and butter all exist in reality. You can touch them; but you cannot touch information. Information begins and ends in human minds. From among the "bumbling, blustering confusion" that is reality, a giving mind makes *distinctions* and attempts to share them with a taking mind. Information, therefore, is what giving and taking minds observe, imagine, remember, analyze, compare, relate, rank, organize, intuit, or integrate.

Because information is a mind-based human entity, it is manipulated in a different way than are tangible items. Data—strings of symbols—may be manipulated physically, electronically, or optically; but information—the sense we make of the symbols and the meaning we attribute to them—results from an inherent psychological process and is moved, shaped, built, and destroyed by the human mind.

Information Is Expandable. Information tends to expand with its use as new relationships and possibilities are realized. Abundance and overload are greater problems than scarcity. As Professor Russell E. Ackoff (1967) noted in an article aptly titled "Management MisInformation Systems,"

> Most MIS's are designed on the assumption that the critical deficiency under which most managers operate is the *lack of relevant information.* I do not deny that most managers lack a good deal of information that they should have, but I do deny that this is the most important informational deficiency from which they suffer. It seems to me that they suffer more from an *overabundance of irrelevant information.* (p. 147)

A quarter of a century later, the problem Ackoff identified still persists according to an article in the July 11, 1994, issue of *Fortune* entitled "Surviving the Information Overload" (Russell E. Ackoff, cited in Tetzeli, 1994). Because it is expandable, information can become a burden as well as an aid. Expandability also means that the ethical issues that any item of information produces can be easily multiplied.

The primary limits to the expandability of information is the amount of time the giving and taking minds have available and their capacity to observe, reflect, analyze, and integrate. Attention is our most valuable psychological resource. When one can devote psychological energy to a stream of varied information, however, amazing things can happen. This is why intellectual property rights lawyer Anne Branscomb refers to information as a "synergistic resource"—"the more we have the more we use and the more useful it becomes" (quoted in Cleveland, 1982a, p. 7).

Information Is Compressible. Complex messages can be compressed, concentrated, consolidated, compiled, integrated, and summarized. Entire video movies, for example, can be transmitted using only a fraction of the binary bits originally required to capture them. By employing the intellectual processes of coding, compression, and distillation, "We can store many complex cases in a theorem, squeeze insights from masses of data into a single formula, capture lessons learned from much practical experience in a manual of procedure" (Cleveland, 1982a, p. 8), or even distill a lifetime of experience in a "knowledge-base" of rules. In the process, some "uncertainty absorption"—a term coined by Herbert Simon (1957)—may occur, and some of the original information may be lost. Users of information should be mindful of this possibility because this, too, can be the source of unexpected ethical issues. For the most part, however, the unique ability to compress this almost infinitely expandable source of power gives it enormous flexibility.

Information Is Substitutable. It can replace labor, capital, or physical materials in most economic processes. As was revealed vividly during the "Desert Storm" war in Iraq, information can be substituted for weapons and make them "smarter." During World War II, a B29 had to fly to within about 3 miles of a target to drop a bomb that could hope to land within 1 mile of it. The Norden bombsight was the innovation that made even this level of accuracy possible. In contrast, laser-guided bombs delivered during the Persian Gulf war were deployed about 50 miles away, and most landed on average within 20 feet of their target. As a result, fewer bombs were needed, and fewer pilots and civilians were killed (Steward, 1991).

Intellectual capital is now corporate America's most valuable asset because it permits trade-offs to be made between materials and information. To cite one example, information is replacing aluminum in beverage can production. From 1972 to 1990 the number of cans produced per pound of aluminum increased almost 40% due to scientific developments. "The beer has a head, but the can has brains," author Thomas Steward (1991, p. 45) quipped. Another illustration is in intelligent plant breeding. Corn hybrids, for example, have experienced a threefold increase in yields per acre between 1959 and 1990, and they are still improving. Substitutability is one of the major sources of information's power. It can be used to improve the human condition, as these illustrations suggest, or it can be used for harm.

Information Is Transportable. It can be moved around the globe today at nearly the speed of light. The ancient Greeks used carrier pigeons to warn authorities of upcoming battles. Using modern technology, the same message can be sent farther, faster, and considerably cheaper. One measure of this improvement, on which remarkable progress has been made, is the cost per unit of time required to travel a unit of distance. With the advent of the telegraph in 1850, for example, message transmission improved to 1,400 miles per hour per dollar compared to the much poorer performance of the pony express or the railroad. By 1960, using analog telephone lines, the figure had jumped to 1.4 million miles per hour per dollar—a thousandfold increase. Around 1980, when the digital infrastructure became operational, this figure vaulted to 38 million miles per hour per dollar. Fiber-optic technologies currently being installed promise even another quantum leap in performance. So information is not only transportable; it is explosively so. In less than a century, we have witnessed a major dimensional change in both the speed and volume of the movement of information, a change in transportability of resources greater than the multimillennial shift from foot travel to supersonic jets. This means that today the evil as well as the good that information does can be realized quickly, virtually anytime, anywhere on the globe.

Information Is Diffusive. It is hard to contain. It tends to leak. Because it is intangible, it naturally oozes through the pores of things and radiates, spreads out, and disperses. Like a heat-seeking automaton, information tends to act as though it is searching for minds that might be able to use it—for whatever purpose, good or evil—while the taking minds with their own set of motivations seem ever more eager to acquire it. This is one of the reasons that many traditional methods of containing the flow of information, such as provisions for confidentiality, secrecy, and intellectual property rights, are, in practice, so difficult to apply effectively today. This, too, is a subject in which ethical analysis has become important.

Information Is Shareable. Perhaps the most significant economic feature of information is that it is *not* depleted with use. Indeed, it can even be enhanced with use, as with training, propaganda, or advertising. Cleveland (1982a) comments that the noted Canadian communications theorist Colin Cherry, shortly before his death, concluded that "information by nature cannot give rise to exchange transactions, only to sharing transactions." Cleveland adds,

> *Things* are exchanged: if I give you a flower or sell you my automobile (or a book or video tape), you have it and I don't. But if I sell you an idea, we both have it. And if I give you a fact or tell you a story, it's like a good kiss: in sharing the thrill, you enhance it. Conversely, if my kiss carries a disease (information harmful to your mental health) the sharing transaction may be infectious. (p. 9)

So with information, the bad is shared easily as well as the good.

◩ ANCIENT ORIGINS OF INFORMATION

These seven characteristics describe how information differs from other resources and other sources of power. The use of information as a source of power has a long history—one that goes back at least 16,000 years to the time when early cave dwellers called Cro-Magnon inhabited the Dordogne River valley in France. There, in Lascaux, some innovative soul, an original information giver, descended into a dark, limestone cave, powdered some nearby clay, and using a bone as a stylus began to paint marks on the walls. In time, these marks became a magnificent frieze more than 30 feet in length that depicts ibexes, bulls, horses, and deer with remarkable fidelity. Archaeologists believe that the paintings were used as part of a ceremony in which magic was conjured up to assure success in the tribal hunt. Many of the friezes show animals that are pierced with arrows and scored with inverted Vs, suggesting that the paintings were used to instruct others in the art and science of the hunt.

Cro-Magnon's experience illustrates each of the seven features of information, and it demonstrates how information processes can become deeply embedded in the fabric of a society. Cro-Magnon had previously developed primitive spears and knives with which to hunt; but the use of these tools was significantly energized and focused by the messages contained in pictures on the wall. This vital knowledge, thus encapsulated, could now be substituted for the use of raw energy and for costly trial-and-error learning, perhaps even for the eventual loss of the teacher. Years of experience and knowledge about the hunt were compressed into just a few drawings, and the information was presented in a form so that it could be shared and acted on by all members of the community. Most important, this information had significant survival value. It is likely that the more Cro-Magnon used the information, the more successful at hunting they were, and, consequently, their appetite for the information contained in the drawings grew. We know little about the social structure of Cro-Magnon or whether they competed directly with other clans of cave dwellers for their prey; but we can imagine that the information painted on their cave walls was quite valuable to them. We can also imagine that some forms of secrecy were employed to keep other clans from acquiring their precious information. Perhaps a small social elite was formed from among the clan of Lascaux consisting of those who possessed the intellectual keys to interpret the drawings and control communications. They could then use the information to keep their power from being diffused more broadly. In summary, even in the ancient caves of Lascaux we see that these seven key features of information are at work.

It should be apparent that these unique characteristics of information play a key role in some of the ethical issues inherent in the use of information. Consider again the case of credit reports. Because the information they contain can be substituted for some of the time-consuming and costly efforts otherwise involved in credit and lending decisions, they are of considerable economic value to some people in a variety of different walks of life. They are used, for example, to pinpoint more clearly the risks or the opportunities involved in doing business with these people. Most times, this makes it possible for consumers to receive credit quickly and easily. With electronic access, a person can instantly qualify for a loan or a credit card. Because these records are compressible, not much energy is required to move them nor much space required to contain them.

Because credit reports are readily shareable and transportable—at one point, Cleveland (1982a) describes information like this as being inherently "leakable"—they are made available electronically to many different businesses located throughout the United States and used for a range of permissible purposes specified by law. Electronic access, however, also makes it quite easy for credit reports to be obtained for questionable or illegal purposes. All that matters is that someone wants to know something about the subjects.

Herein lies a source of information temptation. Credit report information is among the kinds of valuable information about people and their behavior patterns that tend to be, in Cleveland's (1982a) words, "aggressive, even imperialistic in striving to break out of the unnatural bonds of secrecy in which thing-minded people try to imprison it" (p. 9). It is valuable, moreover, because agents pursuing their own self-interests are motivated to acquire it. Recall *Business Week* reporter Jeffrey Rothfeder's (1992) warning: "People can't be trusted with information about each other; they'll do harm with it" (p. 23). So managers at American Express, for example, were tempted by a database of transaction records on about 25 million credit card holders and sorted them by spending patterns and sold the resulting lists, complete with names and addresses, to other organizations, ranging from retail stores to insurance companies (Schwartz, 1992).

Because people rely on information in making decisions that affect their lives and those of countless other individuals, inaccuracies can also create problems. For example, when a lender acquires a credit report containing errors and, consequently, rejects the credit application, it can wreak havoc on the life of the borrower. The word could be passed around that this person and his family are not very reliable and do not make good customers, associates, or friends. As discussed later, this is not as outlandish a scenario as it might first appear.

For the present, however, it is important to note that the unique characteristics of information summarized earlier facilitate its use in developing impressions and making decisions. This relates directly to the central role that information plays in decision making, the subject of the next chapter.

SUMMARY

There exists an intangible thing called information that is the symbolic means by which one mind—the giving mind—influences another mind—the taking mind. The separate giving and taking minds that form an information relationship, however, are not always directly connected. There may be many orchestrators and gatekeepers between them.

Because information derives originally from one or more minds, it is inherently and fundamentally human. It is also expandable, compressible, substitutable, transportable, diffusive, and shareable. This makes information quite different from tangible resources, such as iron or coal, that are consumed and destroyed when they are used, take up physical space, and are more bulky and generally awkward to manipulate.

Information evolves through five fundamental processes that, collectively, make up the information life cycle. First, there is the intellectual process of observing or imagining something, expressing it in symbols, and gathering the symbols together. This is the task assumed by the giving mind and is called the acquisition phase. Second, is the processing phase in which technology is used to capture the symbols in a medium, manipulate them, and perhaps alter their form. In this process, symbols are compared, subjected to mathematical and logical operations, moved, and ordered. Third, the medium that holds the symbols is retained or stored so that the symbols can be retrieved later. Fourth, the symbols are moved through time and space in a process called dissemination. Finally, there is a second intellectual process—a second mind—that receives those symbols and converts them to ideas and actions. This using phase also involves a productive process during which decisions and actions are taken by the taking mind, all of which have consequences for stakeholders.

The activities conducted in information life cycles are the root origin of many ethical issues. In the process of acquiring, processing, storing, disseminating, or using information, people and organizations can either materially harm or significantly benefit people—givers, takers, and orchestrators alike. Although significant ethical consequences may result from any of the information cycle processes, the more important ones stem from the using of information. The next chapter discusses an important aspect of the using phase—decision making.

🖉 NOTE

1. All excerpts from Rothfeder (1992) reprinted by permission from Brockman, Inc.

3

Information and Decision Making

◪ INFORMATION TECHNOLOGY CREATES TOUGH CHOICES

Mrs. Bonnie G was about 21 weeks into a trouble-free pregnancy when to her delight she learned that modern technology could tell her the gender and condition of her baby. When the sonogram tests showed that her baby, which was a boy, had a blockage of his urinary system that had probably caused permanent damage to his kidneys, however, much of her joy turn to despair. Mrs. G and her husband were soon immersed in a set of whipsawing events:

> With only three weeks before it was too late to abort, doctors jumped in with a grueling afternoon of tests: another sonogram to look for kidney damage; an amniocentesis to see if her son's problem could be related to a genetic abnormality; another needle passed through her abdomen and uterus, into the bladder of the fetus to see if the fluid there would yield clues to the degree of damage.
>
> "It was the most devastating day," she recalled. "At that point we had very little information and we were hearing the worst-case scenario."
>
> The roller-coaster ride continued over the next week as each test result returned. The amniocentesis revealed that the fetus did in fact have a minor chromosomal abnormality whose effect on their child no one could predict. The couple thought more seriously about an abortion.
>
> But a later blood test showed that Mrs. G. carried the same anomaly and since she was normal, doctors said it probably did not cause the problem in the fetus. Once again the pregnancy went forward. Then the fetal urine showed that the kidneys were functioning but that some degree of injury had already occurred. Again they hesitated.

As the couple pondered their options, their families weighed in. Mr. G.'s parents are born-again Christians who oppose abortion. "My mother-in-law said she was praying and that the baby was going to be born fine," Mrs. G. recalled. "My husband said, 'Look, you don't have to live with it; it's our decision.' "

At the suggestion of Dr. Berkowitz the couple also met with a kidney specialist, who discussed with them the test results as well as the rigors of caring for a young child with kidney disease, from dialysis sessions to kidney transplants. "Three weeks ago I knew nothing about this, but in this situation you are desperate to absorb it and understand," said Mrs. G.

The tests were repeated. Just days before the deadline for abortion the couple got a bit of good news: The blockage had partly opened and showed that kidney function was improving.

"I think we now know that he won't get into trouble in the early infant period," Dr. Berkowitz said. "But how much time he will spend in the hospital? How many infections he will get? And whether he will need dialysis or how long before he gets a transplant is anybody's guess."

Still, the 11th-hour improvement was enough to make up the couple's minds: "At that point we breathed a little easier and decided to continue," Mrs. G. said. "Technology has been nothing but a help, so far." (Rosenthal, 1994, pp. A1, A13)[1]

Or, has it? One thing is absolutely clear in this case: Technology can change the timing and characteristics of moments of truth. Before prenatal diagnosis was available, Mr. and Mrs. G would have had to wait until the baby had gone full term and was delivered before they were faced with a decision on his treatment. At that time, their decision could have also been made with fairly complete information. Very likely, termination of the pregnancy would never have been considered as an option. The information produced by the new medical technology, however, complicated their situation and extended the range of possibilities. On the one hand, by acquiring the test results when they did, Mrs. G's doctors were in a position to take actions that might improve the condition of the baby, and they also could form a prognosis to inform Mr. and Mrs. G's decision about termination and prepare them for the situation they would face when the baby was delivered. Also, the couple now knew with considerable certainty that the baby was a boy. On the other hand, the Gs were confronted with a soul-wrenching choice, one that was fraught with guilt, moral doubt, and a whole new set of uncertainties.

Information, as this case illustrates vividly, plays two key roles in decision making. It creates moments of truth at which decisions must be made, and it is used by decision makers to consider options and inform their choices.

▨ INFORMATION USE AND DECISION MAKING

Information generates value through the decision situations it creates and the decisions it informs. This occurs during the last stage of the information life cycle: *use.* At this stage the taking mind perceives a set of possible states of the real world and generates a number of possible courses of action for dealing with them. These are then evaluated in terms of the taker's goals, and a particular course of action is adopted. Information instructs and helps guide in making the choice. The process of decision making revolves around five key components that make up the *information value-adding chain* (see Figure 3.1):

1. The first is an original *source* consisting of people, events, physical activities, and objects that are relevant to the person making the decision. Mrs. G herself, her fetus, and the doctors were sources in the preceding case.

2. Next is the observation, measurement, and recording of *data* from the source—that is, making distinctions about items and activities in the source and capturing them in some symbolic form. This is the initial and primary role of the giving mind and generally the end stage of the information life cycle. The sonogram and other test results compose the basic data in the Mrs. G case.

3. Third is the drawing of *inferences, predictions,* and *interpretations* from the data. This involves applying assumptions and perspective to the data. This is an activity of the taking mind. Some theorists define the output of this interpretive process as *information,* reserving for the input the word *data.* Put succinctly, information is produced from raw data interpreted from some point of view. It "is the result of somebody applying the refiner's fire to the mass of facts and ideas, selecting and organizing what is useful—to somebody" (Cleveland, 1982a, p. 2).

The doctors provided the inferences, diagnosis, and prognosis for Mrs. G and constructed the worst-case scenario, thereby serving as the gatekeepers and orchestrators for the Gs. Performing this service also gives the doctors relative power over the Gs and establishes a need for professionalism, a topic that will be discussed in Chapter 7.

4. The fourth component is the evaluation of inferences with regard to *values* (objectives or goals) of the taker or decision maker and the *choosing* of

a course of action. At this stage, personal and social values are brought to bear on the information, and one's mind is made up as to which course of action to take. This, of course, was primarily the responsibility of the Gs in their role as information takers and decision makers, but they also received inputs on values from their doctors and especially from Mr. G's parents. The doctors were also following a principle called *informed consent*—a term used to indicate that a person's approval of procedures, treatments, or other actions is based on his or her possession and understanding of all relevant information.

5. Finally, there is the actual *engaging in a course of action* by an agent. Generally, this is the work of the taking mind. The decision maker's responsibility is based on the changes in the real world that result from the action he or she takes. The value of information derives from its actual or potential use. It is rooted in the chain of events that flows from its source to its ultimate conversion into human behavior. The ethical implications flow from the actual behavior the information induced.

The G's final action was to continue the pregnancy. This decision was significantly influenced by the information they received from their doctors. Consequently, although the Gs are primarily responsible for the decision, the doctors share responsibility for the information they provided and the processes they use to communicate with and to advise their patients.[2]

Two features of the information value-adding chain are worth noting. One is that information develops through several qualitatively different levels. The other is that the flow of information from source to action is often characterized by points of articulation between different parties.

Information Develops Through Qualitatively Different Levels. Although we use the general term information to describe most activities that deal with facts and ideas, some crucial distinctions were made earlier. Information itself is produced by means of stages in an *epistemic hierarchy*—epistemic because the term means to know or to understand and hierarchy because it forms a graded series. The hierarchy is summarized as follows:

$$\text{data} \rightarrow \text{information} \rightarrow \text{knowledge} \rightarrow \text{wisdom}$$

Beginning at the source, things starts out in a raw, crude, nebulous form—the "blustering confusion" to which William James once referred. Distinctions are made from this by the giving mind, thereby creating data.

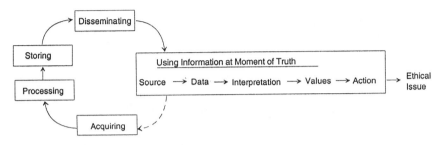

Figure 3.1. Relationship Between Information Life Cycle and Decision Making

Orchestrating and intellectual processing now come into play as information is generated by interpreting the data from some point of view. That is, a viewpoint, which derives from one's cultural, social, psychological, and moral attitudes and beliefs, is used for selecting data, comparing it, organizing it, and casting it into a meaningful framework.

Knowledge, then, is information that has been authenticated, validated, or thought to be true. According to Russell L. Ackoff, knowledge includes practical skills (to know how to do something), and it also "consists of an individual's true beliefs or what he [or she] is aware of" (Ackoff & Emery, 1972, p. 46). People can reliably base their behavior on knowledge.

Finally, wisdom refers to knowledge that has been integrated into a society, a culture, or a value system. Wisdom is "integrated knowledge—information made super-useful by creating theory rooted in disciplined knowledge, but crossing disciplinary barriers, to weave into an integrated whole something more than the sum of its parts" (Cleveland, 1982b, p. 34). The route to wisdom, then, is highly selective—it focuses on fundamental human values—and is not as data intensive as items found lower in the hierarchy. Wisdom includes forgetting as much as remembering and is made up of insights and understandings as to what is true, right, and lasting. "All we know is that we know nothing," writes Tolstoy (1886/1966) in *War and Peace*.

And that's the height of human wisdom. The highest wisdom is not founded on reason alone, nor on those worldly sciences of physics, chemistry, and the like, into which intellectual knowledge is divided. [The highest wisdom is] but one science—the science of the whole—the science explaining the whole creation and man's place in it. (p. 432)

Wisdom also has strong survival value. "Knowledge comes, but wisdom lingers," Tennyson (1842/1962, line 141) observed. Information in any of these four forms is valuable; but its value tends to increase rather substantially as it goes up the epistemic hierarchy and approaches wisdom.

In this book, and in common usage, we frequently use the term information to describe all four stages in the epistemic hierarchy. Occasionally, however, precise distinctions are useful. This is undoubtedly true in your own work. Let's say that you are using a spreadsheet to develop a budget for your organization. You collect cost figures for various activities your organization undertakes, such as renting space and using electricity. These figures are your data. The data are then run through a spreadsheet program that contains assumptions you have made about relationships between categories and monthly and seasonal differences. Some figures, such as total costs per month by category, are produced by the software. That's information. You now take the total cost figures and test them and verify them by checking with other sources or comparing with other organizations. You are now on your way to producing knowledge. At some point, you may discover a pattern of relationships that is consistent and reliable. You decide to put that relationship back into your spreadsheet so that you can draw on it over and over again. In the process, you have constructed a knowledge-based computer system—a form of artificial intelligence—that captures that piece of your knowledge and makes it available for future use. Finally, you evaluate the resulting budget in light of how it fits into the broader context in which you work. Your wisdom is now consulted to determine how to use this knowledge in your negotiations with others in your organization. You use it to modify the results and to develop a strategy for implementing it in your organization.

In preparing this budget spreadsheet, you have worked with data, information, and knowledge. At each stage, you have contributed more intellectual effort to the original data. During the process, presumably, you made the wisest choices you could. This is typical of most so-called information- or knowledge-based jobs. When we examine this kind of work carefully, these epistemic concepts are absolutely necessary. In normal discourse, however, it is usually satisfactory to simply call it information work or, alternatively, knowledge work.

The Flow of Information Is Characterized by Points of Articulation. The connection between information and decision making forces us to articulate clearly the relationship between giving, gatekeeping or orchestrating, and taking minds in a given situation. Fiercely independent decision makers who collect all of their own data, for example, embody both the giving and taking minds in a single agent—namely, themselves. In the spreadsheet budget scenario, for example, you played both the giving and taking roles. Any ethical problems your behavior creates, consequently, can be attributed to you for the most part. That is, you bear moral responsibility in the sense discussed in Chapter 1. (Even in this seemingly autonomous situation, however, you probably acquired your data from other people, and you may have given your total budget figures to someone else who acted on them. You are still morally responsible for your work, but you may share some of that responsibility with others.)

More frequently, however, separate givers and takers (and very likely orchestrators) are involved. Information is handed off between them like a baton. It is passed between the giving and taking minds throughout the value-adding process described earlier. At one extreme, the giving mind makes a decision (i.e., completes the first four phases in the sequence described earlier) and issues it to the taking mind as a command. If the taker treats the command as a mandate and acts on it, it is likely that the giver bears some of the responsibility for any ethical issues that result from the taker's actions.

At the other extreme, a giver may pass just an elemental piece of data to the taker. "A plane is approaching at 2 o'clock," for example. The fact that the taker then shot the plane out of the sky—that is, took this datum, interpreted it, inferred from it, and concluded that it constituted a warning of impending danger—indicates that the taker participated heavily in the decision. In this latter case, the information taker bears a great deal of the responsibility for the action he or she has taken.

Most information usage, however, falls somewhere between these two extremes. In practice, many giving and orchestrating minds can be involved before the final taking minds use the information. The intricacies of the networks through which information work is accomplished add complications to the ethics of information. Information ethics is replete with problems of attributing moral responsibility for outcomes, resulting in the context of many giving and taking relationships in which—to use Cleveland's (1982a, 1982b) description—many intangible, human-based, expandable, substitutable, transportable, diffusive, and shareable symbols are exchanged.

Mrs. G's case illustrates how complex some giving, orchestrating, and taking relationships can be. As the story unfolds, different parties play different giving and taking roles. An important aspect of Mrs. G's case, however—and this is also true of most innovations in information technology and information provision—is that the ethical responsibilities shifted as the information processes proceeded. Note, for example, that the doctors did not make a recommendation to the Gs. They did not provide them with a decision that they could either accept or reject. Rather, they formulated inferences from the data and let the Gs bring their own values to bear in choosing and taking their ultimate course of action. So the doctors left off at Step 3 in the sequence of the information value-adding chain and let the Gs take it from there. In so doing, they followed the principle of informed consent.

▧ INFORMED CONSENT AND THE MAKING OF INFORMATION PERSONS

The notion of informed consent, as revealed in the G's case, is becoming increasingly important in the information age. It spells out the principles by which giving minds with superior information should share it with takers. It tends to shift the burden of responsibility for decision making from the giving and orchestrating minds to the taking minds. This enhances the autonomy and dignity of the information takers while at the same time placing them under considerable stress.

Three basic principles of informed consent have emerged. One is following *customary practice.* Under this standard, the traditional, historical way of providing information to people and making decisions is identified and accepted as normal practice.

The second standard is based on a court case in medical ethics: *Canterbury v. Spence* (1972). Sometimes called the *reasonable person* doctrine, it is based on moral considerations of autonomy.

> When a given procedure inherently involves a known risk of death or serious bodily harm, a medical doctor has a duty to disclose to his patient the potential of death or serious harm. . . . The patient's right of self-decision is the measure of the physician's duty to reveal . . . all information relevant to a meaningful decision process. (p. 787)

According to this standard, information givers should provide enough information to takers for reasonable people to make decisions about procedures, treatments, experiments, or other actions that will affect them.

The third, and more recent, standard is called the *subjective standard*. Rather than referring to an objective reasonable person, as the previous standard does, this standard acknowledges the uniqueness of each individual taking mind. Special fears, backgrounds, education levels, and social conditions are taken into account so that each taker individually understands that he or she (a) is authorizing certain specific actions to be taken, (b) is fully aware of what the risks are, and (c) has an opportunity to say no and stop certain actions from being taken. In the extreme, the subjective standard requires that the giver or user of information include any factors particular to the taker's need or desire for information that the giver could reasonably be expected to know or to discover.

The reasonable person doctrine harks back to the assumptions of economic man. It appears that the doctors in Mrs. G's case at least adhered to this standard. The case suggests, in addition, that the doctors dealt with the Gs in a dignified way and crafted their advice to take into account the Gs unique situation. They approached the subjective standard. In so doing, they were treating Mr. and Mrs. G as *information persons*. As a result of living through this drama, both Mr. and Mrs. G were changed. They became quite different people for having participated in this information-intensive relationship.

Some situations involving information exchange and informed consent are not as dramatic as the G's case, but nevertheless, they are quite important. Many center around the releasing of personal purchasing and credit information and the like. Concern for this practice has led to legislation. In 1973, for example, the U.S. Department of Health, Education and Welfare proposed five new principles for fair information practice. Sometimes summarized under the heading of "knowledge, notice, and no" the five principles are as follows:[3]

1. There must be no personal record-keeping systems whose existence is kept secret.

2. There must be a way for an individual to find out what information about him or her is on record and how it is being used.

3. There must be a way for an individual to correct or amend a record of identifiable information about him or her.

4. There must be a way for an individual to prevent information about him or her that was obtained for one purpose from being used or made available for other purposes without his or her informed consent.

5. Any organization creating, maintaining, using, or disseminating records of identifiable personal data must assure the reliability of the data for the intended use and must take reasonable precautions to prevent misuse of the data. (Laudon, Traver, & Laudon, 1994, pp. 520-521)

Essentially, these principles require that all original information givers must have knowledge of the information that takers have collected about them. Furthermore, the givers must be notified about the purposes to which the information is to be put, and they must have an opportunity to correct invalid information. That is, they must be able to say "No!" and stop unwarranted use of information. Fair information practices, such as the Fair Credit Reporting Act of 1970 and the Privacy Act of 1974, are examples of existing U.S. laws regulating access to personal information. These acts are discussed in Chapter 9.

These provisions of "knowledge, notice, and no" also form the beginning of a new social contract. When it is completed, the social contract for the information society will spell out the rights and duties of information givers, takers, and orchestrators. It will create a new society of information persons.

▨ THE UNFOLDING OF DECISIONS

A good place to start an ethical examination is with the ultimate taking mind, that is, with the final acting agent in the chain. The Gs assumed this role in the case presented here. If the final information taker could use the information to do something that harms stakeholders (or significantly benefit them), an ethical issue is created. The causes of the ethical issues, accordingly, lie someplace in the information value-adding chain. To pinpoint responsibility we must unfold the chain.

The sonogram case chain begins with Mrs. G's decision to take the tests and includes, importantly, the doctors and the medical technologists who performed and analyzed the tests. The chain bounces back and forth between the doctors and the Gs as the test results come in and are communicated. It then goes to the doctors' final communication to the Gs and their attempts and informed consent. Finally, it rests with the Gs. If the final decision is wrong then the responsibility should be allocated appropriately along the information value-adding chain.

Table 3.1   Unfolding the G's Information and Decision-Making Moments of Truth

Information Event	Giver	Taker	Effect of Information on Decision	Time
Mrs. G becomes pregnant	—	—	Continue pregnancy	0 weeks
Learns sonogram tests available	Media	Gs	Take test (buy information)	21 weeks
Learns of boy's urinary system blockage	Doctors	Gs	Consider termination	22 weeks
Amniocentesis reveals chromosomal abnormality	Doctors	Gs	Consider termination more seriously	22 weeks
Blood tests reveal that Mrs. G has same abnormality	Doctors	Gs	Continue pregnancy	23 weeks
Fetal urine reveals kidney damage	Doctors	Gs	Consider termination	23 weeks
Mr. G's parents oppose abortion	Mr. G's parents	Gs	Continue pregnancy	23 weeks
Kidney specialists stress rigors of caring for disease	Doctors	Gs	Consider termination, change lifestyle expectations	23 weeks
Doctors stress costs, time in hospital, infections, treatments	Doctors	Gs	Consider termination, change lifestyle expectations	24 weeks
Third-trimester abortion is illegal—*Roe v. Wade*	The law	Gs	Continue pregnancy	24 weeks
Baby boy delivered	—	—	Care for child, decide on treatment	38 weeks

Table 3.1 summarizes the key information events affecting the G's decisions. Note that in this case, the Gs were the principal information takers and that the information they received affected their decision as to whether to continue the pregnancy or to abort. A variety of information givers and orchestrators were involved. A reporter learned about the availability of sonogram tests and interpreted and packaged this information in a magazine article that Mrs. G read. The information stimulated Mrs. G to be tested. Medical technicians and doctors interpreted the raw sonogram data and inferred that the male fetus's urinary system was blocked. This information was passed on to the Gs, confronting them with a new decision. Similarly, technicians and doctors acquired, processed, and stored additional test data and interpreted it for the Gs. Mr. G's parents, drawing on moral and religious beliefs, also interpreted the situation for the Gs. This information took the form of a recommendation, one likely bordering on a command. Next, the doctors, drawing on their clinical experience, prepared the Gs for the hardships that might attend a

kidney-diseased child, but they offered no recommendations. The law, in the form of the precedent of the *Roe v. Wade* decision in 1973, was interpreted as evidence in favor of continuing the pregnancy following the 24-week limitation. Ultimately, a baby boy was born. In addition to the obvious and important biological processes involved, this infant is also the product of a series of information-processing and decision-making activities. All of these activities have contributed to any ethical issues that may pertain to the birth and subsequent care of the child. Unfolding the information and decision-making processes and identifying key moments of truth helps pinpoint responsibility.

Other kinds of situations, of course, will play out differently. In exceptional cases, such as those involving misinformation, propaganda, or the divulging of confidential information, the taker may be immediately and directly harmed or may use the information to engage in actions that are very damaging to others. The taker in this event, however, did not act alone. The messages she received were also handled by orchestrators and givers. They, too, should bear some of the responsibility. Whenever you are faced with a moment of truth, tracing the information process back to its source will help you uncover the chain of contributory factors that led up to this crucial decision point.

SUMMARY

Information is used in the context of a value-adding chain. The chain consists of sources, data, inference making, valuing, and action taking. Information's ultimate value is measured in terms of the uses to which it is put, including decision making, entertainment, education, and idea generation. Its use is motivated by needs such as the pursuit of wealth, security, recreation, and control.

Because information has value, the possession and dissemination of information can change an information taker's moments of truth. Information not only influences individual decisions, it can also radically change the context and timing in which decisions are made.

For these reasons, information orchestrators, gatekeepers, and givers have a responsibility to respect the dignity and autonomy of the ultimate takers of their information. One mechanism for doing this is informed consent. Under the edicts of informed consent, a stakeholder is informed about the information processes that can affect his or her decision making or alter his or her moments of truth and approves the actions on the basis of having received and understood the relevant facts.

The concept of informed consent underlies the principles of fair information practices discussed earlier in this chapter and repeated here:

1. There must be no personal record-keeping systems whose existence is kept secret.
2. There must be a way for an individual to find out what information about him or her is on record and how it is being used.
3. There must be a way for an individual to correct or amend a record of identifiable information about him or her.
4. There must be a way for an individual to prevent information about him or her that was obtained for one purpose from being used or made available for other purposes without his or her informed consent.
5. Any organization creating, maintaining, using, or disseminating records of identifiable personal data must assure the reliability of the data for the intended use and must take reasonable precautions to prevent misuse of the data. (Laudon, Traver, & Laudon, 1994, pp. 520-521)

Decision making, informed consent, and principles of fair information practices take on more importance when a powerful agent controls the flow of information. This kind of power can be amassed by effective organizations by means of information systems. In strategy, this is called "information systems for competitive advantage." Although they create economic advantages, information systems also create ethical issues. The next chapter addresses this topic.

▨ NOTES

1. Copyright © 1994 by The New York Times Company. Reprinted by permission.
2. This case was adapted from Mason (1981).
3. Representative Ed Markey is believed to have coined the expression "knowledge, notice, and no."

4

Information Systems and Power

◩ INFORMATION SYSTEMS WIELD POWER

A sign welcoming visitors to the U.S. Department of Commerce Trademark Exposition in October 1994 announced that "Information means power, and in the 21st century, the NII (National Information Infrastructure) will be the greatest conduit to entertainment and information resources that we have ever known." The NII, pamphlets claimed, would provide new goods and services that would make the United States an even more powerful nation in this, the information era.

This is only one instance of information resulting in power. Consider also the following case:

> A Midwest sportswear manufacturer is informed by her major customer, a large retailing chain, that her company must invest in an electronic data interchange (EDI) system if she wants to continue selling to them. She learns furthermore that her firm must now be in a position to deliver substantial amounts of inventory "on demand" because the retailer tracks every sale on a point of sale recording and places orders electronically—using the retailer's data format—only when it absolutely needs replenishment and "just-in-time" delivery.

This is power in action, but it is a special kind of power. The retailing chain is using its information system to "lock in" the sportswear company and force it to do business with them in a way that minimizes the retailer's costs but not necessarily the manufacturer's. In effect, the retailer is using technology to shift some of its cost burden to the manufacturer. In the process, the balance of power is changed in favor of the retailer. This scenario is typical of today's information intensive retailing industry. Major "power retailers" such as Wal-Mart, Kmart, Target, Toys 'R' Us, Home Depot, Costco, Dillard's, and Circuit City are all using information systems to identify their customers' needs and to force their suppliers to provide inventory when they want it. "And they expect suppliers to act quickly on that knowledge," states *Business Week* in an article appropriately titled "Clout!" (Shiller, Zellner, Stodghill, Maremont, & Bureau Reports, 1992). "At Wal-Mart, for instance, more than half of its 5000 vendors get point-of-sale data. At Kmart, 2600 of 3000 suppliers have some sort of electronic linkup" (p. 69).[1]

Some of these retailers require their suppliers to put price stickers on individual packages so that the stores don't have to do it. "And one warned [their supplier that] it would impose a fine of $30,000 for errors in bar-coding on products" (Shiller et al., 1992, p. 69). As a consequence, many vendors have had to reconfigure their information and warehousing systems, install bar-coding systems, and automate their processes just to do business with these big retailers.

This is an example of a power asymmetry created in part because the giant retailers have an information advantage. In information relationships, two fundamental types of asymmetries of power arise: (a) Givers and orchestrators can control information that takers are dependent on to meet their own needs; (b) takers (or orchestrators) can force givers to provide them with information they would otherwise not have. The power retailers identified earlier are examples of the second possibility—takers who have a power advantage. As a result of the ascent of information, computer-based systems have become a major source of commercial power for these firms and for many others in many different industries.

How are we to understand this concept of power? Essentially, power is capability. In the final analysis, power is the ability to achieve one's goals. Parties with power use it to bring about consequences they desire. According to the 19th-century philosopher, Friedrich Nietzsche (1887/1924), the "will to power" is humankind's most basic drive. The pure form of this will to power is a person's will to bring to perfect fruition all of his or her capabilities. Ideally, this results in creativity; but if people fail to be creative, Nietzsche believed, they will tend to substitute power over others for their original goals. Thus, power has a kind of aphrodisiac quality to it. And because information increases one's capabilities, it, too, conveys power and is highly sought after.

Power derives from four kinds of competencies: (a) the ability to choose one's own ends, (b) the ability to acquire resources and the means needed to achieve one's ends, (c) the capacity to develop knowledge about how means can be employed to reach desired ends, and (d) the ability to overcome conflicts and barriers that stand in the way. The retailer in the case opening this chapter was in possession of all four capabilities.

There are three key characteristics of power: (a) It derives from a source called its *power base;* (b) it assumes a certain *form;* and (c) it becomes a means of securing *ends.* The source of a person's power may be derived from various bases, including authority, the use of force, charisma, wealth, status, or information and knowledge. In an information society, as we have seen, information and the systems used to acquire, process, store, disseminate, and use it have emerged as the most important base of social and personal power. This evolution can be traced throughout the history of civilization.

Second, the forms power takes include *coercion, control,* and *influence.* All of these have the effect of changing stakeholders' behavior and decision making so that they act in accord with achieving the ends. An economic threat was posed by the retailer, in effect, to coerce the sportswear company to invest in technology and inventory and to implement systems that served the retailer's needs. It is apparent that the retailer was in control of major aspects of their business relationship.

Third, typical kinds of ends include personal goals, community goals, political goals, social goals, or economic goals. For the power retailers, cost reduction and efficiency were among the strongest goals they sought. Note that it was the retailer's ends—*not* the sportswear company's ends—that dominated their relationship.

◩ HISTORICAL PERSPECTIVES ON THE EVOLUTION OF BASES OF POWER

In *Powershift: Knowledge, Wealth, and Violence at the Edge of the 21st Century* sociologist Alvin Toffler (1990) offers a grand theory that depicts a history of the social evolution of power. The development of civilization, in his view, is characterized by three major "powershifts." The first occurred when peaceful cave dwellers, such as Cro-Magnon, and other hunting and gathering societies developed weapons. Weaponry provided them with a new base of power rooted in the threat of force and violence. Indeed, the advent of force and violence as a base of power led to one of Western civilization's first recorded ethical principles. As Thucydides (1954) observed in *The Peloponnesian War,* the ancient Greeks believed that "might makes right." That is to say, the person or persons with the most power in a situation are justified to use it as they see fit. Modern ethics questions this principle by placing more emphasis on the stakeholders who are affected by the blatant use of force and violence. Nevertheless, for most of the history of civilization, the threat of violence, often supported by a might-makes-right philosophy, has served as the fundamental basis of power.

The 15th century witnessed the emergence of a new source of power—monetary wealth. During this period, the French historian Fernand Braudel (1981-1984) observes, modern market and monetary economies developed. In a monetary economy, one's ability to use money and credit (and the things they can buy) becomes a potent source of power. And it has some other advantages. Monetary wealth is a more flexible, mobile, and globally effective source of power than is violence. It can always be used to buy or sell weapons if violence is called for. So in Toffler's view, the rise of capitalism and the advent of industrial society resulted in wealth replacing violence as the predominant form of power.

Although the seeds of the information age were planted in antiquity, it was not until the later part of the 19th century that information became a widespread and coherent basis for power. To be sure, the likes of the Medicis and the Fuggers during the 16th century used their resources to develop information advantages from which they wielded enormous amounts of economic power. In a fascinating historical episode, Nathan Rothschild, a British government agent, in June 1815, dispatched messages to London by means of carrier pigeon informing his agents that Wellington had defeated Napoleon at Waterloo. His pigeons arrived well before the news traveled by conventional means, and Rothschild capitalized on this advantage to make a sizable fortune.

The exploits of these great merchants, however, are exceptions. The pursuit of wealth, especially in Europe from the 15th century on, stimulated the growth of industrialization, transportation, and urbanization, but despite this stimulus, economic growth was not widespread until about 1850 or later. About this time, a strong demand for information processing materialized and the ascent of information really began to take off.

The social and economic problems created by the rapid simultaneous growth of industry, transportation, and urbanization placed many new demands on society. The new enterprises that operated in this expanded environment needed to have larger-scale operations, faster response times, an ability to handle greater volumes, and a capacity to cope with increased complexity. All of this, sociologist James Beniger (1986) argues, created a "crisis of control"— an inability for the new society to satisfy its pressing social goals. Thus began a social revolution. The many innovations in information processing and communication technologies that appeared during the later half of the 19th century were created to provide the control required for business and government to function properly. Largely because these technological innovations were successfully integrated into it, our society was radically and irrevocably changed. As a result, information became a potent source of power.

What are the implications of this shift? The answer is straightforward and quite revealing. In this era, people and organizations can acquire, process, store, disseminate, and use larger quantities and greater varieties of information than ever before in the history of humankind. This means that agents who possess this information and who control the technologies required to handle it have much greater capacity to do what they want to do, that is, to exercise their will over others. The major tools they use for this purpose are information systems.

▧ INFORMATION SYSTEMS

An information system, according to Steven Alter (1992), is a combination of "work practices, information, people, and information technologies organized to accomplish goals in an organization" (p. 7) or in a society. Information systems are made up of hardware, software, people, data, and procedures used to perform the activities in information life cycles. In an information society, the primary function of an information system is to perform the orchestration and gatekeeping process (see Figure 4.1).

The overarching purpose of an information system is to secure improvement in a social system by means of deploying information and information technology. Both technology and information are intrinsically involved. The concept of information has already been covered in some depth in Chapter 2. Information technology is essentially its complement. It is the tangible "medium" for carrying information's intangible "message." Just as there is no information system without information, there can likewise be no information

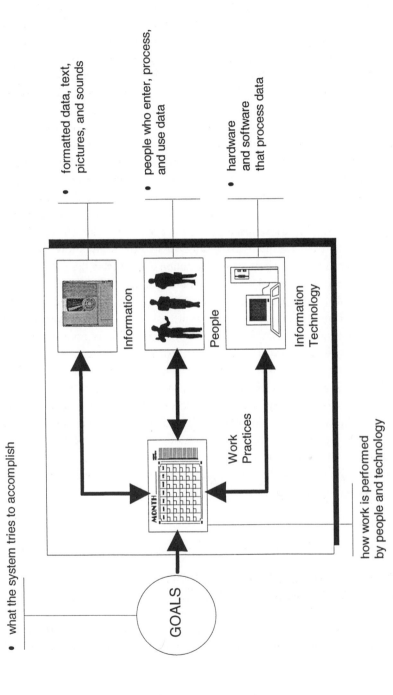

- what the system tries to accomplish

- formatted data, text, pictures, and sounds

- people who enter, process, and use data

- hardware and software that process data

Information

People

Information Technology

Work Practices

how work is performed by people and technology

GOALS

Figure 4.1. Definition of Information System

SOURCE: From *Information Systems: A Managerial Perspective* by Steven Alter. Copyright © 1992 by Addison-Wesley Publishing Company. Reprinted by permission.

without a tangible, objectified means to capture messages and record them in symbols so that they can be acquired, stored, manipulated, moved, displayed, and used. Performing these functions is the task of information technology.

The widespread use of information technology is a distinguishing feature of the information society. Our society has been shaped by a virtual explosion in the speed and capacity by which information can be handled. As these technological innovations have come into common use, information systems have become more central to our social structure and have taken on greater significance in molding people's lives at home as well as in business.

An effective information system is a formidable base of power. It can be used to change individuals and social systems by influencing people's decisions, actions, and ideas. Dictators and despots understand this fact very well. They inevitably practice information gatekeeping by seeking to control newspapers, radio broadcasting stations, telephone systems, printers, and television stations, as Hitler and Goebbels did in Nazi Germany. Most autocrats instinctively know that it is generally easier to control the flow of information by capturing the media or the technology than it is to control the content of the messages. The messages themselves are readily shareable as we have seen. Consequently, some dictators go to extremes. Stalin and his successors, for example, as part of an aggressive program to control information, took the rather excessive precaution of ordering that all typewriters in offices be registered and locked up every evening so that they could not be used to produce any unapproved messages. For the same reason, they ensured that all long-distance phone calls in the former Soviet Union were directed through (and monitored by) a central switch in Moscow. By controlling the technology, they sought to control the information. This was possible because, although they are distinct items, in application, information and information technology are intricately linked to each other. An illustration of the control of information by means of information systems and the exercise of power is found in the case of computerized airline reservation systems.

▧ AIRLINE RESERVATION SYSTEMS: A CASE OF ALLEGED MISUSE

After World War II, there was a growing awareness of the possibilities of commercial passenger flying because more people wanted to travel farther and faster. The new aircraft could potentially satisfy this new demand, but the airline companies could not process passenger reservations fast enough or accurately enough to manage the flights. A flight from New York to Los Angeles, for example, took 3 days in 1931, 21 hours in 1934, 8 hours in the mid-1950s, and 5 hours in 1958. It sometimes took more than 5 hours to accumulate and transmit the passenger information. As a result, passenger information arrived at the destination well after the plane had landed and the passengers disembarked. Aircraft capacity was getting larger, too. Planes in 1931 carried 5 or 6 passengers. By 1958, they carried more than 100. Jet aircraft offered the possibility of tripling the number of seats and halving the flying time, but they also foreshadowed a management nightmare. The crucial management process was to match the seats available on a flight with passenger reservations. The manual system was slow, cumbersome, and error prone. It was hardly adequate for the aircraft of the 1950s and would be totally inadequate for the jet age.

Cyrus Rowlett (C. R.) Smith headed American Airlines during the 1950s and was eager for it to be the first airline to enter the jet age. His enthusiasm, however, was dampened by a deep concern about his airline's ability to manage the necessary reservation systems. At C. R. Smith's instigation, American Airlines entered into an agreement with IBM to develop a computer-based information system that would solve this problem. The result was American's SABRE system. The original SABRE controlled the seat inventories maintained at each flight's point of departure and provided inventory information on all connecting flights from other cities. It also maintained a record of passengers that included name, telephone number, itinerary, and other pertinent information. SABRE was soon followed by United's APOLLO, and TWA's PARS. These computerized reservation systems (CRSs) not only solved the problem of matching passengers with available seats but also provided significant amounts of additional information that was useful for operations and for marketing.

In the early 1970s, the majority of reservations were made in airline offices or at airport counters. Travel agents made relatively few reservations and did even less ticketing. What ticketing travel agents did do was written out by hand after making one or more telephone calls to the airline to confirm availability, fares, and restrictions. Typically, travel agents used the Official Airline Guide (OAG) as their primary source of information. As long as the schedules and fares did not change very often, the OAG was a satisfactory information source, but as the number and diversity of flights increased, the "OAG plus telephone" system became sluggish and more cumbersome.

In 1976, American Airlines led a move (following United's premature announcement) to distribute CRS capacity to travel agents. SABRE was transformed from a passenger services system to a sales distribution system. Travel agents, now feeling the pinch of increased volumes, generally responded positively. Shortly thereafter in 1978, the airline industry was deregulated, and this brought about a proliferation of fares and schedules that made the need for better and faster processing acute. Now the travel agents were eager for the CRS systems. Further improvements in CRS computer capacity, software performance, and communication network efficiencies also made the systems more attractive to them. Some travel agents reported that their employees could make reservations using the CRSs in about one third the time it took to look up the schedules in the OAG and complete the necessary telephone calls. Travel agents clamored for CRSs, and as they put them into use, the number of stakeholders potentially affected by CRSs became significant.

By the early 1990s, the vast majority of airline reservations were made by travel agents using CRSs. The airlines' travel agent CRS programs were so successful that by 1982, the airlines came under the heavy scrutiny of the federal government and had attracted charges of unfair competition. The CRSs had proved to have substantial economic power.

We can get a glimpse into the nature of this power by reflecting on a couple of issues raised by the use of CRSs. One issue was called "display screen bias." When the travel agent calls up a desired destination, between 4 and 10 flights are displayed on the screen at a time. If none of the flights on the first screen are suitable, the agent can call up a second screen and so forth. Studies have shown, however, that between 70% and 90% of the bookings decisions are made from the first screen. So not surprisingly, the carriers that provided the CRS tended to ensure that their flights were prominently displayed on the first screen. Complaints were lodged by disfavored carriers claiming unfair competition. Consumers (and, of course, themselves) were being treated unfairly, these carriers argued, because they were prevented or discouraged from learning about flight offerings and fares that were superior to those of the CRS carrier. That is, the information takers are likely to make decisions different from what they would make had they been given full information.

Information distortion was another issue. CRS carriers controlled the information that is loaded into their systems. Charges were made, however, of the following abuses:

> delays in the input of information on an attractive low fare until the host carrier had had an opportunity to decide whether to match the new low fare;

the consistent omission or misstatement of flight information, particularly on
hotly contested routes;

displays showing flights as full when, in fact, many seats remained available, or vice
versa; and

disregard of directions to close a capacity-controlled low fare, resulting in far more
people traveling on the flight at a low fare than the airline had intended.
(*Note on Airline Reservation Systems,* 1985, p. 26)

▨ THE PARADOX OF POWER

These ethical issues reveal a great deal about the power of information and
its potential for abuse. First, there is the *paradox of power*. SABRE, APOLLO,
and PARS were attractive to travel agents because these systems solved pressing
information-processing problems for them. They helped travel agents become
more efficient and more effective. Consequently, they had a strong economic
incentive to acquire their CRS services. Initially, both parties benefited as more
and more volume was put through the systems. In fact, the more business that
was placed through a CRS, the more services and better cost structure the CRS
owner could provide. In the process, however, the travel agents became very
dependent on and vulnerable to the CRS carriers because the CRS owners now
offered a service that the agents needed and few, if any, alternatives were
available. The CRS carriers also had access to considerable amounts of information about the travel agents and their businesses. This meant that the CRS
carriers had gained a substantial power advantage in their marketplace, and
they could use this asymmetry to compel travel agents and others to do things
they would not otherwise have done. Generally speaking, the same thing
happened with the power retailers. The vendors who made investments in
systems to do business with the power retailers benefited substantially until
they became too dependent on a single large customer and had changed a way
of doing business to one that was very specific to only that retailing firm. Both
the vendors and the travel agents faced crucial moments of truth when they
decided to enter these business relationships.

The CRS providers used their power in several ways. Because they had control
of the technology, they determined the sequence with which available flights would
appear on the computer screens. Competitors claimed, however, that the information screens were biased and therefore consumers and, perhaps, even the travel

agents themselves were harmed. Because the information services available in the CRSs was so valuable, it was alleged, the CRS carriers were in a position to charge inflated rates for participation. The CRS carriers, consequently, had preferential access to the revenue stream and secured the advantages of float and breakage. That is why they were willing to install their systems in travel agents' offices at rates below cost. These, too, were important moments of truth.

In the process of buying market share, the CRS carriers also shut out other competitors while they were enhancing their own power. Their success meant that other non-CRS carriers were virtually forced to have access to their CRSs so that their flights could be listed and booked. This made it possible for the CRS carriers to charge high booking fees or to use booking fee rates as a factor in negotiations with the airline. The CRS carriers also secured an advantage in service and marketing information. First, they were in a position to omit, delay, or distort their competitors' information to their advantage. Second, they could get access to proprietary information about a travel agent's businesses and use that information to their own advantage.

The story of airline computer reservation systems is a remarkable chapter in American business history. By means of information technology, an entire industry was transformed. Large numbers of stakeholders benefited, for the most part. CRSs made it possible for the airlines to offer more flights and services at a variety of price levels. Passengers and travel agents alike benefited. And as American Airlines executive Max Hopper (1990) points out, the airline made a considerable "up front" financial investment just to bring SABRE into existence. This economic disadvantage could only be overcome by using the system effectively.

Paradoxically, however, by providing all of these benefits, the CRS carriers were able to secure considerable power over their customers. Some of the ways this power was used are ethically questionable. At a key moment of truth, the providers of SABRE, APOLLO, and PARS decided to control the information that the travel agents received and thereby influence their decisions in ways that were not entirely consistent with the travel agents' or their passengers' best interests or goals. Because they were in control, the CRS carriers could sell their services at prices above the market, knowing that the travel agents and other carriers needed these services if they were to stay in business. As a result, the very social and economic success of the computerized reservations systems raised some classical issues in the ethics of information. In one highly publicized case, Frontier Airlines filed suit against United Airlines claiming that

United's unfair use of its APOLLO system drove them out of business. The case was finally settled out of court.

These CRS issues reveal the considerable power that can be accrued by using information systems. Whenever you work with information—be it to develop a budget with a spreadsheet, produce sensitive information about medical tests, or manage a large-scale travel reservation system—you are exercising power. The criticality of your moments of truth surrounding information depends a great deal on the power behind the choices you make. A revisit to the process of credit reporting illustrates further how this can affect people in everyday life.

◣ CREDIT REPORTING: INFORMATION POWER AT WORK

When Ron Martin (a fictitious name but a true story) was transferred by his company from Portland, Oregon, to Sacramento, California, he and his family found a house they liked and could afford in a subdivision called Foothill Farms. It had three bedrooms and was just 1 block from a respected grade school, about 2 blocks from the community "cabana club" swimming pool, and a brief 10-minute drive to his office. In addition, a large tree braced the front yard, shielding the house from the hot, late afternoon summer sun. All things considered, it seemed like the perfect place. The Martins made an offer and it was accepted. But soon some strange things began to happen.

At first, everything seemed to be in order. A sizable "earnest" money payment was in escrow, the necessary down payment was in the bank, proof of employment and income level was satisfactory, and the appropriate insurance policies had been requested. The real estate agent and the mortgage banker gave every indication that it was, as the agent put it, "a done deal." But one detail remained. The mortgage lender wanted a credit report "for the record." With the Martin's permission, a credit report was ordered.

A few days later, the lender's agent called to say that, unfortunately, the bank couldn't approve the mortgage application. The credit report showed that "Ron Martin" was a swimming pool contractor who a few years earlier had deluged Sacramento with a special discount on backyard pools. After a successful sales blitz he had disappeared, leaving a lot of angry homeowners with partially dug holes in their yards and a lineup of creditors with unpaid bills. The woman said that she was puzzled at this turn of events, but bank policy precluded her granting the loan unless the matter was cleared up. After numerous days of frantic phone calls and searching for records, Martin was able to provide enough documentation to convince the mortgage bank that he was not the same Ron Martin. The loan was finally granted, but not until, paradoxically, Ron Martin signed a small ream of papers stating that he was not "Ron Martin." For several years afterwards, his records carried an alert stating that he might be "Ron Martin," deadbeat swimming pool contractor.

This is the power of information in action. The credit report was virtually decisive in determining whether or not the Martins would get a loan on their new house. In fact, the Martins were powerless in their efforts to buy a home until the information error was corrected. The mortgage bank, in pursuit of its legitimate goal of assuring itself that there was a high probability that the loan payments would be made in a timely manner, used the information on the credit report to make its decision. But because this information was inaccurate, the Martins were almost thwarted in achieving their own equally legitimate goal of purchasing a home that met their needs. Furthermore, the Martins had not been previously informed about the discrepancy. The fault, in this particular instance, lay in the information itself and in the system that produced it. Accuracy and quality of information is a fundamental issue in an information society. Understanding the forces and effects of inaccuracy requires an examination of the systems that produced the problem as well as identifying its effects.

The use of credit reports can create ethical issues that range far beyond just credit-granting decisions. During the last decade or so, the credit bureau business has expanded well beyond its original intent of helping credit grantors make lending decisions. Today, credit reports are used for many other purposes, such as preemployment screening, insurance underwriting, monitoring customers' accounts to increase or decrease their credit limits, and targeted marketing of prospective customers for credit cards. These uses, too, influence many important decisions that in turn affect people's lives. Moreover, because all of these uses are made without the original giver's knowledge or informed consent, they may result in an invasion of people's privacy.

The information contained in credit reports is an example of information with very powerful consequences. As a citizen in the information society you, too, are likely to work with information such as credit reports, airline reservations, bank accounts, personal records, customer transaction records, books, records, videos, or any of a number of information sources that also have powerful consequences. This work takes you into the realm of information fields, power fields, and their ethical implications.

▧ POWER FIELDS AND INFORMATION FIELDS

Some theoretical concepts are useful for exploring the ways in which information affects people's lives. The extent of the power of any item of concern is defined by the field in which it is used. A *field* is an idealization that is used to encompass all of the relevant factors related to an agent, item, or activity. Conceptually, a field comprehends the span of time, space, and form in which an agent's or item's influence is felt. In the ethics of information, we generally focus on three basic fields: the information field, the power field, and the ethical field.

Power Fields

The term *power field* is used to describe the extent of the influence of the power. The idea is familiar in other contexts. In the military, for example, it is common to describe weapons in terms of the range, velocity, and force of their destructive impact. A pistol has an effective range measured in tens of yards, whereas a mortar's range may extend to hundreds of yards. A Howitzer has a higher trajectory, and its range is measured in miles. These ranges and the number of affected parties, of course, may be extended if we take into account the mobility of the agents who make use of them and the methods used to deploy them. Formulating military tactics and strategy, however, depends substantially on the strategist's understanding of the characteristics and field of impact of the weapons at his or her disposal. The idea of a power field is merely an extension of this familiar approach.

A power field describes all of the parties and activities affected by a particular kind of power base. A weaponry field, for example, includes all those affected by the force of a particular weapon within a certain geographical region and a certain span of time and the kinds of effects inflicted on them. Similarly, a wealth field includes all those who have an interest in, or who might be affected by the use of, a definable accumulation of assets and resources. Agents' power, therefore, may be measured by their ability to achieve their goals when they are operating within a specific field (i.e., their power field) as defined by a discernible matrix of space, time, and form.

This set of concepts takes on more practical meaning when one focuses on particular kinds of fields. A different range of possible outcomes and effects pertains rather uniquely to each different field. Possessing weapons, for example, opens up one set of possibilities with respect to threats, violence, and force, whereas having wealth makes available another set, one focused on economic outcomes. Holding information has yet a third set of possibilities. The principal defining characteristics of an information field include the information it contains and the relationships that it has with a set of stakeholders. This leads us to a fundamental principle:

- The ethics of information is concerned with how agents make use of the power of information within a describable information field.

Information Fields

An *information field* is the collection of all stakeholders (and this includes all of their minds) who in any way participate in an information system or any information activity. Included in an information field are all of the givers, takers, and orchestrators who are part of an information system plus, importantly, all of the stakeholders affected by information giving, taking, and orchestrating processes. An information field encompasses the reach of influence of an information system and includes the system's agents and stakeholders. Ron Martin's credit record field, for example, includes him, all of the retailers and credit grantors he has done business with, all of the people and organizations that have accessed or potentially will access this data, and all those who have worked to produce and disseminate his record. It's a pretty substantial group. The information field of one large credit bureau, for example, encompasses the information fields of all of the 150 million or so people it has files on. It's a massive group. The entire credit reporting industry's information field is larger still. The story of CRSs also illustrates just how large this range of influence can be. As we will see later, ethical thinking about information and information systems is based on a determination of the relevant information field.

Who, for example, is affected when Ron Martin's credit report is in error, and how are they affected? Martin, his family, his employer, the real estate agent, the bank, the mortgage company, and other retailers who may want to sell him merchandise are among the first wave of those affected. Among those affected by secondary and tertiary effects are the community as a whole, others who seek mortgages, and, perhaps, the other Ron Martin himself. Only with this general knowledge of the situation can one determine the kinds of actions that might be taken on the basis of items of information and what the results might be. This fact finding and problem scoping, as will be discussed more thoroughly later, is essential for all ethical thinking.

The idea of a field is important because when you are making an ethical judgment, you should understand the full range of the flow of information and the full impact of the power it carries. It is essential for making effective policy and for thinking effectively at the moment of truth.

Ethical Fields

Finally, an *ethical field* is a collection of all of the values, rights and wrongs, goods and bads, just and unjust considerations that pertain to agents and stakeholders in the information and power fields. As will be covered in more detail in the next two chapters, ethical fields contain corrective vision considerations about what ought to be the case.

▨ INFORMATION POLICY: WHAT IS TO BE DONE?

The ability to accumulate large amounts of power by means of information systems raises questions about institutional structure and regulation. If the result of using these systems is unethical, should some of the power they wield be restrained or channeled in some more socially desirable way? How are people's rights to be protected?

For the most part, Western societies have answered these questions implicitly by adopting a philosophy of laissez-faire. But this means that technology companies will continue to develop more hardware and software, designers and systems integrators will put together more systems, and organizations will deploy them to achieve their own goals and objectives. Many of us, of course, understandably balk at the notion of curtailing this process of free enterprise. Gatekeeping and censorship are generally undesirable actions to take, and

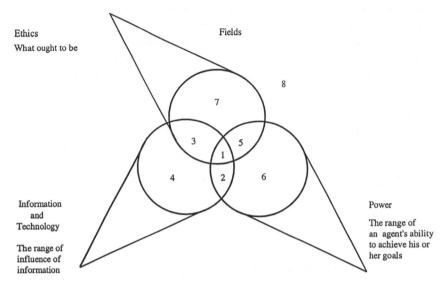

Figure 4.2. Three Primary Perspectives in the Ethics of Information

usually, they are based more on fear than on understanding. Bureaucratic regulation is often inefficient. At times, it can be downright asinine. Nevertheless, certain abuses of the power of information systems likely require some form of social control. We should recognize that not to have a policy—to pursue laissez-faire—is itself a policy decision and that as the CRS and credit bureau cases bear out, disadvantaged parties have been harmed and have been reduced to seeking relief from the courts, legislators, and regulators. Chapters 9 and 10 expand on this point.

Figure 4.2 provides some conceptual guidance for developing policies. Basically, information policies should have the effect of pushing the information and the power fields upward so that Area 1 in the diagram is expanded and that Areas 2, 4, and 6 are reduced. Area 2—information with power behind it that is unethical—is an especially good candidate for elimination. Table 4.1 provides some illustrations of situations falling within each of the possible combinations of fields.

Table 4.1 Using Fields to Classify Situations: Some Hypothetical Examples

1. Info	Power	Ethical	The information emanating from an information system is energized with power to achieve ethical goals. Example: Lotus MarketPlace: Households data are used to help small businesses contact willing customers.
2. Info	Power	Unethical	The information emanating from an information system is energized with power to achieve unethical goals. Example: Lotus MarketPlace: Households data are used to reveal personal information about individuals.
3. Info	Without power	Ethical	Information with ethical potential fails to have an effect because it is not energized with power. Example: Lotus MarketPlace: Households data with potential to improve the delivery of government services is not used.
4. Info	Without power	Unethical	Information with the capability to do harm lies fallow because it is not energized with power. Example: Lotus MarketPlace: Households data that might be used to bribe a person is not used.
5. Noninfo	Power	Ethical	Wealth or violence is used to achieve ethical goals. Example: Lotus and Equifax use this economic wealth to create a distribution network.
6. Noninfo	Power	Unethical	Wealth or violence is used to achieve unethical goals. Example: Lotus and Equifax develop a plan to bribe government officials to make favorable decisions on sales locations.
7. Noninfo	Without power	Ethical	Items with ethical potential fail to have an effect because they are not energized with power. Example: Lotus and Equifax use their economic wealth to make funds available for homeless children but do not provide the advertising funds or management guidance necessary to make the program work.
8. Noninfo	Without power	Unethical	Items with unethical possibilities do not materialize because they are not energized with power. Example: Nothing bad happens.

SUMMARY

As a citizen of the information society, whether you like it or not, you are in the power business. Rather than wielding a stick or a fist, you wield some intangible, symbolic stuff called information. Its effect, however, can be every bit as strong as violence or money for achieving your goals or those of your employer. As the information age matures, the power of information is increasing. This is due in part to the marvelous range of technologies and systems that can be used to control the flow of information. Most likely, you are familiar with some of these technologies and systems or use them in your daily work or studies. Most of us, however, do not tend to think of them as tools of power. But they are. For this reason, we need to understand something about information, information technologies, and information systems as a basis of power. Several concepts that are helpful in this task are summarized next.

Information technology is the tangible means by which information is manipulated and carried to its ultimate users. An information system is a collection of information and information technology—including hardware, software, people, data, and procedures—designed to deliver services intended to improve a social system. An information system begins with the giving processes, comprehends the orchestration processes, and ends with the taking processes. Throughout all of these processes, multiple minds are linked. The full range of effect of an information system—and hence of the information and information technology it contains—defines an information field. All significant physical and psychological changes that result from an information system are included in its information field.

Because power is the ability to bring about desired consequences in the form of physical and psychological changes, an information field can also be compared to its related power field. Information serves as a base of power informing the decision, influence, control, and coercive actions used to achieve one's goals. Information that is energized by power can be used in either ethical or unethical ways. Consequently, an ethical field consisting of considerations about what ought or ought not be the case is needed to evaluate its situation.

The ascent of information starting with Cro-Magnon and moving forward to the present reveals a history of an ever-increasing accumulation of power leading to additional ethical concerns. Several case histories highlight some contemporary dimensions of this concern.

The credit reporting industry story shows how information about people collected for one purpose can be used for purposes not originally intended. It can result in an invasion of privacy, the receipt of unwanted marketing solicitations, and people made considerably more vulnerable due to inaccurate information. The airline computer reservation systems story demonstrates that once organizations gain control of large amounts of valuable information, they can also control the flow of that information to their own advantage. Screen bias, information distortion, violation of proprietary property rights, and unfair marketing tactics were alleged. All of these allegations revolved around the use of the power the CRS providers had accumulated by means of the information, technology, and systems they developed and controlled. Finally, the power retailers are using information systems to force their vendors to change their business processes and to invest in technology to do business with them.

All three situations reveal the paradox of power. The information systems deployed by the organizations in these industries provided enormous benefits to many parties. These parties, in turn, wanted more of the benefits generated by the information and this, in turn, served to enhance the power of the organizations that controlled the provision of information. For the most part this power has been used for the benefit of a wide range of parties. But this power has also been abused. The power of these information-intensive industries is now so great as to warrant legislation and regulatory action and made the potential for information power an important factor in forging a new social contract. The policies that will lead society toward this new social contract will have the effect of pushing information fields and power fields farther within the circle of ethical behavior. Yet we have left unanswered what this ethical behavior is and how it might be discovered. This is the subject of the next two chapters.

▨ NOTE

1. Reprinted by permission of *Business Week*.

PART II

Fundamentals of Ethics

Throughout history, humanity has tried to develop values and beliefs to guide successfully the morality of our conduct. We have asked questions such as, What is right or wrong, good or bad, fair or unfair, just or unjust, acceptable or unacceptable behavior? The products of these struggles are theories and principles that can be applied to the variety of situations we face. This part summarizes the results of this long struggle in a manner that makes them applicable to ethical issues raised by the information age. Chapter 5 provides an overall method for thinking about ethical issues and arriving at decisions. Chapter 6 presents a general framework for selecting ethical theories that are relevant to the issues you face and delves more deeply into specific ethical theories.

5

Ethical Thinking

Dealing with the ethical issues that surround information requires ethical thinking. Ethical thinking is the cognitive means we use when we pause to reflect on ethical issues. It helps us make good judgments at a moment of truth. *Ethical thinking* is defined as the systematic examination of ethical issues at a moment of truth to determine whether an agent's actual or contemplated behavior is ethical or unethical or whether, alternatively, there are no ethical considerations involved (see, for example, Figures 1.2 and 1.3). Ethical thinking is required whenever an agent's behavior might materially affect a stakeholder's ability to achieve his or her goals. That is, one should pause to reflect whenever his or her behavior might impair a stakeholder's dignity, welfare, or sense of justice. Simply put, ethical thinking is required whenever one might harm or significantly help another person, and it involves sorting out moral goods from moral evils.

⬚ MORAL GOODS

Moral goods, philosophers Grisez and Shaw (1980) explain, are things that foster "human *being* and *being more,* human living and living more fully" (p. 2). This means that the good, wherever we find it—in art, health, technology, or intellectual activity—has a future component attached to it. Good actions open up new possibilities for people. Stakeholders' capabilities to function, for example, are expanded or improved. Acts that create moral goods are often called "praiseworthy" and are commonly said to be ethical or moral acts.

Ethics tends to get a bad rap. People often use the term to describe only unsavory behavior. Fortunately, all ethical issues do not involve doing bad things. Ethics deals with good, right, and just behavior as well as with evil, wrong, and unjust behavior. A potentially praiseworthy act occurs whenever an agent makes an exceptional effort to help a stakeholder reach his or her goals and to foster that person's humanity.

This is the tradition of the Good Samaritan, the one who provides aid and succor to sojourners in need. The Good Samaritan story illustrates Jesus' extension of the concept of "Love your neighbor as yourself" to include giving love to pure strangers. In Luke 10:30-32 (Revised Standard Version [RSV]), a man traveling from Jerusalem to Jericho is robbed, beaten, and left for dead. A priest and a Levite traveling down the same road see him but ignore him and pass him by.

> But a Samaritan, as he journeyed, came to where he was; and when he saw him, he had compassion, and went to him and bound up his wounds, pouring on oil and wine; then he set him on his own beast and brought him to an inn, and took care of him. And the next day, he took out two denarii and gave them to the innkeeper, "Take care of him; and whatever more you spend, I will repay you, when I come back." (Luke 10:33-35, RSV)

The information age has already produced a few technological Good Samaritans. Al Ross is one of them. Each year, thousands of children are born with severe physical handicaps, such as cerebral palsy, that keep them from communicating with others and participating in society. Al Ross, a research engineer at the University of Washington, refused to pass them by. While videotaping students in a special education class developed to teach them how to type using a head wand, he agonized over their frustration. This was for him a heartfelt moment of truth. There must be a better answer, he thought. The result of his reflection was a plan that included a portable, microprocessor-based, alternative communication system featuring earphones equipped with sensors and a Morse code tapping device. With this system, handicapped people could "talk" to the world. Steve Harper, a 13-year-old mute with cerebral palsy, used the new technology to send a thank-you letter to the president of the United States. As writer Joel Schwartz (1983) observes, "The moving letter was one young boy's celebration of freedom—the freedom to express himself clearly and to be understood after a lifetime without communication" (p. 115). Others shared in the joy. Tina Nott, the mother of 15-year-old Tania Nott, another participant in the program, exclaimed, "This machine is irreplaceable, the best thing that ever happened" (Goodnow, 1982, p. E4).

◩ MORAL EVILS

A *moral evil,* on the other hand, is anything that "puts limits on human beings and contracts human life" (Grisez & Shaw, 1980, p. 87). It cuts off a stakeholder's further possibilities. Evil activities carried to the limit ultimately result in a kind of existential suicide. The stakeholders affected by a potentially unethical act may, for example, be killed, maimed, insulted, embarrassed, dishonored, compromised, frustrated, made anxious, troubled, or confused; they may lose money or simply be inconvenienced. In some cases, the affected party may not even be aware of the harm, at least for some time. Behavior that results in a moral evil is frequently said to be unethical or immoral.

◩ NONETHICAL BEHAVIOR

There is a vast middle ground between unethical behavior and praiseworthy behavior. This area does not admit to fine moral distinctions. Yet it describes most of our normal day-to-day behavior, most of which raises no significant ethical issues at all. Many acts we take during the course of everyday life simply do not deprive parties from reaching their goals. Nor do they exceptionally assist them. As LA Laker sports broadcaster Chick Hearn says, "No harm, no foul" (or "No help, no praise"). We tend to call these acts "nonethical" or "*a*moral" because they do not raise questions of either praiseworthiness or blame.

Understanding this midground of ethical behavior, however, is important. Normal behavior includes typical behavior and behavior that is consistent with the norms of society. *Norms,* as sociologists view them, are sets of implicit social rules that describe standards, models, or patterns of behavior expected of members in a society. They are mental models that tell us what *should* happen in a given situation. They serve as the basis for mutual cooperation and reduce conflict among people. A society's norms are part of its *social contract.* They are part of an unwritten agreement between its members to behave with reciprocal responsibility in their relationships with one another. Good societies try to establish and promote norms that encourage what they consider to be good or even praiseworthy behavior. Breaches of these norms or other violations of the

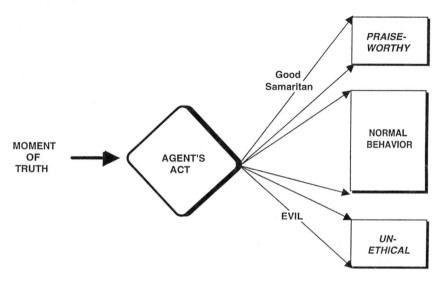

Figure 5.1. Domain of Ethics

social contract—unless they are legitimated by even stronger ethical norms—are unethical. Generally, they call for sanctions of some kind.

When you make a judgment on an ethical issue you are in effect placing an agent's act on a continuum running from praiseworthy (or angelic) at one end to evil at the other. Nonethical and normal behavior fills a large segment in the middle (see Figure 5.1).

▧ ETHICS AS CORRECTIVE VISION: ACTUAL VERSUS THEORY

Ethical theories and principles are tools to use for ethical thinking. They help us reflect on the facts of a case. Ethical theories provide standards for behavior that help us compare "what is" with "what ought to be." Thus, as ethicist William F. May (1983) proposes, ethical thinking involves *corrective vision* (see Figure 5.2). "Ethics supplies a type of *corrective* lens" and "relies heavily on the distinction between what is and what ought to be" (p. 13). Only

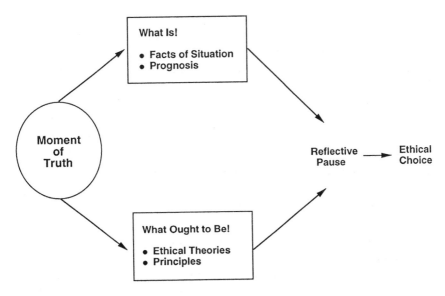

Figure 5.2. Corrective Vision

after comparing what is to what ought to be, can an ethical judgment be rendered.

The intellectual process of ethical corrective vision is not unlike the physiological process an optometrist uses. If you wear glasses, you know what it is like to try to see without them. Things are blurry and out of focus. But that is what you *actually* see. In the ethical language of corrective vision, that is "what is." You go to an optometrist to see better than you could without an aid of some type. You want, say, 20/20 vision. The optometrist sits you down in a large chair and affixes a contraption over your head. The optometrist asks you to look at a line of letters and numbers on the wall, chooses a lens, rotates the contraption, and asks you to look at the line. "Is it clearer?" he or she asks, noting your response and trying another lens. The process is repeated, perhaps many times, until you say that the lens is "just right." If you have an unusual problem, it may take a combination of lenses for you to achieve 20/20 eyesight, that is, until you can see "what ought to be."

Ethical thinking generally follows the same steps. The facts of an ethical issue are established. This is what is. Then various principles or theories of ethics are applied to the facts to see what light they shed on the case. These theories are the lenses through which you gain a better idea of what ought to be. After trying out various theories in various combinations, you find the solution that best resolves your ethical issue. This becomes the basis for an ethical judgment. Chapter 6 summarizes some of the major ethical theories that can be used to make these judgments.

How might ethical thinking be applied in the ubiquitous, networked, multimedia information age in which we live? Let's look at a couple of scenarios.

◩ IT MIGHT HAPPEN TOMORROW

The phone rang in Bill Daniels's office. He punched "Command S" on his keyboard to save the project he was working on as he turned from the screen to the phone and picked up the receiver. "Hello. This is Bill Daniels."

"Good morning Bill. Masterson Cosimo, here. I need to ask you a few questions."

Bill gulped. Why was the corporate chief financial officer calling him? he wondered as he said, "Sure, how can I help you?"

"First a few background questions. Is your job description product manager for our StoreWell database product?"

"Yes."

"How long have you held this job?"

"About one and a half years."

"How old are you?"

"Thirty-three at my last birthday."

Puzzled, Bill thought to himself, "Why is he asking these questions? Surely he has access to my file and knows the answers." Then the bombshell hit.

"Have you ever smoked marijuana?"

"Well, ahh, When? What do you mean? What difference does it make?"

"I just need a yes or no answer, Bill."

"Not while I have worked for SoftWell Products."

"Noted! Now another question. About your trip to California last month to meet with the users' group. I note a $276 entertainment charge for Saturday night. Was this all business?"

"Why, yes. Am I being investigated or something? Should I consult my lawyer?"

"Bill, I must inform you that everything you say is being recorded and analyzed on the company's 'truth phone.' "

Bill gasped, set the receiver back in its cradle, slumped in his chair, put his head on his desk, and tried to think through the implications of what he had just experienced.

A truth phone converts the speaker's voice messages to a stream of bits that when fed into a microprocessor can produce running digital voice stress analysis readings. These readings, in turn, can be used to determine whether or not the speaker is lying. At least one American company, Communications Control Systems, is gearing up to market truth phones. "Insurance companies are reportedly among the first customers for the truth phone, using it to determine whether claims from clients should be investigated" (Harper, 1993, p. 13). As the preceding scenario suggests, however, some people will find many other "creative" applications of truth phones. Several ethical issues are raised by these applications. Many of these issues will be discussed later, but first let's look at another scenario—one a little closer to home.

◣ IT COULD BE HAPPENING TODAY

Denise Dederik veered to the lane marked Toll Tags Only, slowing to about 15 miles per hour. She began picking up speed as her Accord passed the unattended glass stall. Behind the scenes, an electronic transmitter continuously showered the tollbooth's entryway with a barrage of radio signals. A small credit-card-sized tag mounted on the windshield of the Accord received a signal and reflected Denise's account number to the lane controller, which, in turn, flashed it back to the main computer where her prepaid account was debited. Simultaneously, the time, location, and other particulars of the event were stored in the computer's files. Denise triggers these events every weekday at about 11:40 a.m. when she commutes to her job at XTN Transportation and again about 8:30 p.m. when she returns. Periodically, of course, she triggers them again when she drives into town for shopping, dinner, or to attend the symphony.

Last week, Denise received a letter from Hartford Honda Service Company offering her a special new service. Because she was an "early-evening-shift worker" who had a very fine credit rating, she was encouraged to drop off her car about noon at a service center near her office when its 90-day checkup or other maintenance was required. She could pick up the car again at 8:00 that evening, and her account would be automatically billed for the service. She would be mailed a statement once a month. The letter also noted that because she commuted about 46 miles each way every day, she would receive regular reminders about buying gas, getting oil changes and brake checkups, and purchasing other products or services that depended on automobile usage. The letter also reminded her that she could facilitate the service when she arrived if she called the company's 800 number from her cellular phone on her way to work.

At first, Denise was delighted. The service helped solve a problem she had doing business with organizations that were not open when she finished work. But her delight soon turned to anger and fear as she realized what the contents of the letter implied. "How did they know my work schedule?" she wondered. In fact, Hartford Honda Service knew quite a bit about her. She had purchased the electronic toll tag service because of the convenience it offered. Now, this company was offering her additional conveniences. "But at what price?" she thought. She was suddenly aware that she had unwittingly revealed a great deal about herself and her daily habits to Hartford Honda Service, a company with which she had had no previous relationship. How many other organizations had acquired information about her, she wondered? Were the benefits she received from the electronic toll tag worth this threat to her privacy? Was she now vulnerable to other nefarious, perhaps very evil, uses of the information about her? Were there any safeguards in place to protect her?

◩ THE NEED FOR ETHICAL THINKING IN THE SCENARIOS

Several ethical issues are raised in the preceding scenarios. Both Masterson Cosimo and Hartford Honda Service (and perhaps also the Toll Booth Authority) are takers who were using information about Bill and Denise (the givers) in a way that potentially violates their right to privacy. If this is true, Bill's and Denise's future freedom of choice will be limited. Both will be thwarted in their attempts to realize as fully as they might their possibilities as human beings.

There are several crucial moments of truth in each of these scenarios. The SoftWell Products Company faced a moment of truth when it decided to install the truth phone system, thereby opening up a new set of technological possibilities. Masterson Cosimo faced a moment of truth when he decided to use the truth phone when he called Bill. He will face another very crucial moment if he decides to use the information he collected about Bill. Bill also faced moments of truth as he responded to Cosimo's call. The Toll Booth Authority (and its systems designers) faced a moment of truth when it decided to implement a system that collected transaction data for identifiable individuals and a significant moment of truth when it decided to sell that data to Hartford Honda Service. Hartford Honda's crucial moment of truth came when the company decided to use the data to embark on a targeted marketing program.

How might the operative vision at these moments of truth have been corrected?

In these scenarios, neither information giver was offered a choice to participate in the decisions that influence the collection and use of the data. There was no informed consent. Bill was subjected to what is in effect an electronic lie detector test without his knowledge. Denise was similarly uninformed about the additional uses made of data about her. In neither case was the giver's consent solicited. An agent can justify his or her behavior in part by notifying givers of possible uses and gaining their consent. Had Denise been informed fully about the possible uses of the data generated about her driving habits she might well have decided *not* to participate in the electronic toll tag program. That is, she might have made a conscious trade-off and decided that her privacy—not revealing information about herself and her behavior patterns to others and not placing herself in a situation in which she was vulnerable to the misuse of information collected about her—was much more important than any conveniences the system provided. These harms may well have outweighed the benefits, but she was not offered the opportunity to decide for herself. The principle of informed consent requires that she be informed of this new use of the data she has supplied.

The principles of fair information practices, as discussed in Chapter 3, also pertain in this case. They require that there be no secret personal record-keeping systems, that both Bill and Denise have a way to find out what information is being kept about them, and that the organizations involved adopt procedures for correcting their records if they are in error. Furthermore, the information takers should not use the information for any purposes other than those for which it was originally collected, without the subjects' consent. Neither Hartford Honda, the Toll Booth Authority, nor SoftWell Products had adopted these procedures.

Invasion of privacy, lack of notification, accuracy, property, and entrapment are among the ethical issues that require ethical thinking in these two scenarios. Each of these issues was generated by the use of new technology and the information it generated. In the process, the implied social contract that exists between Bill and his institution and between Denise and hers was altered. Introducing new technology into a social system changes the social relationships between its members and thereby affects the existing social contract. Frequently, existing norms are challenged. Generally speaking, new technologies have the capability of increasing agents' breadth of options for action. New technologies enhance agents' power and redefine the balance of power among stakeholders.

The use of electronic toll booths for example, raises a vital ethical issue: What information about a person should be collected and how should it be used? The facts of the case include the capturing and storing in a computer's memory detailed data about automobiles that pass through the booths, linking that data with other information about the driver, and providing the information to other users. Most of the data collected is needed by the toll booth authority to do the necessary accounting required to offer the service. This aspect of what is versus what ought to be presents minor, if any, ethical issues. Most people would agree that few if any people are materially affected by these actions.

Issues arise, however, when the information is shared with others or put to uses other than only those needed to provide the service. People's "will to power" and the unique characteristics of information discussed in Chapter 2 suggest that both the motivation and the capability exist to share the information with others. When the data is used in this manner, the possibility of materially affecting some givers or stakeholders, such as Denise, is greatly increased. Subscribers can be harassed or compromised, for example, and speeders automatically ticketed. Consequently, this additional use of the information requires careful ethical examination.

Some observers of the electronic toll booth situation believe that the threat to privacy is, indeed, significant. "We think there is a real privacy concern [with the use of electronic toll systems]," says privacy advocate Marc Rotenberg of Computer Professionals for Social Responsibility. "Creating mountains of personal information about where people drive is not good" (quoted in Sharn, 1993, p. 1). Others downplay the threat. "Who would care how many times you crossed the bridge?" counters Randal Paisant of the Crescent City Connection in New Orleans (quoted in Sharn, 1993, p. 1).[1] A third perspective is

Investigative reporters, for example, who turn up an occasional moral lapse or indiscretion on the part of a community member actually smear the entire community. They tar everyone with a brush intended for just a few. Muckrakers, in their search for wrongdoing and corruption, these dissenters go on to say, usually end up discrediting all of the very good and beneficial things that a person or organization has done. In their view, ethical thinking raises unnecessary apprehensions, fears, and anxiety. Some who take this view even question that information used for purposes other than those for which it was collected creates any ethical issues. "So you get a little extra mail. What's the fuss?"

In discussions about the relative merits of the use of information or information technology, you are likely to hear one or more of these viewpoints expressed—sometimes moderately, occasionally in the extreme. As is true of most debates, each of these three criticisms contains a grain of truth. But that doesn't mean we should "throw out the baby with the dirty bath water." Those of us who believe in the value of ethical thinking have a deep and abiding belief in the potential of ethical reflection for improving the human condition.

Proponents of ethical thinking believe that (a) the agent with the most power—be its source violence, wealth, or information—is not necessarily always right; (b) the social and cultural institutions that our society has created, as good as they may be, are not ethically pure or perfect; and (c) there are clearly times when responsible citizens must point out and make public what they believe to be unethical behavior, regardless of who the perpetrator is. For these reasons there is a role in society for ethical norms and standards of behavior. Why?

Because normlessness creates havoc. Letting each individual pursue his or her own interest wantonly and without constraint leads to an intolerable condition, one that the 17th-century philosopher, Thomas Hobbes (1651/ 1839), summed up as "a war of every man against every man" (p. 112). Society needs norms and moral standards to avoid this chaos. Indeed, there are times during which an individual's unrestrained pursuit of his or her own interests is itself destructive of that person's own aims. That is, people can act in ways that actually harm their own interests. Ethical norms and moral standards help us cope with these kinds of ongoing dilemmas. They provide the essential basis of trust and cooperation on which to build a good society. Ethical dialogues are valuable means for helping us arrive at principles, norms, and standards for guiding our behavior and for pursuing the illusive social goal of mutual cooperation and trust.

◩ FOUR TYPES OF ETHICAL ISSUES

Active, Pressing Issues

Temptations

A *temptation* occurs at a moment of truth during which an agent is faced with making a choice, and the agent can determine which choices are morally good and which are morally wrong, but he or she is tempted to choose the wrong. For example, to lie, steal, or cheat simply to promote one's own self-interests are typically considered to be wrong behaviors in most cultures; yet there are times when people have a desire to do these things. This notion begins in the Garden of Eden with Adam and Eve's succumbing to partake of the forbidden fruit, the classic biblical story of temptation.

We all face temptations of some sort almost every day. They come in all sizes, big and small. One of the roles of ethical thinking is to help us recognize temptations and thereby avoid them. Some temptations are more obvious than others. If you go to your local computer store and steal a copy of the new word processing software you wanted, that is clearly wrong—and you know it. It's a temptation easily averted. But to copy the same software from your organization's computer system for your own use is equally tempting and perhaps, initially at least, a little less guilt ridden. That is, until you reflect on it awhile. Somehow, copying software does not appear to be so bad and may seem to have only a faint tinge of wrongdoing associated with it. It's a temptation more easily given in to but one that should be equally averted.

These kinds of information temptations abound, as staff writer Victoria Shannon (1994) maintains in an op-ed piece for the *Washington Post*. Consider the following scenarios:

A. Your term paper is about Michelangelo, and you know you'll get extra credit by including a laserjet print of the sculpture of David that you transferred to your computer from American Online service.

B. Your multimedia presentation at work gets a round of guffaws when people hear a line from "Star Trek" that you copied from CompuServe a few months ago: "He's dead, Jim," Dr. McCoy deadpans in answer to a question you've asked about your competitor.

C. You send to your sister by electronic mail Consumer's Reports' latest ratings of video camcorders from Prodigy. (p. 12)[2]

Using commercial information services, it is easy to download art, sound, or text. But in the preceding scenarios, these materials are the product of someone else's work, so this act can generate several different kinds of moments of truth. Your fee entitles you to access but not necessarily to reproduction or commercial use. Additional considerations for intellectual property rights and appropriate attribution should guide any decision to reproduce the material accessed. Private use for one's own education and entertainment is often distinguished from commercial use in which the material becomes part of a product or service sold to others. For example, a Southern Methodist University student in a summer intern program created an icon to represent the company who sponsored her work and placed it on the World Wide Web so that it was accessible by anyone with access to MOSAIC or other interfacing programs. Her icon was appropriated by others—it was a good one—without attribution or compensation and is now available to the world. There is a great temptation to claim information available on Internet or other services as one's own—it is so readily available—but it is a temptation best averted.

There is a good test to use whenever you are faced with a temptation, especially a very small one. Ask yourself, "If I took the same course of action over and over again would it still be acceptable?" This is known as the *slippery-slope rule*. An act may be negligibly unacceptable now (or even appear to be acceptable) and bring about only small changes in the ethical field. If, however, the same act is repeated, in the long run it would bring about unacceptable, unethical changes. "Once you start sliding down the slippery slope," the adage goes, "you may not be able to stop." "So don't start," is the ethical advice.

An information society is replete with information-based temptations. Sellers of information services have a commonplace industry saying: "People have three motivations for acquiring information: fear, greed, and curiosity—and the first two far outweigh the third." The employee who makes a clandestine copy of her firm's customer database likely knows that what she is doing is wrong, but greed or some other motive compels her to do it anyway. Agents who become information takers do so because they believe that the information will help them achieve some of their goals. It has value for them. And because information exhibits the seven characteristics identified by Harlan Cleveland (see Chapter 2), it is usually hard to restrain and contain the information. That's one reason why information temptations are prevalent. Unfortunately, in most cultures and organizations—perhaps even in our superegos—we do not have the same kinds of ethical mechanisms to safeguard us against these temptations as we have developed, say, against the unethical use of force, wealth, or other sources of power. One of the challenges of the information age is to identify these temptations and to develop guidelines for dealing with them.

Some ethicists believe that the leaders of societies and organizations have a moral obligation to safeguard their members from common temptations. Creeds and codes of ethics are one mechanism for doing this. In fact, auditors and sellers of cash control technologies have a saying that captures the flavor of this obligation: "There are two conditions that must be met for someone to steal cash: the need for money and the opportunity to take it. We all have the need. So we must take away the opportunity." This maxim recognizes a temptation and also indicates that the managers should take some action to forestall those who might succumb to it. Managers and other responsible parties are partially culpable if the proper safeguards are not put in place. We will return to this point later in the book with the question of what safeguards a good society is morally obligated to implement.

The ethical issues surrounding temptations are more profound than they often appear at the outset, but they are comparatively easy to resolve. They simply involve distinguishing right from wrong. But what happens when we must choose between competing goods or competing evils? These situations arise occasionally. Dealing with them requires relatively deep ethical thinking. We call this occurrence an ethical quandary.

Ethical Quandaries

An ethical *quandary* is created whenever an agent faces a moral bind between competing goods and competing evils. Some people may call this a "dilemma." Literally, however, the term *dilemma* describes a choice between just two equally unwelcome alternatives. A quandary, however, is a richer, more perplexing state in which there may be many different directions to turn, each of which is laced with bad and good implications. Dilemmas are nested as a special case within the broader notion of quandaries. "Damned if you do, damned if you don't, damned all around," is an old Missouri expression that captures the essence of a quandary. In the biblical tradition, the story called the "Agony of Abraham" describes a classical quandary. When the Lord commanded Abraham to sacrifice his only son Isaac as a test of his faith, Abraham was confronted with a quandary. He loved his God, he said, but he also loved his son. Any choice carried excruciating pain as well as pleasure.

Resolving a quandary often requires arduous ethical thinking. We encounter them frequently. Imagine that you are an executive in a consumer products company and your head of information systems has just presented a "business case" for a new distribution and marketing management "executive information system" (EIS). The primary benefits of the EIS will be obtained by flattening the organization and eliminating several hundred middle-management jobs. These managers have been working associates for years, and many are friends whose families you know well. Most, you are sure, will have difficulty in finding another job, at least for some time during these periods of soft employment. In fact, any job they might find will probably not be at the economic and status level they now hold. Each of them will surely experience uprooting, confusion, frustration, and the type of isolation Durkheim (1951) called "anomie." This is a terrible prospect for you. Yet your company is facing stiffer competition and is losing market share. Its profit margins are plummeting. The company must, you know, get "leaner and meaner." The executive information system completes a large step towards that goal. What should you do?

This presents a true quandary. If the executive information system is successfully installed, your company will have a better chance of surviving, perhaps of prospering. In the process, however, you will have inflicted some suffering on the dismissed middle managers and will have likely kept them and their families from achieving their goals as human beings. On the other hand, if the system is not installed and the company's economic condition deteriorates, the remaining employees and, ultimately, the stockholders will be hurt and denied an opportunity to achieve their goals. So either direction you take—even in a case as abbreviated as this—is fraught with challenging ethical issues. As will be developed more fully in the next chapter, quandaries of this nature require a full examination of the facts of the case and an application of moral principles to them so that a reasoned and principled decision can be made.

Proactive, Nonpressing Issues

Criticism

Agents face not only temptations and quandaries, but they also face passive situations, ones in which they must take the initiative. Organizations and social systems, for example, have policies and procedures (or the lack of them) that may encourage unethical behavior. How should a corporation be structured so that confidential information is safeguarded and important information rises to the top? What kind of laws and institutions does the nation need to ensure that an individual's privacy is protected? Answering these questions also requires ethical thinking, and, generally speaking, the taking of proactive action. Chapters 8, 9, and 10 take up some of the dimensions of this type of ethical thinking. It goes under the general heading of *criticism*. It requires an evaluation of a situation, judging its ethical merits and faults, and suggesting means for improvements.

Professional Self-Regulation

Every person in an information society is also responsible for his or her fellow information persons' behavior. "Bad apples" must be eliminated; unethical performance confronted and regulated. This is the problem of *self-regulation.* Policing and disciplining others is an unpleasant task, but it is a vital one in an ethical society. Some considerations with respect to self-regulation in the information professions are discussed in Chapter 7.

These four types of moments of truth—temptation, quandary, criticism, and self-regulation—create ethical issues that require resolving. An approach for dealing with these follows.

▧ RESOLVING AN ETHICAL ISSUE

At the moment of truth, when you are faced with a temptation, quandary, or other ethical issue, you should begin a dialogue with yourself about it. Ideally, you will include others in your discussions as well. Like most dialogues, ethical dialogues are inevitably dynamic. They move from point to point in a nonlinear fashion, focusing on various considerations as they come to mind or as they unfold in the process of discussion. Nevertheless, it helps to have a structure in mind, a track to run on. Guidelines to ethical thinking should not be used as a rigid sequence of steps to follow but, rather, as a checklist that ensures that every important element of the issue is being considered. The following six considerations should be taken into account when resolving an ethical issue:

1. What Are the Facts? What are all of the morally relevant considerations? First, this requires a scoping out of the pertinent information field, an understanding of the information life cycles involved, and an identification of the key decision-making processes at work. Second, it requires identifying all of the key agents—givers, takers, and orchestrators—and the relevant acts, results, and stakeholders. It also includes an understanding of agents' and stakeholders' values and motivations and of all agents' and stakeholders' personal, social, and physical history. In the language of corrective vision this first step establishes "what is."

2. What Ethical Principles, Standards, or Norms Should Be Applied? That is, "what ought to be?" In this step, the relevant ethical considerations are applied to the facts. This is where the ethical theories and principles described more thoroughly in Chapter 6 come into play.

Steps 1 and 2 provide the necessary basis for corrective vision and for resolving a given issue. The ethical principles and standards brought forward for consideration at this point can be used to interpret the facts of the case and arrive at a preliminary moral judgment. But the job is not yet complete. The next four steps are required to round out the decision-making process and place it in the broader context of the community it affects.

3. Who Should Decide? Who should take the actions necessary to bring about what ought to be? There are two general considerations at this step. One deals with the need for participation of all relevant parties and for expanding perspective. The other addresses issues of sovereignty, legitimacy, and the ability to affect a resolution.

The first consideration is informational. There is a tendency for individuals and organizations to make ethical decisions in isolation from other parties. So an immediate consideration is whether or not all of the relevant players are participating in the resolution of the issue. Are all of the appropriate voices and points of view being heard? Beyond this, there is the notion that exposing an issue or one's contemplated behavior to public discussion serves as a kind of test of its ethical basis. Would you tell your mother or father? Your spouse? Your boss? Someone whom you respect and whose respect you want? Would you be comfortable if the actions you are contemplating were reported in the newspapers, radio, or television? In a video prepared by Arthur Andersen and Co. (*Ethics in Business,* 1991), a noted retailer recalls how he applies this approach to his own decisions. When making important decisions, he tries to anticipate what his father might say. Would he say, "attaboy, son"? He also asks himself, "Would the boy I was be proud of the man I am today?" This personal, internal dialogue illustrates an important point. Not all of the ethical voices need to be present or even alive at the time their message is included in the dialogue. They only need to be heard. Listen to voices from the past—perhaps in acknowledgment of piety—and most important, listen to voices from the future. What will future generations say about the actions you are about to take?

The second consideration is instrumental. In modern society, some people assume roles, especially in organizations and institutions, that have the duty or responsibility to deal with the issue under consideration or at least some part of it. Still other parties may have the resources required to resolve the issue. These parties, too, need to be made part of the decision-making process.

4. Who Should Benefit From the Decision? Often, many stakeholders are affected by an ethical decision. Their voices provide insights and make claims as to what the decision should be. In arriving at a final decision, these stakeholder claims should be examined and weighed. Whose values should predominate? Who has the strongest claim? To whom do we have the most compelling duties or responsibilities? What are the long-run considerations?

5. How Should the Decision Be Made? Unfortunately, decisions and the methods by which they are made are not totally separable. The process used to arrive at an ethical judgment is also a part of the judgment itself. The familiar notion of a right to *due process,* for example, rests on the belief that the method by which any ethical decision is made must be fair and follow established procedures, if there are any. In some cases, it is more important that the method of arriving at a decision be perceived as fair and ethical than the decision itself. Often, conflicting parties or parties with competing claims can agree only on the method by which a decision will be made—while they continue to contest its substance bitterly.

In response to this need, societies have created many different procedures to promote fairness in decision making. One is to establish, *before* a decision is made, a set of procedures that clearly prescribes which parties will be consulted when a decision is at hand. Such procedures identify the parties who have the authority to comment, examine procedures, recommend courses of action, decide, or veto decisions. Voting processes and secret ballots are sometimes required. When the limits of deterministic procedures are reached, a decision is sometimes left to a prescribed form of chance. Toss a coin, draw straws, or pick a random number. In extreme cases, as Shirley Jackson (c. 1949/1980) describes in her chilling short story *The Lottery,* a rather complicated probabilistic process can be used in making decisions. All of these methods are employed for the purpose of achieving due process.

Due process is necessary, but it is not enough. There must be *due respect* as well. Respect comes from the style and integrity of the decision makers and other parties involved. It is not inherent in the methods used. Primarily, it requires that the dignity of all the parties involved be honored and preserved. This calls for prudence—showing discretion and foresight—wisdom, and above all, love. Love is hard to describe but easy to recognize:

> Love is very patient and kind, never jealous or envious, never boastful or proud, never haughty or selfish or rude. Love does not demand its own way. It is not irritable or touchy. It does not hold grudges and will hardly ever notice when others do wrong. It is never glad about injustice, but rejoices whenever truth wins out. If you love someone you will be loyal to him no matter what the cost. You will always believe in him, always expect the best of him and always stand your ground in defending him. (I Cor. 13:4-7, Living Bible)

Love and due respect in ethical decision making result from a caring for all parties who may in any way be affected by a decision and the way it is made and carried out. In general, people's dignity should be preserved and negative effects minimized. Appropriate tone of voice, attitude, and patience are among the attributes of an ethical way of going, and this can be as important as following an ethical set of procedures in making decisions.

6. What Steps Should Be Taken to Prevent This Issue From Occurring Again? The late legal philosopher, Thomas Cowan (personal communication, fall 1965), emphasized that all decisions we make become part of society's historical transcript. They become precedents carried on to perpetuity and not just answers to contemporary or pressing problems. An analogy from the medical profession will help make the point clear. Physicians draw a distinction between acute care and preventive medicine. Acute care deals with the immediate crisis; preventive care is applied to keep such crises from happening again. Ethical decisions have the same characteristics. An acute ethical issue often needs to be solved at the moment of truth at which it occurs. In the process of resolving it, however, there are other things to take into account. Will the proposed solution generate even worse problems in the future? What sort of precedent is being set? Do we need to restructure our institutions to keep this issue from occurring again? Do we need procedures that will make it possible to deal with this kind of issue more effectively in the future? In summary, what course of action will put us in the best position for the future? What kind of social transcript do we want to write?

The last four of these six considerations have a common thread. They require an ethical decision maker to think beyond just the presenting ethical issue. The four latter considerations expand the ethical field by bringing in additional voices, focusing on procedures, concentrating on style, and looking to the future. They make us consider ethical decisions as a whole, including the love we bring to them.

These six considerations apply to each of the three levels of agency: individual, organizational or group, and societal. In fact, applying these considerations tends to raise an issue from a lower level (i.e., the individual level where it is usually first encountered) toward the societal (i.e., systemic) level. Suppose John, a student at a local university, is tempted to make a copy of an educational software package for his own personal use. Whether he should be allowed to copy it and use it for personal purposes begins as an individual issue. It concerns the ethics of John's behavior. As we reflect on this issue, however, some other key questions are likely to be raised: Who is affected by this issue and its resolution? Who should make the decision? What procedures and processes should be used? How should John and others be treated in the process? What policies and norms should be put in place and publicized so that this issue doesn't arise again? Our thoughts range from John himself to his classroom professors, to his university, to the software publisher, to the broader economic and social milieu. Ultimately, we are forced to consider the society as a whole. Thus, wide-ranging concerns for a community's culture, norms, standards, and policies become an inevitable part of the ethical thinking process.

SUMMARY

Ethical thinking is the cognitive means we use when we pause at a moment of truth to reflect on ethical issues. It requires systematic examination of an ethical issue and determining whether an agent's actual or contemplated behavior is ethical (creating moral goods) or unethical (creating moral evils) or whether, alternatively, there are no ethical considerations involved. Moral goods expand and improve on the human condition, whereas moral evils degrade it. Behaviors that are nonethical do not affect the human condition in any material way.

The fundamental approach to ethical thinking is to compare what is—the facts of the situation and the prognosis they imply—with what ought to be, as determined by ethical theories or principles. This approach is called the model of corrective vision. It is essential in an information society because (a) the agent with the most power—be its source violence, wealth, or information—is not necessarily always right; (b) the social and cultural institutions that our society has created, as good as they may be, are not ethically pure or perfect; and (c) clearly, there are times when responsible citizens must point out and make public what they believe to be unethical behavior, regardless of who the perpetrators are.

A tension always exists at a moment of truth between what is and what ought to be. Temptations and quandaries result from this tension. Temptations occur when agents are faced with situations in which the pursuit of their own goals or self-interests would lead them to choose acts that are wrong, and they know it. Quandaries exist when agents experience moral binds in which every available alternative results in mixtures of good and bad, right and wrong, or just and unjust.

In addition to these active and pressing tensions, two more passive, nonpressing circumstances create moments of truth calling for proactive action. For one, a good citizen in an organization or a society should be ready to criticize rules and institutional arrangements that he or she believes are unethical or that tend to encourage unethical behavior. For another, a good citizen should also point out and attempt to correct the unethical behavior of his or her peers or fellow citizens, especially if that person is a member of an information profession that has ethical guidelines. This responsibility to be proactive is part of the social contract and flows from the covenant, discussed earlier, that exists between givers and takers and that establishes a need for self-regulation and professionalism. A good citizen in an information society—a fully developed information person—should stand ready to criticize or regulate the behavior of others, as appropriate.

Dealing with these four types of moments of truth—temptations, quandaries, criticism, and self-regulation—requires an ability to think through and resolve the ethical issues they raise. Six considerations should be taken into account when doing this:

1. What are the facts?
2. What ethical principles, standards, or norms should be applied?
3. Who should decide?
4. Who should benefit from the decision?
5. How should the decision be made?
6. What steps should be taken to prevent this issue from occurring again?

These six considerations for resolving an ethical issue, especially the second—what principles to apply—have evolved through several thousand years of reflection. Beginning with the ancient Greeks and running through biblical times and up to the present, many wise and reflective minds have contributed their thoughts to an ongoing conversation on ethics. All of this thought is potentially relevant to any given ethical issue or for understanding the activities taking place in any specified ethical field. An overview of this body of thought is the subject of the next chapter.

NOTES

1. Copyright © 1993, *USA Today*. Reprinted with permission.
2. Copyright © 1994, *The Washington Post*. Reprinted with permission.

6

Ethical Theories and Principles

◼ PROMISE CLUB: THE ETHICS OF INFORMATION EXCHANGE

In 1989, Cheryl Flannigan, an accountant and mother of two young children, joined the Tom Thumb supermarket Promise Club program, a frequent-shopper membership program. She received a membership card with a personal identification number (PIN) that made discounts and debit card privileges available to her. In addition, she received advance information on impending specials, additional product information, free recipes, and health and nutrition advice. Each time she checked out, she simply "swiped" her card through a Promise Card terminal at the counter, which read her membership number from a magnetic strip embedded in the card. Her account number was instantaneously transmitted to the store's back office computer, and in less than 2 seconds her authorization was established and her account approved.

> As the clerk scanned the grocery items, the point-of-sale system automatically checked for membership specials, crediting Cheryl with the promised savings for appropriate items. As the items were accumulated, their universal product code (UPC) identifier, quantity, and price were transmitted to the store-controller computer in the store. The computer appended the time of day to the item data and then stored all of it on an attached hard disk. As Cheryl wheeled the grocery cart out of the store, the total amount of her purchases for the day was transmitted to the store-controller computer. Here the amount was added to a running total of the Flannigan's purchases for the month that was stored in a "household" file. (Ives, 1989, p. 3)

Every evening, Cheryl's and hundreds of other customers detailed purchasing data were transmitted to Citicorp Information Services Incorporated (CPOS) where it was merged with similar information from other stores located throughout the country and used to build a national purchase behavior database. Citicorp planned to build a database representing at least 10 million households. CPOS acquired the data from the stores, merged it together, repackaged it, and among other things, sold it to consumer package goods manufacturers and direct marketers. The database also contained substantial personal and demographic data about each household. Some of this information was obtained from the Promise Card application form. Buried in the small print of the application, just below the signature line, was the statement "I agree to allow Tom Thumb & Page and their data processing supplier to record and make use of information about the products I purchase" (Ives, 1989, p. 14).

Citicorp insisted on exclusive marketing rights to the data and, although they paid some stores to share their customer purchase information, the contract called for the grocers to pay for the use of data generated from their own stores. CPOS sold the data for direct-marketing purposes. An advertisement in the November 18, 1991, *Dallas Morning News* claimed that "this state-of-the-art system identifies valuable purchasing information by household name and address.... [It] contains key purchasing data that qualifies these consumers for all kinds of direct mail offers—and all of these qualified buyers have indicated an interest in receiving promotional offers!" By late 1991, CPOS was advertising to all potential buyers the availability of consumer database lists of over a half million weight-conscious consumers, over a half a million health-conscious consumers, over a million coupon clippers, nearly 700,000 pet owners, and over 300,000 cosmetic buyers as well as offering to produce, for a price, virtually any especially tailored list the database made possible.

As CPOS began to put their database program into effect, complaints were lodged against the system. Grocery store customers complained about third-party use of information that identified them individually and about their purchasing behavior. In their view, potential use of this data constituted a threat to their privacy. Their wine and liquor, flowers, Wheaties, and Pampers purchases were nobody's business but their own. Some supermarkets, too, complained that they had been pressured into making an unfair deal with CPOS in which they relinquished with little compensation the use of their valuable consumer profile and shopping data.

Among the various acts to assess in this case, two stand out:

• The first is CPOS's selling of customer profile and purchasing pattern data to third parties, such as direct marketers. Consumer data complete with names, addresses, and other information was being formed into complete profiles and made accessible to third parties who planned to sell products to these consumers.

• The second is CPOS's using of its power advantage to require participating stores to convey ownership rights in the data to CPOS. This is, on the surface, a business-to-business issue, but it indirectly involves consumers because the data being sold is personal data about them. The larger issue is, "Who owns this data?" What are the consumer's rights to it?

Two benefits of the Promise Card program should also be acknowledged: The customer gets discounts and better information with which to shop, and the businesses involved get better information with which to manage their affairs.

◾ MORAL IMAGINATION: THE ROLE OF ETHICAL THEORIES

Any case involving ethical issues such as the events surrounding the CPOS Promise Card may be interpreted in the context of ethical theories and principles. As described in the previous chapter, to carry out the second step in resolving an ethical issue—What principles, standards, or norms should be applied?—one must draw on ethical theories. Imagining "what ought to be" requires access to concepts and theories. But what theories? Where do these ethical precepts come from? There is a long and diverse history of ethical ideas from which to draw. This chapter summarizes and illustrates some of the most important ethical ideas that have been developed. To begin with, the tradition can be divided into one of two great streams of ethical thinking—teleology and deontology.

◾ MORAL OBLIGATION VERSUS SEEKING OUTCOMES: TWO SOURCES FROM WHICH ETHICAL THINKING SPRINGS

The Greeks, concerned with creating an ideal society, debated and struggled with the concepts of goodness, fairness, and justice. The word *telos,* meaning goal or purpose, was coined by them, as was the word *deon,* meaning duty or to bind. The first is used to talk about the "targets" or purposes of actions; the second to talk about "rules" used to guide moral behavior. From their origins in these two Greek words, two great ethical traditions, and sets of theories for each, have emerged: *teleology* and *deontology.*

A theory, according to the *American Heritage Dictionary* (3rd edition), is a "systematically organized [body of] knowledge applicable in a relatively wide variety of circumstances, especially a system of assumptions, accepted principles, and rules of procedure devised to analyze, predict, or otherwise explain the nature or behavior of a specified set of phenomena." Theories are used to identify the relevant factors in a situation and to think or reason about them. They help you decide what to consider and what to exclude from your thinking. Ethical theories, in addition, direct your reasoning toward the good and bad, right or wrong, or fair or unfair in agents and their actions.

Teleological ethical theories focus primarily on the *consequences, results, ends, goals,* or *purposes* of agents' acts. Teleological theories center on one of two factors: either the agents themselves or the results of agents' actions.

Agent-oriented theories, on the one hand, focus on an agent's moral responsibility, intentions, state of knowledge, virtues, and self-interests. The principal agents in the Promise Card case are the Tom Thumb executives who decided on the program and the Citicorp executives who sold it to them and provided the data services. Agent-oriented theories are used to examine such things as their motives; what they knew at the time; whether they were honest, truthful, prudent, courageous, and fair in their dealings, and whether they should be held responsible for their actions.

Results-oriented theories, on the other hand, focus on public interest. Results-oriented teleological reasoning is used to interpret the results of an act in light of its consequences for stakeholders. This is usually done by measuring the utility of the act for each stakeholder—that is, by netting out the costs and benefits that flow from the act. Similarly, theories of justice are also teleological and depend on the overall effects of actions on stakeholder interests. Justice is served when an agent's dealings with other stakeholders is fair. This is usually achieved by comparing and weighing the conflicting claims of each stakeholder and striking a balance between them. Standards of justice, as we will see, are generally taken to be more encompassing and important than utilitarian considerations. The stakeholders in the Promise Card case include consumers, manufacturers and direct marketers, Tom Thumb executives and employees, and Citicorp personnel. Result-oriented theories are used to assess the overall outcome of the program and its effects on each of the stakeholders implicated. In general, they are used to balance the benefits that flow to the stakeholders, such as discounts and better purchasing information, against the cost they incur, such as the loss of privacy.

Deontological ethical theories center on the *act* taken by the agent and the duties, rights, privileges, or responsibilities that pertain to that act. In deontological reasoning, an agent is obligated to follow the rules. These rules, most of which are familiar to us all, are incorporated in moral statements, such as the Golden Rule, or codified in doctrines, such as the Ten Commandments of the Judeo-Christian tradition. On the surface, deontological reasoning appears to be straightforward, simply "follow the rules." Difficulties arise, however, when different parties hold different views or attempt to apply different rules. Frequently, more than one rule applies in a given situation and they are in conflict. What then? As will be discussed later, deontological theories have a way of dealing with this question. One rule that applies to Tom Thumb executives in the Promise Card case is, "Do no harm!" Because their privacy was invaded, some harm was done to the supermarket's customers. If deontological reasoning is used and only this rule is applicable, then Tom Thumb (and Citicorp) acted unethically. But as we will see, applying deontological theories is somewhat more complex than this.

⌗ A MODEL FOR ETHICAL REASONING: FOUR FUNDAMENTAL FOCUSING QUESTIONS

Understanding the two wellsprings of ethical reasoning is important, because depending on whether teleological or deontological theories are applied, a different assessment can be made of a situation. From a practical point of view, ethical analysis rarely employs only one mode of reasoning. In most cases, several modes are used to assess the ethicality of a circumstance. When you assess an ethical situation, there are four key questions to ask (see Figure 6.1). The answers to these questions will guide your choice of theories to apply and help you determine what ought to be. As information professionals, these questions will help you interpret the facts of a case and guide your thinking about a particular situation. Asking the questions is an essential part of the process of corrective vision. The answers serve as lenses for choosing ethical theories and applying the processes of corrective vision.

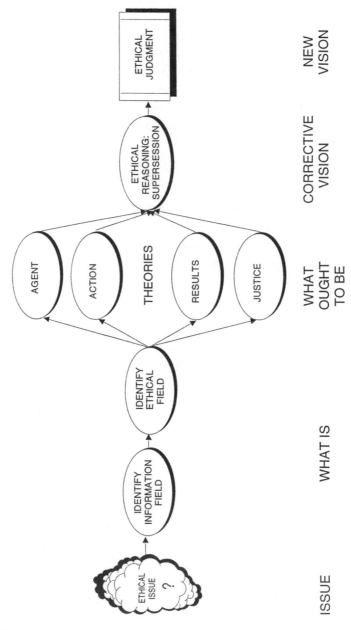

Figure 6.1. A Model for Ethical Reasoning

1. Who Is the Agent? Was the agent responsible for causing the issue to occur? What are the motives, interests, and character of the agent? Drawing on teleological theories and reasoning, the answers to these questions are used to assess the agent's position and to clarify the nature of the goals that the agent is pursuing.

2. What Action (or Actions) Was Actually Taken or Is Being Contemplated? Does the agent have a duty to perform it? Is the agent forbidden from performing it? Does the agent have a right to perform it? Is the agent free to perform this act in this particular situation? Drawing on deontological theories and reasoning, the answers to these questions are used to determine the "rules" or moral obligations that apply and to assess how these have been followed or violated.

3. What Are the Results or Consequences of the Act? Which stakeholders are affected and how are they affected? Who are the winners and losers? Is the greatest good being done for the greatest number? Drawing on teleological theories and reasoning, the answers to these questions are used to weigh the outcomes or results of an act as they affect stakeholders.

4. Is the Result Fair or Just? Are all parties involved being treated in a just, equitable, and fair manner? Are the burdens and benefits being distributed fairly? Are appropriate punishments and penalties being meted out to those who did wrong? Are those who were wronged being compensated adequately? Drawing on teleological theories and reasoning, the answers to these questions are used to determine the overall correctness, fairness, or equitableness of the entire situation.

The answers to these questions point you toward relevant ethical theories and principles that draw on the insights of thinkers down through the ages. They provide guidance as to what ought to be and are used to interpret the facts of a case and guide your thinking about it. Moreover, it turns out that most of the major theories in ethics focus primarily on just one of these four components—agent, act, results, or justice. Focusing attention on each of these components in turn therefore simplifies the reasoning process while providing access to a very substantial ethical tradition. Figure 6.1 shows the role of each of the four centers of ethical theory in the overall thinking process of corrective vision.

▧ APPLYING THE MODEL

At a given moment of truth, you apply the model in Figure 6.1. First, identify the relevant information field. As discussed in Chapter 4, this is accomplished by identifying all of the major stakeholders who participate in the information system and the information they want or need. This is the process for getting the relevant facts—"what is" or Step 1 in the process of ethical thinking covered in Chapter 5. Next, you identify the values, goods and bads, rights and wrongs, just and unjust considerations that pertain to agents and stakeholders in the field. This involves reflecting on several ethical principles and theories. The categories of agent, act, results, and justice covered in this chapter are helpful in this regard. For example, in the CPOS Promise Card case, among the agents to be considered are CPOS (Citicorp) and Tom Thumb; among the actions to be evaluated are CPOS's selling of personal purchasing information to third parties and CPOS's use of its power advantage to acquire ownership rights to the store's data; and among the stakeholders to consider are CPOS, the stores, the individual customers, consumer package goods manufacturers, and direct-marketing organizations that were purchasers of or prospects for the lists. This is the what-ought-to-be phase. Finally, you interpret the facts in light of the various principles and theories. Sometimes the application of different principles will result in conflicting advice. Because ethical reasoning requires identifying the principles on which you base your ethical conclusions, you should select the principle or principles that are most compelling in this case. This "trumping" process is called *supersession.* Supersession means using one principle to trump or outrank another and is discussed more fully later in this chapter. The final result is an ethical judgment that includes a preferred course of action and the ethical principles that support and defend it.

Ethical theories are abstract and general, but they form the broad context in which ethical judgments are made. A hierarchy exists that connects theories with judgments and actions. In increasing order of generality, ethical judgments and actions are based on rules, guidelines, or codes, which, in turn, are based on ethical principles, which, in turn, are grounded in ethical theories (see Figure 6.2). For this reason, a general understanding of ethical theories is useful when dealing with issues raised by an information society.

Some of the ethical theories that are appropriate for examining issues in the information age are discussed next. They are categorized according to the primary focusing question to which they pertain. Because most of us are familiar with thinking about people and their character, let us begin with theories that focus on the agent.

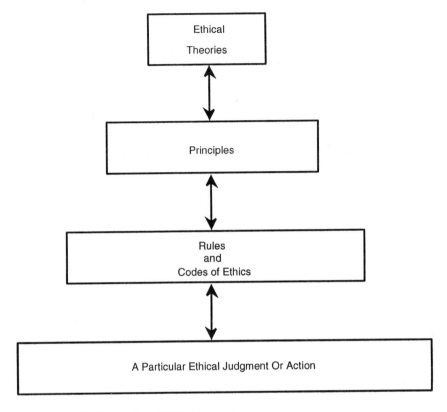

Figure 6.2. The Hierarchy of Ethical Reasoning

▨ CENTERING ON AGENTS: USING THE ANSWERS TO QUESTION I

Moral Responsibility

Ethical inquiry begins at a moment of truth when one party—the *agent*—is faced with an ethical issue. Agents act at several different levels, including as individuals, as a group, as an organization, or even as an entire society. A crucial feature of agency is that, generally, agents act in pursuit of their own self-interests. Indeed, the ethical theory of egoism, discussed later, states that in the long run, this is a good thing. According to the "enlightened self-interest" point of view, if an individual's actions do not promote long-term survival, then an agent is imprudent, perhaps even foolish.

How are we to assign moral responsibility of agents if we focus primarily on agents themselves rather than on their acts or the results that flow from their acts? A good deal of ethical theory centers on this question. It focuses on the character and the virtues of agents. "Being good"—as opposed to the utilitarian's "producing good" or the deontologist's "doing right"—is the teleological ideal toward which agents should strive, according to William May (personal communication, fall 1990). Or to put it differently, agents should pursue moral virtues and avoid moral sins.

The Watergate hearings in the middle 1970s introduced the American public to two key questions that are essential for pinpointing moral responsibility: "What did a person know?" "When did that person know it?" Underlying these familiar queries is an ethical theory that harks back to Aristotle. In the *Nicomacheon Ethics of Airstobles,* Aristotle (1911) explores the nature of virtue by noting that it arises in a context of passions and actions. According to Aristotle, if an agent acts both *voluntarily* and *knowingly,* it is appropriate to assign him or her whatever praise or blame is associated with the act. There are two possible circumstances:

- One, the agent knowingly and freely *performed* the act and knew that it was morally wrong to perform it. As discussed in Chapter 5, if the agent was aware that the act was wrong at the time and engaged in it anyway, the agent succumbed to a *temptation.*
- Two, the agent knowingly and freely *failed* to perform an act and knew that it was morally wrong for the agent to fail to perform it. This we usually call *negligence.*

Harry, for example, is tempted by the vast possibilities of the information contained in the databases of the credit bureau where he works. He voluntarily and knowingly steals a password and uses it to acquire information about Arlo, whom he plans to swindle. Mary Ann knows that he has stolen the password but fails to report the violation to her superior even though she knows that company policy requires that officials be notified in all cases involving breaches of password security. Harry is to blame by the first criterion because he succumbed to a temptation; Mary Ann by the second because she was negligent.

Moral theory is fairly explicit in these relatively clear-cut cases, but what happens if an agent acts involuntarily? Does the agent still bear the same responsibility? In this case, the application of moral theory requires a little more analysis. Aristotle and subsequent thinkers have studied this question in considerable depth. Their conclusion is that the answer turns on two crucial attributes of the agent and his or her situation: (a) *ignorance* and (b) *compulsion* or *inability*. If an agent did not know it was wrong or was forced against his or her will to engage in the action taken, that agent should not be held morally responsible for that action.

Linda, say, is a mortgage banker. She unwittingly receives a credit report that is in error and, on the basis of the erroneous data, denies Smith a loan. Being denied the purchase of a home inflicts considerable pain and suffering on Smith. Linda, in this relatively straightforward case, should not be held responsible because she acted in ignorance. This is a case, according to Aristotle, of involuntary behavior. It deserves our pity and pardon but not moral blame.

Now, let's take Linda's case and treat it *casuistically*—that is, let's manipulate some of the elements of the case and examine their ethical implications. As we do this, we will explore some of the considerations that Aristotle and others brought to bear on more complex situations that feature a fundamental distinction between voluntary and involuntary behavior.

Suppose that it is common knowledge at Linda's bank that some of the credit bureau's reports contain grievous errors and that it is a normal practice for most mortgage bankers to perform checks on the validity of the reports. Linda did not know that this particular report contained errors—to this extent she acted in ignorance—but she had been made aware of the practice of verification in a training program. Consequently, she may still be held responsible for her deeds because, due to her position and training, she should have known that the report was potentially in error. She was negligent and, to use a legal term, she did not practice *due diligence*—that is, she did not pursue all courses of action at her disposal to validate the information before rendering a decision.

There is a related problem that Aristotle raised but St. Thomas Aquinas really pinned down. Aquinas (c. 1270/1952-1956) called it "voluntary ignorance." Today, we often call it *culpable ignorance*. It's a crucial idea for the information age because, with so much knowledge and information floating around about so many people and things and with so much technology to process it, acting in ignorance is not always a defensible excuse. Aquinas has this to say about it:

> Ignorance is said to be voluntary with respect to that which one can and ought to know, for in this sense to act and not to will are said to be voluntary. . . .

> Ignorance of this kind happens either when one does not actually consider what one can and ought to consider, which is called "ignorance of evil choice," and arises from some passion or habit; or it happens when one does not take the trouble to acquire the knowledge which one ought to have in which sense, ignorance of the general principles of law, which one ought to know, is voluntary, as being due to negligence. (pp. 650-651)

The issue of culpable ignorance—unwilling but negligent ignorance—is a pressing issue in the information age. With news services such as Cable News Network (CNN) available worldwide today, for example, it is assumed that the leaders of the some 168 countries of the world will be aware of late-breaking events within minutes after they occur. As a result, heads of state and their underlings cannot satisfactorily plea that they were not informed of a crucial event if indeed it was reported on CNN. The principle at work here is that it is the responsibility of agents to acquire any relevant information made available by public and readily available sources. Following this same rule, corporate executives are expected to know about any crucial corporate activities that can be captured and reported by modern information systems.

Similar to culpable ignorance is the concept of *willful ignorance.* Some agents act out of ignorance deliberately. They position themselves so that it is difficult, if not impossible, for other people to know what they really knew or should have known about a questionable act. Subsequently, when something bad happens, they plead ignorance. We sometimes call this "distancing" oneself or "looking the other way." During the Watergate period, for example, President Nixon allegedly pursued a policy of "plausible deniability" whereby his underlings were instructed to structure their communications to him and their actions in such a way that he could always deny that he knew anything about them with credible and defensible arguments.

The tactics of willful ignorance and plausible deniability were probably being employed in the late 1970s when eight companies in the electrical wiring devices industry were fined for price-fixing. The senior executives at these companies claimed that they didn't know that their middle managers—who were their subordinates and reported to them—were meeting in hotel rooms and colluding to keep their prices artificially high. The middle managers, however, told a quite different story. It was true, they admitted, that they never explicitly told their bosses that they were fixing prices. In fact, their bosses refused to listen to any discussions about competitive pricing. The bosses, in several highly charged meetings, had instructed their subordinates in no uncertain terms that they were expected to achieve some very high profitability goals. These targets were set well beyond what a normally operating competitive market would bring and were virtually unachievable without some kind of market tampering. The bosses made it clear to their subordinates that they must achieve these goals, or else they would lose their jobs or be demoted. The subordinates were further instructed to use "any available means possible" to do so. In this case, the bosses were in fact ignorant of the actual price-fixing, but they were willfully so. Therefore, they are culpable because the systems they had put in place (a) shielded them from information they should have received and (b) coerced their middle managers into performing illegal acts.

Aquinas (c. 1270/1952-1956) went further in identifying situations in which culpable ignorance occurs. On the one hand, he observed, there are situations in which even after an agent such as Linda takes proper and reasonable precautions—due diligence—she might still take an act that she would not have taken had she been more fully informed about all of the surrounding circumstances. Linda exhausted the possibilities for acquiring the information and simply was unable to find it. This is a case of absolutely involuntary behavior and, accordingly, is not culpable.

There is another possibility, however. Suppose Linda tells us that despite the fact that she had taken proper precautions and that she did not know that the record was in error, nevertheless, she would have made the very same decision regardless of the facts. That is, the lack of knowledge about the errors in the report did not influence her decision at all. Ignorance, accordingly, was not her motive or explanation. This is called *nonvoluntary behavior* and must be evaluated on some other basis than ignorance. Let's explore another scenario.

Linda reports to us that the information in the report didn't influence her decision at all because the area in which the home is located is a "redlined." area. She knows that redlining (a form of discrimination) is illegal and that many people consider it to be unethical. Nevertheless, her boss told her "in no uncertain terms" to never make a loan in that section of town. If she made such a loan, she would immediately lose her job. Being a single-parent head of household, this is a rather disastrous prospect for Linda. Furthermore, the boss threatened, if she did not follow his instructions or reported his policies to anyone else he would "toss her into the hot grease"—a phrase used to convince her that, as common parlance expresses it, if he was "fried" she would be fried too. Linda's boss is a very powerful and revengeful man, and she knows that he could carry out this threat and make her life miserable.

This is a case of *compulsion* or *duress,* both Aristotle and Aquinas would agree. It is a situation in which the agent is compelled by external forces to do something that he or she knows or suspects is unethical.

Figure 6.3 summarizes a theory of moral responsibility. It is based on making three key distinctions: (a) voluntary versus involuntary behavior, (b) behavior undertaken with or without full knowledge, and (c) whether or not in the situation under examination there were strong cultural norms for the agent to practice due diligence and be fully informed about the facts. Linda's case can be evaluated by tracing it through the diagram. Consider the redlining scenario. If we conclude (a) that Linda had no choice but to behave as she did (she acted involuntarily), (b) that she acted without full knowledge, and (c) that there was no organizational or cultural reason why she should have known, then she should not be held morally responsible for her actions in this case. If to the contrary, we conclude that despite this pressure, Linda should have had the courage to stand up to her boss and follow her conscience, then her action was voluntary and hence culpable, and very likely, it is unethical. Everything now turns on Linda's virtue.

Figure 6.3 can also be used to determine the responsibility of the key agents in the CPOS Promise Card case. CPOS entered the program voluntarily and with full knowledge of its processes and intent. Because this was an innovative program, the cultural norms that pertained to it were rather weak. Nevertheless, CPOS is responsible for its actions. Tom Thumb entered into the program voluntarily but with what turned out to be less than full knowledge. Yet a strong cultural norm exists requiring retailers to know how information about their customers is being used. Tom Thumb is responsible due to culpable ignorance. With respect to the issue of the transfer of ownership of the data to CPOS, Tom Thumb may have acted somewhat involuntarily, succumbing to Citicorp's superior economic power. But the store did it with reasonably full knowledge and with strong cultural norms to protect their customers. Consequently, they are responsible due to a lack of courage. The direct-marketing organization operated voluntarily and with full knowledge. However, as often happens with new programs, technologies, or innovations, the cultural norms prohibiting their actions were weak. Nevertheless, the direct-marketing organizations should be held responsible for their acts. Finally, a case can be made that the customers entered the program voluntarily but with less than full knowledge. And because the norms are weak, customers, generally, should not be held responsible due to their relative ignorance. (Situations such as this, in which weak cultural norms play an important role in assigning responsibility or in

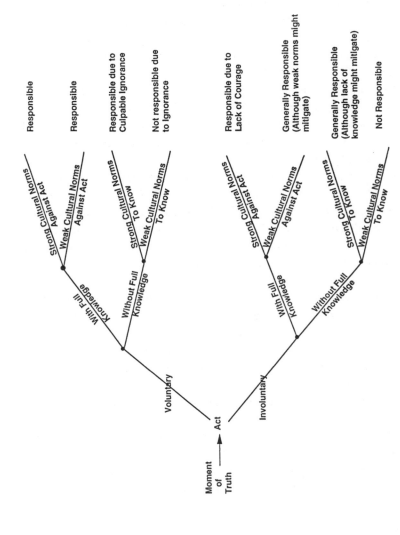

Figure 6.3. Assigning Responsibility

123

which some forms of coercion are used or useful information is withheld, often trigger the need for social policy. This need is discussed more fully in Chapter 9.)

Virtues

The particular way an agent responds to external and internal forces brings us to a consideration of the fundamental qualities of agents themselves—their character. We sum this up with the term *virtues.* The ancient Greeks believed that a good ruler—a good agent—must be a good person. But some of these wise old men (and their followers) had quite different ideas about what it means to be good. The virtues they identified generally fall into two categories.

Homer, Thucydides, and others rooted agents' goodness in their power and strength. These are the so-called *competitive virtues* and are based on the principle that "might is right."

Plato and Aristotle, on the other hand, based their ethics on a set of *cooperative virtues,* virtues that help avoid conflicts between agents and stake-holders. *Courage,* the virtue questioned in the previous scenario about Linda, is one of the four principal virtues they identified. The others are *prudence, temperance,* and *justice.*

To be prudent is to be careful, wise, and well-informed and to have foresight. A prudent person places himself or herself within the full span of time. He or she is true to the past and does not distort it, is open to the present, listens carefully, has a vision of the future, and is ready for the unexpected.

A person with temperance has his or her appetites under control and shows moderation. Temperance tends to stem from one's instincts and, meta-phorically, resides in one's "gut."

A fair and just person appreciates and accepts differences, respects diver-sity, and is not envious. The virtue of justice combines reason with instinct and intuition.

Finally, a courageous person is ready to face conflict and danger in the pursuit of an important, legitimate goal. Courage requires overcoming fear and resides fundamentally in an agent's heart.

Courage, like all virtues, involves behavior between two extremes, a point that Aristotle noted. Aristotle's (1925) concept of the "golden mean" places virtues in the middle of a continuum that places excesses at one of its ends and deficiencies at the other. Courage, for example, falls between the extremes of rashness and timidity. Similarly, temperance falls between the extreme of overindulgence or gluttony at one end and frugality, indigence, total denial, or abstinence at the

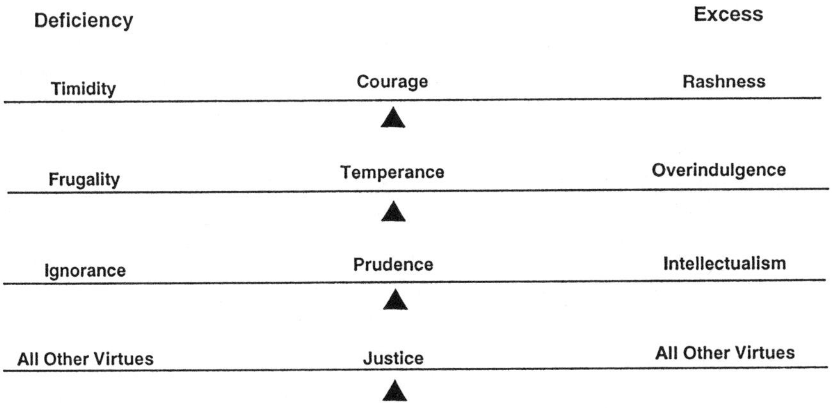

Deficiency		Excess
	Courage	
Timidity		Rashness
	▲	
	Temperance	
Frugality		Overindulgence
	▲	
	Prudence	
Ignorance		Intellectualism
	▲	
	Justice	
All Other Virtues		All Other Virtues
	▲	

Figure 6.4. The Golden Mean of Virtues

other. Prudence falls between ignorance on the one hand and overbearing intellectualism or "knowing it all" on the other. That is, prudent persons are not necessarily characterized by the magnitude of the facts and amount of knowledge they possess. Rather, they are noted for their wisdom and their ability to select just the relevant information required in a given situation and to use it effectively. Justice, some have argued, is the highest of the virtues. Being a just person means that one possesses a balance (a golden mean) among the other virtues and is able to let each of the other virtues take its appropriate part. Justice requires that all of the virtues are working well together (see Figure 6.4).

These four historical virtues continue to this day to serve as fundamental criteria for evaluating the character of agents at their moments of truth. In the meantime, other criteria have been added to the list. Aquinas (c. 1270/1952-1956), for example, noted that the Greeks' virtues were all too worldly and omitted the spiritual. He added *faith, hope,* and *charity* as virtues to be considered due to their biblical roots and more spiritual orientation. The social changes associated with industrialization during the 19th century brought to the forefront three additional virtues: *industry*—working hard, *honesty,* and *trustworthiness* or *integrity.* (In *The Threepenny Opera,* Kurt Weill, 1931/1968, stressed the opposite of practicing virtues by identifying seven sins to be avoided: sloth, pride, anger, gluttony, lust, avarice, and envy.)

Consideration of the virtue and character of an agent is necessary to determine an agent's responsibility at the moment of truth. Generally speaking, an ethical agent should display all of the virtues in reasonable amounts. This means that the virtuous person is constantly pursuing all of the virtues. Modern psychology has largely wrapped this up into single concept: self-realization. Abraham Maslow (1971) and Edgar A. Singer (1959), for example, argue that it is a "good" person's moral responsibility to develop his or her personal capabilities to their very fullest. Maslow (1971) calls this "self-actualization." We sometimes boil it down to a single word: integrity. The term *integrity* is derived from the same roots as "intact" and "untouched." It means that the agent has moral strength, is free from major flaws, is honest, and is a complete person.

In the discussions earlier about the CPOS Promise Card case, questions were raised as to whether Citicorp used its economic power so that might made right with respect to the ownership of the data. On the other hand, questions were also raised as to the extent of the courage and prudence that Tom Thumb exhibited in its relationship with CPOS, especially because the privacy of some of its customers was at stake. Although all of these organizations are generally ethical and law-abiding, these possible lapses raise a question about the breadth of their integrity.

The idea of integrity, however, suggests its opposite. It points to the possibility that an agent who does not pursue the virtues (as described earlier) loses contact with the world and is not to be trusted. Although few ethicists quarrel with the value of integrity there are those who believe that self-interest is an even more important goal. One who lets own self-interests dominate his or decisions is called egoistic. That behavior is defended on other theoretical grounds.

Egoism

The ethical theory of *egoism* essentially argues that it is appropriate—and ethical—for agents to pursue their own self-interests. In the extreme, egoism says, "Only *I* count" and asks, "What's in it for me?" "What's good for me?" It is an "ethics of arrogance" position.

A more considered form of egoism is offered by Ayn Rand, author of *The Fountainhead* (1943), *Atlas Shrugged* (1957), and a variety of novels, plays, and philosophical writings. Rand's "objectivist ethics" promotes what she calls "rational selfishness," which for her is based on

> the values required for man's survival *qua* man—which means: the values required for *human* survival—not the values produced by the desires, the feelings, the whims or the needs of irrational brutes, who have never outgrown the primordial practice of sacrifices, have never discovered an indus-

trial society and can conceive of no self-interest but that of grabbing the loot of the moment. (Rand, 1964, p. 31)

In contrast with altruism and collectivism, Rand emphasizes "man's right to a moral existence," which she believes can be achieved only if one is concerned with his or her own interests and becomes the primary beneficiary of his or her own moral actions.

A somewhat more moderate version of this view is called "enlightened self-interest." One's choices, the enlightened view holds, ought to promote one's own well-being and enhance one's chances of survival in the long run. Not to do so would be foolhardy and eventually self-destructive. In the short run, an agent might be required to make numerous compromises, agreements, bargains, or concessions and thereby pursue something less than absolute and total self-interest. This sacrificing detour is permissible as long as these diversions serve some long-term and higher-order goal, such as the goal of social harmony or the ultimate survival of the species.

Psychologist Abraham Maslow (1971) turns some degree of selfishness into a responsibility. He suggests that human beings have a moral obligation to follow their own self-interest to the extent necessary to realize their maximum potential, as long as they do not inflict harm on others. We should engage in "self-actualization," he argues, but it should also be enlightened.

Closely related to the concept of egoism is the concept of *autonomy*. This is another idea of Greek origin that means "self" (*autos*) "law" (*nomos*). Immanuel Kant (1788/1956), for example, held that the will of a person is autonomous when it acts from its own inner principles and is other-directed (heteronymous) when it accepts principles from outside itself. Politically and economically, one is autonomous when he or she is self-governing and pursuing his or her own goals.

Honoring the customer's rights of self-interest and autonomy often leads to policies of caveat emptor, "let the buyer beware." The principle of autonomy applied to the customers in the CPOS Promise Card case would result in a policy of informing the customers as completely as possible and, then, letting them decide whether or not to participate.

Egoism has its counterparts at other levels of agency. Many economists, following Adam Smith (1776/1986), argue that the best social systems emerge under conditions in which individuals and organizations are motivated by profits and pursue their own self-interests. Modern ideas of corporate strategy and of securing competitive advantage are based on the concept that corporations should have a substantial degree of autonomy, pursue their own goals and objectives, and obtain as much market power as possible. Indeed, economist Milton Friedman (1970) argues that "The Social Responsibility of Business Is to Increase Its Profits."[1] The same holds true in the public sector. Government agencies and not-for-profit organizations, management theorists such as Peter Drucker (1973) aver, should establish missions and pursue well-focused goals that are consistent with these missions. These organizations need to acquire budget power and the power of public legitimation. Finally, at the social level, a society, too, has a right to autonomy and self-interests so that it can establish a culture, develop values, and, of course, survive. All of this amounts to an argument in favor of egoism.

The idea of egoism is also a good place to begin to understand an agent's behavior. It points to the agent's underlying motives and establishes a preliminary ethical defense for his or her behavior. Unbridled egoism, of course, presents problems. "Your right to swing a fist," an old saw goes, "ends at the point of my nose." That is, one's pursuit of his or her own personal interests—such as power, glory, or greed—is likely to conflict with other stakeholders who are operating in the same ethical field and thereby keep them from obtaining their own egoistic goals. Egoism, therefore, must be guided or limited by one or more other ethical principles. A great deal of ethical thinking centers on determining just what these limitations on egoism should be because, as is generally acknowledged, a lack of guidelines or restraints to purely egoistic actions leads to the kind of social chaos that so frightened Thomas Hobbes (1651/1839). Consequently, there are severe ethical problems with unbridled egoism. Rule-based (deontological), utilitarian, and virtue- or responsibility-based ethics supply some of the necessary restrictions on totally self-interested behavior. Indeed, many of the rule-based theories were developed explicitly to rein in unconstrained egoism by requiring acts that led to a more stable social system and prohibiting those that did not.

▨ CENTERING ON ACTIONS: USING THE ANSWERS TO QUESTION 2

Deontology Revisited

Agents take actions. Another major ethical perspective focuses on the acts themselves and evaluates them with respect to a priori rules that specify what acts must, can, or cannot be taken. This point of view goes by two labels. The most familiar one is *rule-based ethics,* which gets its name due to its emphasis on the rules used to guide an agent's behavior. The other more general and philosophical name is deontology. As noted earlier, deontological ethics refers to moral obligations or rules that have the force of commands and thereby dictate an agent's behavior. An agent's acts, for the most part, are considered to be ethical if he or she follows society's rules and to be unethical if he or she violates them.

Deontological reasoning identifies two kinds of ethical behavior: (a) It specifies what acts an agent should or must take. These are called *responsibilities* or *duties.* (b) It specifies what acts an agent is permitted to take. These are called *privileges* or *rights.* Rights and duties have a stronger moral force than do privileges and responsibilities because they are derived from law, tradition, or nature, including one's own conscience. They are timeless and universal and hence not revocable. Privileges and responsibilities, on the other hand, may be revoked. They are accorded to an agent by dint of his or her position, situation, or favor.

Rights, duties, privileges, and responsibilities have prima facie force. Initially, at a given moment of truth, they are presumed to be ethical and binding "at first sight." Only after closer inspection and further ethical thinking might they be disregarded. Furthermore—and this is a crucial requirement—they may be disregarded only when another morally stronger claim supersedes them.

In the language of ethics there are, generally speaking, two kinds of duties. Some acts *must* be taken in a given situation. These are simply called duties. Other acts are specifically forbidden. These are called *prohibitions.* Prohibitions are duties *not* to do something. Duties and prohibitions are a priori rules that are supposed to direct an agent's behavior irrespective of the consequences of the act. A given act is ethical, prima facie, if it follows from a duty (or unethical if it violates a prohibition). The Ten Commandments, for example, contain both duties requiring an agent to do something ("Honor thy father") and duties requiring an agent not to do something—a prohibition—("Thou shall not steal").

Rights specify acts that an agent is inherently and universally entitled to take by reason of law, tradition, or nature. An act taken by an agent who acts within his or her rights is generally considered to be ethical, whereas an act that violates the rights of another stakeholder is generally considered to be unethical. In our society, for example, it is generally assumed that citizens have a prima facie right to their own privacy. Consequently, an agent who violates that right is, prima facie, acting unethically.

Several of the documents written to guide the formation of the United States as a nation contain descriptions of rights. In the Declaration of Independence, for example, Thomas Jefferson described some of a citizen's "unalienable" rights when he wrote, "We hold these truths to be self-evident, that all men are created equal, that they are endowed by their Creator with certain unalienable Rights, that among these are Life, Liberty and the pursuit of Happiness." Similarly, the U.S. Constitution's Bill of Rights safeguards certain political rights. Justice Hugo Black, in a famous case (*New York Times Company v. Sullivan*), argued that the First Amendment—the so-called freedom of speech amendment—provides citizens with "an unconditional right to say what one pleases about public affairs."

Both duties and rights are in principle not revocable. They derive from legitimate sources and have the prima facie force of commands. Historically, the four generally acknowledged legitimate sources of duties and rights have been the following.

From a Deity. The Ten Commandments and the Golden Rule—"Do unto others as you would have them do unto you"—are examples of rules deriving from God.

From Reason and Rational Thinking. Some rules, such as Hippocrates's admonishment to physicians, "First, do no harm," are derived from reasoning. Some ethicist, called *pluralists,* argue that there are multiple rules that agents are obliged to follow. Others, such as Immanuel Kant, claim that there is only one very comprehensive rule for people to follow. They are called *monists.* Both have derived their rules on the basis of logical argument.

From Law. The legal system permits or empowers agents who come under its jurisdiction to act in a specified way, or it may require others to act in certain ways toward the agent. Special kinds of rights and duties, generally enforceable by law, are specified in contracts and other formal agreements between parties.

By Consensus. Societies develop cultural norms that their members are expected to follow. Some of these are coalesced into a social contract. Organizations and professional groups often develop codes of ethics or credos that contain rules and guidelines of behavior that all members of the organization are expected to obey. These rules are agreed to by members of the organization. By means of an "oath of office" and as a necessary condition for membership, certification, or license, the association's members agree to live by its code. Physicians in the United States, for example, are required to take the Hippocratic Oath before practicing medicine.

Privileges are permissions, immunities, or advantages granted to the agent but not necessarily enjoyed by everyone else. They can also be taken away. Privileges can be revoked by the granting source and are therefore not "unalienable" or inherent in the same sense that rights are. The concept of privilege is much broader than the concept of right. It comprehends all of the acts that an agent is ethically permitted to take. A right may be considered as a special kind of a privilege, one that is inherent and nonrevocable.

Responsibilities are acts that, generally, should be performed whenever a certain situation arises. The notion of responsibility lays stress on an agent's accountability for the fulfillment of an obligation. As discussed in Chapter 1, ethical theories use the term *responsibility* in several related senses. In one interpretation, discussed earlier in this chapter, an agent is considered to be morally responsible for his or her acts if they are performed voluntarily and knowingly. Under these conditions, the agent is presumed to be the *cause* of the outcomes that created the ethical issue. This responsibility, accordingly, is determined by examining the state of the agent. In a second sense, responsibility refers to the acts an agent is expected to take in a given situation. In this sense, responsibility is a broader concept than is duty because it comprehends all of the acts an agent is obliged to take. Unlike duties, however, responsibilities may be revoked, modified, or supplanted.

The concepts of duties, prohibitions, rights, privileges, and responsibilities focus on an ideal of an agent's obligation for "doing right," as opposed to "producing good." These ethical concepts are correlative and mutually dependent. For the most part, every right an agent possesses imposes a duty on that agent and one or more stakeholders. For example, if an agent has a right to privacy, then other stakeholders in the field have a duty not to violate that right. Similarly, when privileges are accorded an agent, he or she usually assumes responsibilities to use these privileges in an appropriate manner, and other stakeholders have a prima facie responsibility to honor these privileges. Table 6.1 summarizes the relationship between rights, duties, privileges, and responsibilities.

Table 6.1 Relationship Between Rights, Duties, Privileges, and Responsibilities

	Command Is Nonrevocable	Command Is Revocable
Agent is allowed to do (can do)	Right	Privilege
Agent is obliged to do (must do)	Duty or prohibition	Responsibility

What Are an Agent's Prima Facie Duties?

The relationships people enter into with others also create duties. Relationships, such as employer to employee, promiser to promisee, creditor to debtor, wife to husband, child to parent, friend to friend, fellow countryman to fellow countryman, and information giver to information taker, all carry moral obligations. The philosopher W. D. Ross (1930) argues that all agents bring the demands of all of their previous relations with them when they confront a new moment of truth and that they must honor these demands. He calls these "prima facie duties"—because they are binding at first sight, before a closer inspection—and states that agents are obliged to perform these duties unless there is a strong reason not to. The set includes the following:

1. Duties arising from an agent's previous acts

   Duties of *fidelity*. Agents should keep their promises, foster trust, act with integrity, and be truthful. These duties of fidelity may be overt or implied and, when followed, have the effect of allowing other stakeholders in the field to depend on the agent.

   Duties of *reparation*. An agent should compensate and make amends to any stakeholders he or she has wronged in the past.

2. Duties arising from previous acts taken by stakeholders that affect the agent

   Duties of *gratitude*. An agent should be grateful, thankful, and repay other stakeholders for the good deeds done and from which he or she benefited.

3. Duties owed to stakeholders who have gained benefits beyond what they merit or earned

   Duties of *justice*. An agent should see to it that benefits and disbenefits are distributed fairly across the stakeholders in an ethical field.

4. Duties arising from the fact that an agent can improve his or her own condition and become more virtuous and knowledgeable

   Duties of *self-improvement*. An agent should maintain his or her own dignity and respect, strive to actualize his or her potentialities, and seek to achieve autonomy.

5. Duties arising from the fact that other stakeholders in the field have a right not to be harmed

    Duties of *nonmaleficence*. An agent has a duty not to do harm to any other stakeholder.

6. Duties arising from the fact that there are stakeholders in the field whose condition can be made better with respect to virtue, knowledge, or pleasure

    Duties of *beneficence*. An agent has a duty to improve the life of stakeholders who are worse off or in despair.

Some Prima Facie Stakeholder Rights Concerning Information

With respect to their rights, information stakeholders—givers, takers, and orchestrators—in an ethical field are generally assumed to have the following prima facie rights:

1. A right to know
2. A right to privacy
3. A right to accurate, reliable, unbiased information
4. A right to own or control their intellectual and tangible property
5. A right to fair access to information and information technology
6. A right not to be burdened unduly with the task of producing information or operating technology (including a right to be excluded from having to fill out questionnaires and other bureaucratic forms)

Trumping or Supersession

Frequently, one's prima facie duties come into conflict with one another. Initially, at the moment of truth, it is assumed that an agent should perform all of the prima facie duties attributed to him or her. However, the performance of one duty can, in some cases, prohibit the agent from performing another duty, or, alternatively, it would result in a violation of the rights of another stakeholder. The following example, based on a classical critique, illustrates this possibility:

Amy has a prima facie duty to tell the truth. Darrell knocks on her door one night and tells her he is being pursued by members of a street gang who threaten to kill him despite the fact that he has done nothing to harm them. He asks her to give him a hiding place and not to tell the gang where he is. Amy agrees. Later, members of the gang beat on Amy's door and demand that she lead them to Darrell. Torn between two options, Amy finally tells the gang that she does not know where Darrell is and they leave.

Amy lied. She violated her prima facie duty to tell the truth. But she was faced with a moral quandary. If she told the truth, Darrell would be unjustifiably killed, whereas if she lied, he would be saved. So she chose to lie to respect her duty of nonmaleficence toward Darrell as well as, perhaps, her duties of gratitude, justice, and respect for the rights and privileges of others. A full examination of the facts of the case could very well lead to the conclusion that Amy's behavior was ethically justified despite the fact that she violated a prime facie duty.

This story illustrates a crucial point in pluralist, deontological theory and in ethical thinking in general: supersession. An agent can fail to discharge a prima facie duty or can violate another's prima facie rights *only* if that duty is superseded by a higher-order duty or right. In addition, the agent bears the burden of proof and must be able to demonstrate why the duty respected is more important than the one violated. Quandaries of this type arise frequently in day-to-day decision making.

Applying Deontological Reasoning to the Promise Club Case

In applying deontological reasoning to the CPOS Promise Club case, one would begin with the relationship between the store and its customers. The store has a prima facie duty (nonmaleficence) not to harm its customers, and to the extent that its actions invaded their customers' privacy, it has violated this duty. It also has a duty of fidelity. It holds in trust the data it has collected about its customers with the assumption that it will use this data only for business transactions. How binding this duty is depends on whether or not the statement, "I agree to allow Tom Thumb & Page and their data processing supplier to record and make use of information about the products I purchase," dropped unexplained into the fine print, constitutes informed consent. The store's duty of beneficence includes an obligation to provide services to their customers. The force of pure deontological reasoning is that if any of these duties are not fulfilled, the store is unethical and should discontinue the program. Other relationships between the store and CPOS, CPOS and the list users, the list users and the customers, the list users and the stores, and CPOS and the customers should also be examined.

Supersession applies in several ways in the CPOS Promise Card case. First, within the bounds of deontological reasoning, the store's duties to not do harm to its customers and for fidelity with respect to the data it holds in trust trumps its duty for beneficence, making the program appear to be unethical on a deontological basis. In contrast, however, a utilitarian analysis, described later, may lead to the conclusion that in terms of its overall consequences, the Promise Card program was defensible on an ethical basis. These conflicting rule-based and utilitarian conclusions must now be resolved. A person who believed that any harm to customers was intolerable would judge the program to be unethical, whereas one who weighed all of the consequences may conclude that the program was ethically defensible. In either case, the final judgment would be based on articulable reasons derived from ethical theories and principles.

Is There Just One Universal Right or Duty? Kant's Search for an Ethics of Equity Based on Human Relationships

The philosopher Immanuel Kant in the late 18th century posed a central question for ethics: Does there exist a single moral right (and correlative duty) that is so fundamental that everyone is obligated to pursue it regardless of its outcome or the characteristics of the agents to whom it pertains? Kant reasoned that such a moral law did indeed exist. He called it the *categorical imperative* and argued that it was binding on all members of a community, absolutely, without exception or qualification. The origin of this law is the human will, and its goal is to improve the human condition.

Toward the end of *Critique of Practical Reason* Kant (1788/1956) reflects on the human condition and observes, "Two things fill my heart with never ending awe: the starry heavens above and the moral law within" (p. 162). The human will guided by this moral law operates by its own code. The legislative requirement of Kant's categorical imperative essentially states that every stakeholder must be treated as an equal to everyone else. This means that everyone has a right to be treated as a free person and, accordingly, everyone has a correlative duty to treat all other stakeholders as free persons. Kant offers three interrelated formulations of his categorical imperative, which may be summarized as principles.

1. Principle of Consistency. "Act only according to that maxim by which you can at the same time will that it should become a universal law" (quoted in Newton, 1989, p. 133). Truth telling, for example, is justified by this principle because if everyone were permitted to lie, we could never separate truth from falsehood. Consequently, no one could be trusted and society would become chaotic. Thus, in an information society, if a person could violate anyone else's privacy, steal or copy their intellectual property, limit their access to information, or provide them with inaccurate information, they would be violating the principle of consistency.

2. *Principle of Dignity.* "Act so that you treat humanity, whether in your own person or in that of another, always as an [end in itself] and never as a means only" (quoted in Newton, 1989, p. 135). This principle implies that any policy—such as slavery or coercion—that treats human beings as a means of achieving something else rather than as an end in itself compromises their dignity and is unethical because it is done without respect for their humanity. Kant would consider, for example, that the use of information about an individual without his or her informed consent, such as the secret use of "truth phones," constitutes an assault on that person's dignity.

3. *Principle of Harmony and Community.* If everyone in an ethical field abides by the first two principles, a mutually supporting community is formed, one that Kant called a "kingdom of ends." In this realm, every stakeholder contributes universal laws out of his own free will. He or she is accountable to these laws, and they treat every other stakeholder with dignity. The result is a community based on individual dignity and equality for all members. Operating on this principle, for example, every stakeholder who has access to an information system would will that every other stakeholder would have open access to the same information services and that none of the information provided would compromise the dignity of any other stakeholder.

Kant's vision is glorious. It is a good guideline to always keep in mind. In support of Kant, many observers agree that most of the serious problems that society faces today—pollution, poverty, militarism, information and knowledge provision—are problems of human relations and equity as Kant described them. Certainly, many information issues are illuminated by shining Kant's light on them. But the theory has several shortcomings besides often being simply impractical to implement. Numerous ethicists have offered critiques. They find two general pitfalls in trying to apply his views.

C. West Churchman (1982), an ardent admirer of Kant, points out that Kant's theory of morality "does not permit gradations of morality in human affairs." As a consequence, an act is either good or evil. There is no middle ground, no shades of goodness, no quantification of an act's moral quality.

Furthermore, there is no trade-off principle in Kant's theory. In Kant's view "one cannot 'buy off' evil by subsequently doing good." So, Kant renders the process of supersession, as discussed in this book, irrelevant. The command "Thou shall not lie," for example, must be obeyed regardless of how severe the consequences or how moderate the falsehood.

Applying Kant's Categorical Imperative to the Promise Club Case

A rigorous application of Kant's categorical imperative would find the CPOS Promise Card program unethical. Because its primary purpose is to collect data about customers, it tends to emphasize treating customers as means rather than an end in themselves, although they do receive some benefits in terms of discounts and so on. The principle of dignity is violated. Because at least one customer's privacy is violated and the requirements of informed consent may not have been fully met, it is unlikely that one would will that all customers be treated in this manner thus violating the principle of consistency. As a result of violating the other two principles, the principle of harmony and community cannot be upheld either. It is unlikely that the CPOS Promise Card program leads to a kingdom of ends.

Most ethicists find Kant's categorical imperative inspiring but too restrictive. Churchman's (1982) critique suggests that to deal adequately with the most common needs for quantification and for making trade-offs, one needs to reach beyond the rules—beyond deontology—and bring in consequentialism, a form of teleology.

▨ CENTERING ON RESULTS AND STAKEHOLDERS: USING THE ANSWERS TO QUESTION 3

Consequentialism and Utilitarianism

Acts have consequences. They affect the lives of both stakeholders and the agents themselves. Theories that focus on the consequences of acts are teleological, as described earlier. They hold that the moral worth of an action is determined by the results that follow from it. One historically important result-based notion is called *utilitarianism*. It is part of a larger set of theories called *consequentialism*, all of which focus on the goal of "producing good."

In the late 18th century, a British writer, government reformer, and philosopher named Jeremy Bentham (1789/1823) set out to provide a moral basis for government policy and legislation by posing a new ethical theory. "Nature has placed mankind under the governance of two sovereign masters," he begins his treatise, "*pain* and *pleasure*" (p. 1). All people are subjected to these sensations, he argued, because they are inherent and fundamental to the human condition. He used these two sensations as the basis for a calculus designed to reach objective grounds for coming to agreements on social policies. The key to the calculus is to assess the consequences of acts on the basis of a common unit of measure: *utility.* Utility refers to the effects of an act that tend to produce (a) benefits, advantages, pleasure, good, or happiness and (b) costs, mischief, pain, evil, or unhappiness. It is measured by the sum of benefits over costs or of pleasure over pain. Utilitarians believe that the best policy to follow at a moment of truth is the one that produces the greatest utility; the best social policy is the one that produces the greatest utility for the greatest number of stakeholders. Economic cost-benefit analysis is a modern refinement of Bentham's original idea.

The utilitarian approach involves three steps:

1. Identify the alternative courses of action an agent can take at a given moment of truth.
2. Estimate the benefits and costs of each alternative to each and every stakeholder. Summarize the results of this assessment into a utility measure.
3. Choose the alternative with the highest measure of utility.

This theory is relatively clear and easy to understand, but it is sometimes very difficult to apply. One problem, as Bentham (1789/1823, pp. 17-20) acknowledged, is an agent's tendency to apply the cost-benefit calculus only to oneself. When agents choose the course of action that maximizes only their own personal utility they are engaged in a process called "egoism" because they are exclusively pursuing their own self-interests. In contrast, a truly ethical social policy can be achieved only by applying the principle of utility to the entire community of stakeholders. This adds a new degree of complication: the difficulty in moving from micro- to macro-considerations. This is one of the major pitfalls in applying utilitarianism.

A second problem is the difficulty of adequately measuring utility. Considerable progress has been made in this area by modern economists and operations researchers; nevertheless, the central problem of devising a common measure for valuing outcomes for different people still persists. This is sometimes referred to as the problem of interpersonal comparison of utilities. Aware of this problem, John Stuart Mill—the son of Jeremy Bentham's best friend, the Scottish economist James Mill—made several extensions to the theory of utilitarianism that solved some of the problems of making comparisons. In doing so, however, he complicated the problem of measurement even further. Mill (1859/1956) pointed out that it was not just the quantity of pleasure that had to be taken into account but also the quality of pleasure. All stakeholders have preferences, and they are usually not exactly the same. What is a great pleasure for one person might be an inferior one for another person and vice versa. Following Mill, most utilitarians admit that there is a difficulty in measuring utility precisely, but they also point out that many good approximations are available and are used frequently. Market prices, monetary equivalents, and explicit statements of consequences can be substituted for purer forms of measurement.

Perhaps the most damning charge against utilitarianism is that it is potentially brutal and heartless. It allows for a given individual's rights to be severely compromised to provide benefits for several others. As a result, justice is not served. John Stuart Mill (1859/1956), however, sought to refute this criticism in his classic *On Liberty* by arguing that general happiness—a state he believes can be reached by the utilitarian method—also requires the preservation of all individual rights and justice. If he is right, then the simplistic concept of cost-benefit analysis must be augmented to make provisions for minimal safeguards for every stakeholder.

Applying Utilitarian Reasoning to the Promise Club Case

A plausible utilitarian argument in the CPOS Promise Club case goes as follows: The consequences of third-party use of customer profile and purchasing data inflicts some harm on those customers whose privacy is violated. This may be offset by the benefits derived by customers from receiving discounts, recipes, health and nutrition information, and mailings describing new products and price specials. The manufacturers, direct-marketing organizations, and other users benefit because they can be more efficient in advertising to a smaller, more prequalified set of customers. This improves their profitability and might even result in lower prices for the consumer. Thus the price they pay for the lists is more than recaptured in reduced costs and increased sales. CPOS benefits from selling the service to the users. The stores benefit from having a service that they can feature in competition with other supermarkets and from the goodwill that flows from satisfied customers. On the other hand, the stores are disadvantaged because they have given up ownership of their valuable customer data (they must buy it back from CPOS), and they certainly lose to the extent that their Promise Card customers become disgruntled and disaffected and take their business to a competing store. On balance, it would appear that the greatest good for the greatest number favors continuing the program. The trade-offs between those who are better off and those who are worse off indicate, initially, that the losses the customers and stores bear are made up for by the gains of others. But the crux of the argument rests on the amount of weight placed on the loss of the customers' privacy and the inconvenience caused by additional mailings. If these "pains" are great enough, the balance would tip in favor of assessing the CPOS Promise Card program as being unethical and discontinuing it.

Utilitarianism is a widely used and respected ethical theory. In fact, most approaches to decision making are based on some form of utilitarianism. This theory is also used in conjunction with other ethical theories as illustrated by Mill's broadening of it to include a requirement that the basic rights of all members in a society be safeguarded. This leads us to considerations of justice.

⊠ CENTERING ON JUSTICE: USING THE ANSWERS TO QUESTION 4

Standards of Justice

Justice requires the comparing and weighing of the conflicting claims of all of the stakeholders in an ethical field and arriving at a solution that balances these claims fairly. It encompasses several important social decision processes: (a) how benefits and burdens are distributed among stakeholders, (b) how rules and laws are administered, (c) how competition and cooperation are conducted within the field, (d) how perpetrators are punished for the wrongs they committed, and (e) how victims are compensated for the wrongs they have suffered.

The concept of justice helps us overcome one of the criticisms of utilitarianism discussed earlier. If decisions are always made on the basis of the greatest good for the greatest number, the majority will continue to benefit and the minority will suffer. Exclusive reliance on norms of utilitarianism eventually creates an underclass that is comparatively powerless and comprises some of the least-advantaged members of the society. In extreme cases, the fundamental rights of the underclass are breached. A utilitarian might argue that slavery (or even paying very low wages) is justified on the grounds that the overall output and productivity of the community is improved and therefore everyone benefits—or at least many do. Justice, however, requires that each stakeholder's claim be considered individually and that his or her basic rights and privileges not be violated.

Throughout history, a number of standards for arriving at just decisions have been put forth. These standards assume one of three general forms: distributive, retributive, or compensatory forms.

Distributive Justice

Stakeholders in an ethical field who are similar in all relevant respects should receive similar benefits and burdens. This standard is further refined by additional standards for achieving a "similar" distribution.

Equity. Every stakeholder is an information taker and should receive equal shares of the society's benefits and burdens. "Equal" can also be defined in several different ways. The following examples of standards for equality in information systems capture some of the different definitions:

1. Every stakeholder receives exactly the same information.
2. Every stakeholder has exactly the same information technology.
3. Every stakeholder has access to the same pool of information (or information services) and can be a taker if he or she wants.
4. Every stakeholder has the same budget to spend for information or information services.
5. The response time from the time of a request for information to the time of its delivery is the same for every stakeholder.

Merit. Every stakeholder should receive benefits according to his or her contributions to achieving the goals of the society as a whole. Under this standard, stakeholders would earn the right to take information and information technology based on the results of their efforts in society. In a capitalist or market society, these results would be evaluated by the marketplace, and stakeholders would receive the information they were willing and able to pay for.

Socialism. Every stakeholder should receive burdens according to his or her ability to bear them and should receive benefits according to his or her needs. Under this standard, those who are able to produce and give information of all sorts should do so. The resulting pool of information is then distributed to those who need it. (Most communist countries adopted policies of this sort. More recently, as market forces have reached these countries, their information policies, such as those dealing with intellectual property rights, have been severely challenged.)

Libertarianism. Every stakeholder may bear whichever burdens he or she chooses and may receive whichever benefits come of that choice and what other stakeholders choose to give to or do for him or her. This is a standard based on freedom. Under this standard, stakeholders are free to produce whatever information they are inclined to and to buy whatever information is available in the marketplace without restraint. They are free to subsequently use the information for their own purposes or sell it to others. Censorship is not tolerated. That is, information takers who have accumulated information can give it or sell it without restraint to anyone else they want to.

Fairness à la John Rawls. Every conflict of claims among stakeholders should be resolved by a fair method. The fairest method, Rawls (1971) proposes, is to assume at the outset that every problem is couched in a "veil of ignorance." Suppose, for example that you are just now writing the social contract for a new society. You have no way of knowing whether you will end up in the upper, most powerful class; the middle class; or be relegated to the under, powerless class. What rules would you want in the contract? Under these conditions, Rawls argues, no sensible stakeholder would agree to provisions that would assign him or her to the underclass. People would not want to predestine themselves or their future generations to suffer poverty and powerlessness all of their lives. In this "original position," he concludes, stakeholders would base their rules on two principles:

1. Each person is to have an equal right to the most extensive basic liberty compatible with a similar liberty for others.

2. Social and economic inequalities are to be arranged so that they are both (a) reasonably expected to be to everyone's advantage, and (b) attached to positions and offices open to all. (pp. 60-61)

In a Rawlsian information society, applying the first principle ensures that every stakeholder's basic rights and liberties—such as one's right to know; right to privacy; right to accurate, reliable, unbiased information; right to one's own intellectual and tangible property; and right to fair access to information and information technology—are protected. The second set of provisions, then, describes how inequalities will be dealt with. The second principle's initial condition—called the "difference principle"—acknowledges that there will be inequalities in the distribution of information and information technology but requires that steps be taken to improve the lot of the *least advantaged* members of the society to the greatest degree possible.

The second principle's second condition—called the "fair equality of opportunity principle"—recognizes that an effective society is organized into positions, offices, and roles. Each position has its own somewhat unique information requirements. Accordingly, the distribution of information will be unequal. However, Rawls argues, every stakeholder should be given an equal opportunity to qualify for any position, including the most privileged ones. This implies that training and education in information proficiency should be available to all stakeholders.

Retributive Justice

Any agent who does wrong or is morally responsible (as discussed earlier) for harming another stakeholder should be punished if the following two requirements are met: (a) The evidence of wrongdoing and that the agent caused it must be convincing, and (b) the punishment must be consistent and proportional to the wrong done—"an eye for an eye, a tooth for a tooth."

Compensatory Justice

Any stakeholder who is wronged by a morally responsible agent should be compensated, rehabilitated, and made "whole" to the extent possible. Restitution and reparation should be completed and damages paid to the injured party. This is an important condition of justice, but as we saw in Chapter 2, the nature of information makes this standard difficult to apply in many cases. On the one hand, a person whose software is copied without authorization can likely be recompensed for lost sales; on the other hand, there may be no adequate compensation available for a person whose personal privacy is violated.

In summary, according to the standards of justice, a good society is one in which (a) laws and policies distribute benefits and burdens in a fair manner, (b) violators are punished, and (c) victims are adequately compensated. It is generally expected that people will abide by these laws. But what happens if someone in good conscience decides that the laws themselves are unjust?

When Can Laws Be Violated? The Case for Civil Disobedience

Is breaking the law ever ethically justified? The pure deontological perspective seems to argue "No!" But this ultraconservative belief shields the possibility that a law itself may be unethical. Societies, in fact, make two kinds of law—just laws and unjust laws—St. Augustine observed in about 400 A.D. One of the founders of theology, Augustine (1881) argued that "an unjust law is no law at all" and went on to claim that an agent can justifiably violate an unjust law if (a) it can be demonstrated that the law is unjust, (b) the actions taken to break it do the least harm possible to others, and (c) the actions taken are necessary to correct the injustice.

Martin Luther King, Jr. is the most notable modern exponent of this view. In his "A Letter From a Birmingham Jail," written in his cell after he was arrested for boycotting the Montgomery, Alabama, bus system, King proclaims that the then prevalent laws permitting segregation were unjust. Consequently, they could be ethically disobeyed:

> I hope you are able to see the distinction I am trying to point out. In no sense do I advocate evading or defying the law, as would the rabid segregationist. That would lead to anarchy. One who breaks an unjust law must do so openly, lovingly, and with a willingness to accept the penalty. I submit that an individual who breaks a law that conscience tells him is unjust, and who willingly accepts the penalty of imprisonment in order to arouse the conscience of the community over its injustice, is in reality expressing the highest respect for the law. (quoted in Newton, 1989, p. 153)

If, as King believes, evil, wrong, or unjust laws can be—in fact, should be—broken, then what is to prevent lawlessness and total chaos from reigning? The answer lies, again, in the principle of supersession: One may breach an ethical principle only if he or she can demonstrate that some other principle is superior to it. This is an important principle, but does applying it result in an infinite regress or vicious circle? Many ethicists argue that this is not the case because the ultimate principle from which all other ethical principles flow, they believe, is justice.

Supersession Revisited: Justice as the Highest Order Theory

Justice is considered by many to be the highest-order ethical principle. It runs through the entire gamut of theories. In ancient Greek theory, justice is the virtue used to balance all the other virtues and to permit each to play its proper role in society. For pluralist deontologists, like Ross (1930), justice is a duty that can be, and often is, used to supersede other duties. Kant (1788/1956) included equity and dignity—concepts closely related to justice—as fundamental features of his categorical imperative. For Kant, justice is served by following the edicts of the three formulations of the categorical imperative. Utilitarians argue that properly applied, the principle of the greatest good for the greatest number satisfies the criteria of justice as well, and they used this argument to justify their theory. John Rawls (1971), however, provides the most comprehensive account. His procedural theory, he believes, incorporates the essential features of most ethical traditions: (a) It is based on the Kantian moral principles of consistency, dignity, and harmony; (b) it serves to protect rights and duties; and (c) it satisfies utilitarian requirements as well.

The route to justice through supersession may be summed up as follows: In a morally perfect world, the agent, the act taken, and the results of the act are all ethical and satisfy the requirements of justice. If so, then ethical reasoning need be carried no further. If not—if a virtue must be compromised, if a prima facie right or duty violated, or if an alternative with lower utility implemented—then the act *must* be defended on the basis of some other ethical principle that supersedes it. A chain of reasoning is used to find the moral grounds for the supplanting of one principle by another. The final link in this chain is the concept of justice. The principle of supersession also safeguards ethics from the criticism that it is relativistic.

Epilogue to the Promise Club Case

In the days since its inception, the CPOS program that Tom Thumb and grocers adopted underwent considerable change as ethical issues were raised and dealt with. The company's senior executives became a focal point for the ethical debate on privacy and direct marketing. On May 16, 1990, Jerry Saltzgaber, CEO of Citicorp Point-of-Sale Information Services testified in defense of his company's program before the Subcommittee on Government Information, Justice, and Agriculture of the Committee on Government Operations of the U.S. House of Representatives hearings on Data Protection and Household Marketing. After claiming that "everyone benefits from household marketing," he explained CPOS's policies:

> At Citicorp POS, we have recognized our responsibility for consumer privacy and data protection from the very beginning. At every stage of our development, we have endeavored to find out how consumers feel about our use of their purchase information. And at every stage, they have told us that they feel comfortable with our programs and our use of their purchase information. Based on our experience, we have developed a very pro-active privacy policy which, we believe, insures consumer's the privacy they desire.
>
> The principles of this policy which guide our entire operation are quite simple. We explain our programs, as well as the use of household information, to consumers before they enroll. We tell them that we intend to use their purchase information for additional marketing purposes. And, we inform consumers that they can participate in the programs even if they withhold their permission to use their purchase information. We remind shoppers every year that we are using their purchase information and that they can withdraw their permission and still participate in the program.
>
> We have established a privacy review committee that oversees our operations and reports directly to me on privacy issues. But most important, we do not release the purchase information if we believe it might be detrimental to consumers, and we don't respond to requests for information about specific individuals without their consent or a court order.
>
> With respect to data protection, CPOS maintains control of all names and addresses of customers. We only allow reputable companies, who have executed confidentiality agreements with us, to use our purchase information, and we take appropriate action to insure that they live up to their obligations under their agreement with us.
>
> We subscribe to the Mail Preference Service of the Direct Marketing Association and comply with all customer requests not to receive direct mailings. And we do not allow our purchase information to be used for computer-generated telephone sales efforts. (U.S. House of Representatives, 1990, p. 89)

It appears, however, that Saltzgaber's and CPOS's moment of recognition came too late. Under the headline "Citicorp's Folly?" (1991), the *Wall Street Journal* noted that the point-of-sale unit had "irritated retailers and shoppers"

Table 6.2 Differences Between Various Ethical Theories

Focal Center	Type	Theories and Concepts
Agents	Teleological	Egoism, moral responsibility, virtues, self-interest (Figure 6.3, "Assigning Responsibility," applies here)
Actions	Deontological	Moral laws and commands; prima facie duties, rights, privileges, and responsibilities; categorical imperative
Results and stakeholders	Teleological	Consequentialism, utilitarianism
Justice	Teleological	Fairness, distributive justice, egalitarianism and equality, retributive justice, compensatory justice, civil disobedience

alike and that, despite this reaction, an "overoptimistic executive" [Saltzgaber] had kept spending cash on a "terrific idea" that had missed its targets. The article concluded that "In November [of 1990, Citicorp] abruptly canceled its most ambitious program, fired 174 staffers and shunted aside [Mr. Saltzgaber], a gung-ho chief executive it had brought in 2 1/2 years earlier to run the program" (p. 1).

SUMMARY

Ethical theories are the lenses through which corrective vision is realized. They are used to interpret the facts of an ethical issue—what is—and to indicate what ought to be. There are two broad types of theories: teleological and deontological. Teleological theories focus on the purposes of the social system and the consequences of acts. They are used to evaluate agents, the results of actions taken, and the standards of justice. Deontological theories deal with the acts themselves and the duties, rights, privileges, and responsibilities that pertain to them. Agents, actions, results, and justice are the four focal centers used to differentiate between various ethical theories (see Table 6.2).

Corrective vision requires that the final moral judgment be reached by means of ethical reasoning. In general, ethical reasoning bases judgments and actions on rules, codes, or guidelines, which, in turn, are based on ethical principles, which, in turn, are grounded in ethical theories. At the beginning of the examination of an ethical issue, all relevant theories are presumed to have equally valid moral force. These prima facie claims can be broken only by demonstrating that some other principle supersedes the principle being replaced. This process is repeated, forming a chain of reasoning. The final arbiter in this chain, if no other dominating principle emerges, is the concept of justice. Figure 6.1, "A Model for Ethical Reasoning," illustrates the process.

◩ NOTE

1. Copyright © 1970 by The New York Times Company. Reprinted by permission.

PART III

Applications of Information Ethics in Society

The forces that resulted in the information age were described in Part I. Today, these forces confront people with new moments of truth. The actions people take in response to these forces will set the course for the future and shape the nature of the evolving society. Drawing on the notion of ethics as corrective vision, Part II presented a framework for applying ethical thinking and for gaining access to key ethical theories and principles that can be used to arrive at ethical decisions and judgments.

Implicit in much that was said in Parts I and II is that ethics is essentially an individual matter. The moral life, however, involves much more than individuals and individual behavior. Beyond the challenge of individual ethics are the special ethical problems that confront organizations and entire societies. These problems of "collective" ethics must also be addressed. Hovering between the individual and collective levels of ethics is the institution of professions. Professions are composed of groups of people who provide a common body of expertise to help human beings solve their problems. Professionals operate both as individuals and as members of collectives and, frequently, as employees of organizations also. Indeed, playing these various roles becomes a source of ethical tension for professionals. The chapters in Part III are devoted to ethical issues affecting collectives. In particular, they address the special ethical considerations faced by professionals who work with information as members of a profession, of organizations, and of societies in the information age.

7

Information Professionalism

INFORMATION PROFESSIONALS: AN EMERGING PROFESSION

Professions, in their most general sense, consist of exclusive occupational groups who apply special expertise to help human beings solve particular human problems. Some familiar professions include medicine, law, architecture, and engineering. With the advent of the information explosion, a new kind of profession is emerging, one that seeks to help people by providing them with information and by managing the complex processes—information life cycles—by means of which information is produced and provided. According to Abbott (1988), among the crucial tasks these professionals perform is to "help clients [who are] overburdened with material from which they cannot retrieve usable information" (p. 216). Those working in this new class of professionals are called *information professionals* (IPs). IPs face some difficult and challenging ethical issues, as the following case illustrates.

UNTESTED SOFTWARE: A PROFESSIONAL QUANDARY

A number of years ago, a software engineer who was responsible for coordinating the National Aeronautics and Space Administration's (NASA) contract with major hardware and software vendors to build an onboard flight management system, lost her job because she was concerned about the quality of the software product that was under development. During the project's first complete, formal progress review, this software engineer realized that, although the project was presumably nearing completion and the software would soon be operational, it had not been adequately tested. Nevertheless, the company's senior management wanted the software project completed quickly, delivered on time, and billed according to the contract schedule. Unfortunately, this experienced software engineer felt that the product had not been properly tested or checked, nor had several design change modifications been property verified. All of this, she believed, negatively affected the quality of the product. In addition, the documentation was inadequate. Most troubling, however, was her strong belief that certain modules of this highly complex program were inherently untestable on land and thus must be tested during a space mission. The software engineer repeatedly, and with increasing intensity, reported her concerns to her superiors but to no avail. In fact, she claimed, that after hearing about her reservations, several senior executives both intimidated and harassed her for her concerns, accusing her of incompetence and insubordination. Her job was threatened. A few days later, the software engineer collapsed under the stress. Because she could no longer do her job, the executives dismissed her.

This case illustrates the key ethical problem of professionalism: Professional duties and responsibilities sometimes come into conflict with organizational goals and outcomes. In this case, the software engineer was faced with a true ethical quandary: Either she could follow the course of action dictated by her professional knowledge and experience and hold up the software project until the code was adequately tested, or she could accede to the wishes and goals of her employer. Which should she do? By refusing to go along with management's wishes, she jeopardized her job and her health but lived up to her professional responsibilities. In this case, it turns out, she was factually correct. Subsequent use revealed that the software was indeed faulty. Flaws in the software that would have placed lives and expensive equipment at risk were discovered just before a mission was begun and a testing program, similar to that recommended by the departed engineer, was undertaken that revealed several more.

Most professional decision situations are not as demanding as the one described in this case. Nevertheless, all professionals must be prepared to make these kinds of choices. This chapter discusses professional responsibilities and the close relationship that exists between professionalism and ethical behavior. It begins with a response to the question, What is a professional?

◪ WHAT IS A PROFESSIONAL?

The term *professional* derives from the Latin root words of *pro*, meaning "before," and *fateor*, meaning "to avow." This etymological origin suggests "the notion of a covenant, a declaration or vow to be faithful for something to someone" (May, 1983, p. 3). In most professions, the "someone" is the professional's clients and the "something" is the professional's special expertise.

A profession consists of a group of people who follow a calling, the successful completion of which requires specialized knowledge—knowledge usually obtained after a long, intensive academic preparation. The members of a given profession possess similar knowledge and skills, provide similar services to their clients, and are committed to high ethical standards. Generally, professionals are expected to take an altruistic attitude toward their clients, the services they provide them, and the society in which they live. Importantly, professionals assume a position of social independence. Ideally, they are self-reliant and free from the influence, guidance, or control of any other individuals or organizations. The group is primarily responsible for achieving the stated goals of the profession and for defining ethical, technical, and other standards of conduct. Generally speaking, the group's members avoid conflicts of interest in which an individual's narrow self-interests prevail over a client's or society's interests. Members of a profession are accorded special rights and privileges because they provide valuable services and are given training, status, and power to deliver these services. In return, they are expected to give up some of their freedom and to assume certain duties and responsibilities with respect to their clients and society in general. Consequently, there is a spirit of personal sacrifice in a profession.

Consider the example of the medical profession. Physicians were not always recognized as professionals. As recently as the 19th century, the practice of medicine was characterized by sketchy medical education and preparation and, in some instances, even by quackery. Recognizing the importance of high-quality medical practice, early in this century the Rockefeller and Carnegie Foundations commissioned one of their aides, Abraham Flexner, to study the situation and to make recommendations about the education and preparation of individuals who intended to practice medicine. The Flexner Report, as his completed study came to be known, subsequently revolutionized American medical education and practice, and it clearly defined medicine as a profession. In it, Flexner summarized the nature of the new and expanding responsibilities and privileges of medical practitioners. The American Medical Association used the Flexner Report to undertake far-reaching changes that reshaped the medical profession. These changes were based on Flexner's attributes of a profession that are now recognized as important attributes not only of the medical professional but also of any group that aspires to practice as professionals.

Flexner proposed the following set of criteria for defining a profession that is still in use today:

- A profession possesses and draws on a store of knowledge that is more than ordinary.
- A profession possesses a theoretical and intellectual grasp that is different from that of a technician's practice.
- A profession applies theoretical and intellectual knowledge to solving human and social problems.
- A profession strives to add to and improve its body of knowledge through research.
- A profession passes on the body of knowledge to novice generations for the most part in a university setting.
- A profession is imbued with an altruistic spirit. (Metzger, 1975)

Flexner developed these criteria about 80 years ago to evaluate the medical profession. Later, he applied them to the field of social work. Today, they are also apt and appropriate for the emerging information professions.

◫ WHAT IS AN INFORMATION PROFESSIONAL?

A large number of occupations are being created that are highly information intensive and rely heavily on one's knowledge and skills for handling information. Most of these information occupations are also recognized as professional occupations because they deal almost exclusively with some aspect of information acquisition, processing, storing, dissemination, and use. As professionals, these workers possess specialized knowledge, and, as is true of all professionals, they also employ their knowledge and skills in the service of others.

Information professionals possess specialized knowledge about information, knowledge, and information technology. That is, they are skilled at processing symbols. They deal primarily with codified or objectified information rather than information in a subjective form. Consider a contrast: Two people casually talking face-to-face also exchange information and influence each other's minds. They do not require help from an information professional to do so, whereas a banker who requests credit information from a bureau does. So, too, do those who call on the services of an accountant, archivist, or the like. The relevant distinction is that these IPs deal with information that is objectified and packaged in symbols. Such information has been gleaned from the world, organized, systematized, and captured in some external medium that an IP is able to manipulate.

Technological knowledge is also an important part of information professionals' specialized knowledge. They are not only concerned with moving signs and symbols from one mind to another; they are also inevitably concerned with the means by which the information is conveyed. In fact, a large percentage of many IPs' time and talent is devoted to selecting, managing, and applying the means through which information is handled and transferred.

Information professionals serve as information givers and orchestrators. They interact with their clients, information takers, to improve their clients' intellectual state. All information work, as discussed in Chapter 2 and subsequent chapters, involves, to some extent, influencing other people's minds. Information professionals do this by using their skills and power to help their clients understand and know something they did not know before or help them do something they could not do before. Conveying power from the professional to the client is done by means of signs and routines that the professional uses to influence the client.

This kind of conveyance of power is on the upswing. The demand for information work is growing rapidly and has become a dominant factor of the labor force. Since the early 1970s, more than 50% of the U.S. labor force has been involved in jobs that require an extensive amount of information handling (Bell, 1973; Porat & Rubin, 1977). Included among the kinds of jobs these people hold are those of accountants, archivists, consultants of all kinds, librarians, records managers, information systems analysts, management scientists, museum curators, journalists, computer programmers, and software engineers. Information work, or knowledge work as it is sometimes referred to, is rising in quantity and in centrality to the economy as almost all jobs are becoming more information intensive. The implications of these changes are profound. The global economy and the polity are now more dependent than ever on the performance of information workers. Because organizations and individuals are increasingly dependent on them, information workers are assuming a much more prominent and powerful societal role. Along with this enhanced power, however, comes a greater need for ethical responsibility—a responsibility that derives directly from the social functions they perform.

Thus, the primary "someone" to whom an information professional makes a covenantal commitment includes his or her clients and subsequent information takers. The "something" for which he or she is responsible, is the knowledge, information, and skills he or she uses for managing information throughout the entire information life cycle. These skills include knowledge about the nature of information, about information technology, and about theories of knowledge (i.e., about symbol processing and interpretation). The nature of the covenant can be stated more formally:

• The primary social purpose that IPs pursue is to manage and conduct the activities undertaken during information life cycles to improve their client's intellectual state and hence to effectively influence their client's behavior or state of mind.

The functional knowledge base that IPs draw on to discharge this responsibility is their capability to get the right information from the right source to their client(s) at the right time in the form most suitable for the use for which it is intended at a cost justified by its use. This is the essence of the implied covenant that exists between an IP and his or her clients.

▧ WHAT KIND OF WORK DO IPs DO?

All information professionals have much in common with each other. They all conduct the activities inherent in information life cycles, yet some important distinctions can be made between the different kinds of work that

IPs do. Information work can be identified in terms of nine different specific functions that identify the role and work of specific IPs.

IPs Who Identify, Build, and Safeguard the Operational, Managerial, and Strategic Systems for Organizations With the Intent of Improving These Organizations' Decision Making and Control. These professionals identify useful sources of information and place data collection and sensing mechanisms within these sources to generate and collect requisite information. They then design systems that transmit, accumulate, analyze, process, store, and disseminate this information to users by working with clients who are managers or employees of the organization. They seek to help their clients run their operations better, control their resources more effectively, and develop strategies that help their organizations prosper and survive. Although the activities of the organization itself will generate much of the requisite information, the domain of information sources is broad and varied and necessarily includes aspects of the entity's relevant business environment.

Typically, these IP positions are called system analysts or management information systems (MIS) specialists. The highest organizational position is usually a vice president for information services or chief information officer (CIO). These IPs' power derives from their exceptional understanding of the processes of measurement, analysis, and data processing and from their knowledge of the computer-based and communications technologies used to carry out these functions.

IPs Who Translate Client Information Requirements Into a Set of Instructions That Are Executable by Machines. These professionals work with symbol strings known as "programs" that are produced to satisfy information requirements normally specified by an information system analyst or MIS specialist. The first order of responsibility is to understand clients' needs and to develop effective programs to solve their problems. Clients typically include a company or government agency.

These information professionals include computer programmers and software engineers. Their power derives from their specialized knowledge of computer and communications devices and the internal structure of those devices in addition to their knowledge about software, specific programming languages, and theories of program structures and program development. (This is the knowledge that was questioned in the space shuttle case discussed at the outset of this chapter.)

IPs Who Observe Events and Shape and Report These Events as Observations or as a "Story." These professionals gather and distribute information about events in a manner designed to allow others to make judgments about these events and their implications. Their clients are the public, individual citizens, business people, government officials, and those who seek to understand and interpret events outside their immediate geographical location.

These professionals include reporters, writers, photographers, camera operators, editors, publishers, and broadcasters—in short, the media. Their power derives from their roles as independent observers, distillers, commentators, or analysts of current events and their ability to influence public opinion and affect the public welfare by means of the choices they make as to what stories to publish and how to present them.

IPs Who Report to Interested Parties on the Economic Activities of Organizations and Other Entities. These professionals identify, collect, and prepare financial reports and statements. Some also produce economic and agricultural forecasts. Their intention is to report fairly and accurately to businesses, governments, not-for-profit enterprises, investors and stockholders of public corporations, managers, taxpayers, public regulatory agencies, and all others who have an economic interest in an enterprise.

These IPs include certified public accountants and financial accountants. Their power derives from their understanding of the economic theory of organizations and their in-depth knowledge of a set of principles and procedures for implementing these theories and for reporting the results. They also have a command of the processing technology necessary to derive these results and deliver them to their clients.

IPs Who Collect, Categorize, and Store Information, Usually in the Form of Documents, Images, Photographs, Memoranda, and Artifacts That Reflect and Trace the History of an Entity or of a Field of Interest. These professionals make archival material available to others on request, although restrictions may be placed on access and use of the information, depending on the nature of the material or the clients requesting it. The nature of the entity or field of interest defines the domain of the sources. Often, clients are historians or others who are interested in the entity or field.

These information professionals are archivists or historians. Their power derives from their ability to select those currently available materials that will be preserved for the future.

IPs Who Clarify, Preserve, and Display Cultural Objects That Have Lasting Interest or Value. Typically, these professionals work with objects and artifacts that themselves are tangible and, as such, are not expressly information. They provide meaning to the artifacts by means of their in-depth knowledge of the artifacts themselves and of the context or situation from which they come. By choosing an interpretation of the objects and the setting in which they will be displayed, these IPs give them new significance. Their clients are the public and other institutions that engage in cultural or educational activities.

These professionals are museum curators. Their primary sources are artists, historians, scientists, naturalists, and collectors of items of cultural value. They derive their power from their specialized knowledge of art and artifacts and the methods and procedures used to identify and interpret them. They have a knowledge of the history of the objects and of these objects' potential value to society. They also have knowledge about methodologies for classifying items and their preservation and storage. They are trained in artistic and educational techniques and use these skills to enhance the informational and educational value of the objects and artifacts.

IPs Who Collect, Categorize, and Store Information, Usually in the Form of Books, Documents, Journals, or Databases That They Make Available to Others on Request. The information provided by these professionals may be delimited by the service and client requirements. Typically, clients are individual citizens, the community, government agencies, and companies.

These information professionals are librarians, information brokers, corporate information services personnel, and database administrators. Their power derives from their knowledge of data and publication sources, acquisition procedures, and handling and classification techniques, such as cataloging, indexing, abstracting, and retrieval.

IPs Who Evaluate Organizational Information That Is to Be Produced and Used in Organizational Settings. These professionals seek to systematically organize, store, and save information that organizations have produced or acquired and to control the costs associated with information generation and storage. Usually, their clients are businesses and government agencies.

These information professionals are records managers, and they derive their power from making decisions about the classification, storage, organization, retention, and destruction of information resources and from their knowledge of legal reporting and retention schedules for documents and information resources.

IPs Who Collect Data About Organizations or Operations and Build Models of Them—Abstract Concepts and Relationships That Describe a Portion of Reality in a Way That Permits Its Representation in Symbolic Form—That Can Be Used to Guide Decision Making. These professionals produce symbols that can be manipulated by computer programs. Information that is both internally generated and external is included in these models. The objective is to help clients achieve efficiency goals and to provide analytical and optional solutions to business problems.

These information professionals are management scientists and operations researchers. They derive power from the application of theories and techniques of model building.

Today, the work of the nine types of professionals is relatively distinct. But as the ubiquitous, networked, multimedia era emerges, these roles are rapidly merging together. Eventually, they may culminate in one superprofessional group. Consequently, anyone who plays one of these roles should become aware of the characteristics and responsibilities of the others.

▨ WHAT ARE AN IP's RESPONSIBILITIES?

As we have seen, the information exchange relationship between professionals and their clients also creates a power relationship. Clients and other information takers lack the right information or the means to find the appropriate information in the mass and chaos of the enormous amount of information available to them. Because clients need or want particular information to perform better in their circumstances, they are at an initial power disadvantage; and hence, they are dependent upon IPs to provide the information they need. Power is used here, as before, to describe an agent's ability (see Chapter 4) to produce the desired effect on a client. In this asymmetrical power relationship, the professional is superordinate and the client is subordinate with respect to the information required. A banker, for example, who needs a credit report to make a loan decision is at a power disadvantage until he or she receives the information. A manager who requests a computer program is at a disadvantage until the company programmer designs and writes the program. The manager may continue to be dependent on the programmer to keep the program running over time. As this chapter's opening scenario indicates, a highly trained astronaut is dependent on software engineers to produce the programs necessary to run the onboard flight management system required to navigate the space shuttle in space.

The ability to influence a client's mind or behavior at a time of need bestows considerable power on information professionals. Their ethical responsibilities derive directly from this power advantage, and therefore, they must guard against using their power to serve their own, more narrow, self-interests. Although many of the information professional's responsibilities are directed toward information takers, the covenant applies with equal force to information givers. An information giver's rights to property, privacy, confidentiality, and relief from undue burden must be counterbalanced with such things as a client's right to have access to needed and accurate information.

Working in organizations further complicates the ethical responsibilities of information professionals. As employees of organizations, they have two masters to serve. On the one hand, they should be dedicated to achieving the goals and objectives of the organization that employs them and to following the instructions provided by their superiors. On the other hand, they are expected and have a duty to exercise judgment and independent assessment in a given situation, in addition to being faithful to their professional covenant and the ethical codes of their profession. These competing duties, to the organization and to the profession, can and sometimes do, come into conflict, as the space shuttle case illustrates. At moments of truth when such quandaries arise, professionals must weigh the pros and cons of each alternative course of action and determine which supersedes the other. The covenant and most professional codes of ethics, however, make it very clear that one's professional responsibilities generally take precedence over other duties. Thus, one is ethically permitted to break the ethical standards of his or her profession only under exceptional circumstances. For this reason, professionals working in organizations can become "thorns in the side" of management; in extreme cases, they may become "whistle-blowers"—that is, ethical resisters who publicly disclose unethical or illegal practices in the workplace.

Generally, the essence of a profession's covenant and responsibilities are captured in a code of conduct or code of ethics for that profession. A code of ethics holds the profession as a whole and its individual members accountable to the public. In return, the profession and its members earn the public's trust, confidence, and respect and an opportunity to obtain increased social benefits and economic rewards. The American Medical Association Code for physicians, the American Bar Association Code of Ethics for attorneys, and the American Society of Mechanical Engineers Code of Ethics for engineers are typical codes that summarize the promises these professionals made to regulate themselves in the interest of society.

As the number of types of information professionals has grown, each professional group has developed its own codes of ethics. For example, the Association for Computing Machinery (ACM) is a professional society with more than 86,000 members, mostly computer programmers, software engineers, scientists, and information analysts. Their stated purpose is to foster understanding about information technology and to promulgate standards for its use. In addition, there are other codes such as the Code of Ethics and Standards of Conduct adopted by the Data Processing Management Association and the Librarian's Code of Ethics, which was first adopted in 1938 and then updated in 1975 and 1981. Examples of a number of the codes of ethics are found in the Appendix.

Overall, the key ethical principles in the different professional codes vary little across different professions. Typically, codes of ethics provide guidance on (a) responsible professional behavior, (b) competence in execution of duties, (c) adherence to moral and legal standards, (d) making public statements, (e) preservation of confidentiality, (f) interest in welfare of the customer, and (g) development and maintenance of professional knowledge.

Codes of ethics are useful aids to individual decision making. They help identify ethical issues. Some of the codes suggest possible courses of action to take at identifiable, significant moments of truth. The codes, however, supplement—they do *not* replace—the general standards for behavior for the society as a whole. One of the drawbacks of ethics codes is that in unique, novel situations that frequently arise with new technology, they provide only minimum guidance.

◪ A FRAMEWORK FOR IDENTIFYING AN IP's RESPONSIBILITIES

Professional Responsibilities

Every profession has a central social purpose and a distinctive functional knowledge base. Each profession also has distinctive responsibilities that flow from its social purpose and its special corpus of knowledge. These responsibilities are generally of two types: (a) professional responsibilities that derive directly from professional activities and (b) social responsibilities that derive

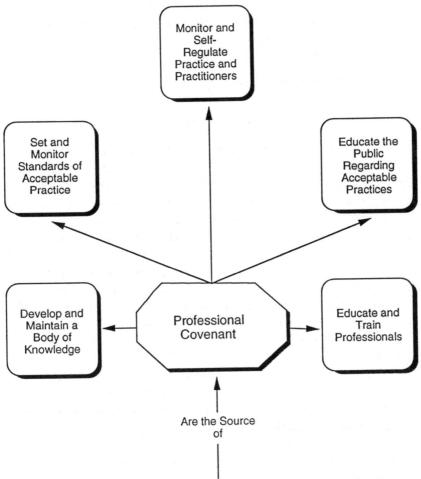

Figure 7.1. Professional Social Responsibilities

from the profession's obligations to the public in general and society at large. Figure 7.1 summarizes these responsibilities. The collective responsibilities that a profession assumes as a whole derive from the expectations that society has of the profession and the privileges society accords it. Five such social responsibilities can be readily identified.

Five Major Social Responsibilities

Develop and Maintain a Body of Knowledge

As discussed earlier, the foundation of information professions is a functional knowledge base by which the IP acquires for the client the right information from the right sources at the right time in the form most suitable for its intended use at a cost justified by its use. This is a unique kind of expertise that draws on concepts and theories describing the nature of information, its economics, the psychology of its use, and technological and methodological means by which systems are designed and implemented. A substantial portion of this knowledge is conveyed to aspiring practitioners by colleges and universities. In addition, most professional groups conduct substantial amounts of "in-house" training; many individual professionals are also obliged by their organizations or encouraged to take courses to "self-learn" (or "self-teach" themselves) new methods and technologies as these emerge as state-of-the-art practice.

The moral obligation of information professions is to continue to invest in research, develop and test new theories and frameworks, and conduct studies and postmortems to evaluate the validity of theories and concepts relevant to their practice. The resulting new knowledge must be integrated with the existing corpus of knowledge in a way that makes it accessible and applicable. This knowledge is then used to educate and train practitioners and new professionals.

Educate and Train Professionals

There are several dimensions of education for IPs. Most important is that every IP master the theories, methods, techniques, and practices of the profession as supported by the profession's body of knowledge. Each IP must understand deeply the profession's covenant and its professional responsibilities. Professionals must be able to recognize crucial moments of truth and respond to them effectively and ethically. (One of the missions of this book is to help professionals do this.) The moral obligation of a profession is to ensure that all of its practicing members are adequately educated and trained. Certification is one way of meeting this need.

Monitor and Self-Regulate Practice and Practitioners

Not only must information professionals produce knowledge and impart it to their colleagues, they must also ensure that their colleagues use the knowledge appropriately. This, in part, was the quandary that the software engineer faced in the case discussed at the beginning of this chapter. She believed, based on her professional education, training, and experience, that her colleagues and managers were not applying the knowledge of their field appropriately or ethically. In this case, her attempts to correct the situation failed, but she did try. Some critics of the professions would argue that she was further obligated to become a whistle-blower.

Self-monitoring of a profession by its members is essential, but it is also very difficult to accomplish when controversy or contradictory information presents itself. For example, a controversy erupted recently when two art historians by the names of Moran and Mallory came into conflict with the librarians at the well-respected Kunsthistorisches Institut in Florence over the attribution of a famous Sienese fresco, the Guidoriccio fresco (see Swan, 1991). For many years, the art institute as well as most of the Italian art community, had believed the Guidoriccio to be the work of Simone Martini, a founding father of Western painting. Moran and his colleague, Mallory, produced evidence that argued that Martini could not have been the artist because, they believed, the fresco postdated his life. According to Moran and Mallory's claims, the librarians at the Kunsthistorisches Institut failed to recognize their theories in their indexing of art periodicals, reports, and books and instead consigned information on their alternative designation of the fresco to a file labeled "Miscellanea Moran," which isolated their writings from the mainstream and made them inaccessible to any interested parties. Even an institute scholar admitted that he was unable to find information on the Moran-Mallory theory when asked to do so. The two art historians first resorted to complaints to the College Art Association, the International Federation of Library Associations, and the American Library Association's Office of Intellectual Freedom but got no results. Feeling that the library community had closed ranks against them, they claimed that their ideas had been censored and that, consequently, the art community was being deprived of accurate information. Ultimately, the issue was presented in lawsuit Moran and Mallory.

Set and Monitor Standards of Acceptable Practice

To adequately monitor the activities of its members and to regulate their activities effectively, a profession needs a set of standards of acceptable practices by which to compare and contrast professional behavior. Usually, this takes the form of a code of ethics.

One information professional group in particular has taken the issue of developing a meaningful code of ethics seriously and attempted to make the code relevant to the membership as well as to the client body at large. The ACM first adopted an ethics code in 1972, which was known as the Code of Professional Conduct. The 1972 code established the association's status as a profession and made the assumption in the code that all members would acknowledge and follow the code. In effect, the code was imposed on the membership, but over the years, the association found that many members either ignored the code or did not find it compelling. In 1992, the ACM attempted to correct this problem by developing a new code, the Code of Ethics and Professional Conduct. In developing the new code, the ACM used a grassroots approach. The association conducted a set of discussions with its members during which it emphasized the importance of commitment and consensus in developing the code principles. Education and socialization are stressed as being of primary importance rather than enforced compliance. Unlike the 1972 code, the new ACM code is based on the assumption that the membership will follow a code of behavior so long as it sets standards of acceptable practice that are in line with the values and beliefs of the membership. (See Appendix for the ACM and other codes.)

Educate the Public Regarding Acceptable Practices

A profession must not only develop and regulate its own standards; it must also set realistic expectations for its clients and the lay public as to what the standards are and how they will be monitored. This is necessary to establish social legitimacy and to continue to receive the privileges society accords the profession. A code of ethics and various kinds of public relations activities also help to achieve this objective. As one writer puts it, "To the extent that a code confers benefits on clients, it will help persuade the public that professionals are deserving of its confidence and respect, and of increased social and economic rewards" (Frankel, 1989, p. 110).

Individual Professional Responsibilities

In addition to general social responsibilities, every IP has a moral obligation to carry out a variety of individual responsibilities. Seventeen such responsibilities can be identified. Figure 7.2 summarizes these responsibilities.

Do No Harm

Individual ethical behavior is concerned both with helping other people and, specifically, with not hurting them. This principle is captured by the code of ethics of medicine, the Hippocratic oath, which states, "First, do no harm." As with physicians, IPs interact closely with clients—it is their most important and challenging relationship—and they must know their clients' needs very well. They must frequently seek out sources of information and knowledge to satisfy their clients' needs. As a result, they come into close contact with information givers as well. The close association between IPs and the client brings rewards as well as posing challenges. The key elements of this relationship must stress the need for IPs to operate effectively within this relationship through exercising good judgment and demonstrating empathy with their clients and sources.

Be Competent

An information professional must exhibit professionalism in knowledge and demeanor. A professional has a responsibility to master the complex body of knowledge that constitutes the functional knowledge basis of his or her domain of practice. This is particularly challenging for IPs who practice in a rapidly developing and evolving technical and commercial realm.

Consider, for example, the difficulties Staff Sergeant Jones faced. In January 1990, a $12 million A-4 attack jet crashed in Willow Grove, Pennsylvania, reportedly due to fuel line problems. Four Marines were discharged or given "career-ending reviews" as a result. One of those discharged was Staff Sergeant Jones, the librarian in charge of the Technical Publications Library at the aircraft's home base. Officials claim that he failed to update a maintenance manual used by inspectors. Jones contends that the new manual was on order and that the one actually used by inspectors was labeled "training only—not for aircraft maintenance." Nevertheless, a court-martial upheld that Jones had not discharged his responsibilities in a competent manner, and he was dismissed ("Disturbing Developments," 1990).

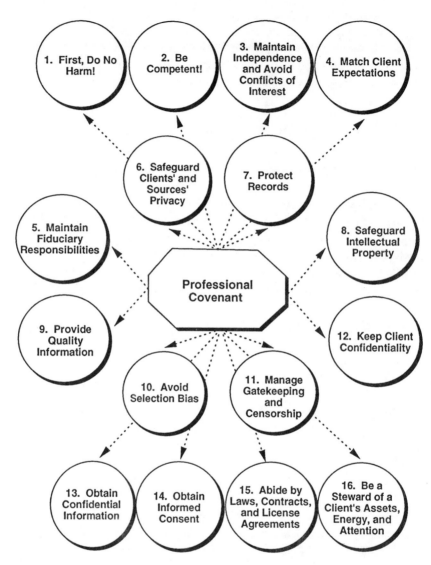

Figure 7.2. Professional Practice Responsibilities

When serving as an employer or principal of a firm, an IP should hire
qualified IPs as employees and should ensure that employees receive appropri-

ate training and educational opportunities to keep abreast of the latest sources of information. As a principle, an information professional should guard against misrepresenting, being dishonest, or being defensive about an employee's mistakes or capabilities when questioned by a client. Failure to ensure that information work is performed by a qualified employee can have a negative effect on a firm's future. In a recent case, for instance, a lawsuit was filed against Dun & Bradstreet in which it was contended that Dun & Bradstreet had not provided high-quality research. The plaintiff discovered that a 16-year-old summer intern had provided inaccurate information in response to a request for corporate performance data and that, furthermore, this information was now included in Dun & Bradstreet's Business Information Reports database. In a situation like this, it is ethically responsible, as a general principle, for an IP to make restitution to the injured client, such as refunding search or programming costs or even compensating for damages incurred, if the data is incorrect and actions can be traced directly to the information error.

Information professionals have a responsibility to make sure their peers and employees act in an ethical manner. An IP should introduce employees to industry and professional codes and expect employees to honor these standards of conduct in their work.

Information professionals should also guard against returning continually to only those sources they have become comfortable with using. Interviews with database searchers, for example, have found that in some cases, professional searchers have avoided using complicated technical databases because they are unfamiliar with the sources and find them "hard to use." It is not unusual for an IP to use a general-purpose and easily accessible source to search out information for the client rather than a more appropriate technical database. As a consequence, the client's costs were usually higher than necessary and the information not as complete or precise as possible.

This raises the question of professional liability. Professional competency is linked to professional liability because it is seen as a question of personal competency or misconduct. One writer provides this definition: "unreasonable lack of skill in the performance of professional duties through intentional carelessness or simple ignorance. . . . One must assume that a professional person must be a responsible individual" (Nasri, 1986, p. 141).

Some observers have taken the point of view that recent court cases have further defined professional liability to mean that a professional must exercise "reasonable care or prudence." For instance, the failure of a professional to use state-of-the-art information technology and methods can lead to liability. The courts have already ruled in a number of cases that medical personnel who failed "to use information technologies, such as the use of computers to gather data or to provide medical information from medical databases," failed to exercise prudence and that "[this will] eventually result in findings of negligence in certain areas of medical practice" (Froehlich, 1992, p. 302). The conclusion drawn from examining the issue of professional liability is that prudent information professionals should take steps to ensure that their clients receive accurate information from up-to-date sources and that acquisition and provision is conducted appropriately. In this regard, it is likely that one's ethical responsibilities exceed those required by existing laws.

Maintain Independence and Avoid Conflicts of Interest

Information professionals have a complex relationship with computers, telecommunications, publishers, and database vendors. They must guard against any improper influence on the part of vendors on their professional judgments. Information professionals must exercise independence and objectivity in selection of their tools and services on behalf of the client. Their private interests should never supersede their public and professional obligations. In the exercise of their professional duties, they should be free from the influence, guidance, or control of any other parties. The ethically responsible position for the professional information manager is to take action and make decisions based on the merits of the situation.

Match Client Expectations

Information professionals must ensure that their ability to perform work is reasonably equivalent with their clients' expectations. It is unethical to misrepresent either your qualifications or the ability of your firm to produce a product or service in a timely or competent manner. It is an ethical requirement that you have the education and background to perform the work requested by the client if you accept the engagement. For example, Chris Dobson (1991-1992), a Dallas-based independent information broker, points out in her company's newsletter, that it is irresponsible behavior for an information professional to "learn on the job" when that person has represented to the client that he or she knows how to perform the requested task and has the necessary skills and resources to carry it out. Also, information professionals should make sure that their clients understand whether they are acting in the capacity of a generalist or specialist. As John Everett and

Elizabeth Crowe (1988) write in *Information for Sale,* "It is also helpful to examine the distinction between generalists and specialists. A generalist might research kumquats today, the cost of kites tomorrow. . . . A specialist is geared to one subject area such as economics" (p. 4).

Maintain Fiduciary Responsibilities

All information professionals are provided some information to hold in trust. A part of acting ethically is ensuring the safety of the information entrusted to one's care. Archivists and records managers, for example, regularly consider their responsibilities for the records they manage. In one recent case, the Illinois Historical Library decided that the public interest in certain historic documents was more important than the wishes of certain persons when they decided to release sections of the diaries of U.S. Senator Orville Hickman Browning (1806-1881). The Illinois Historical Library had been keeping the existence of the diaries secret since 1920, in accordance with the wishes of a Browning descendant. The expunged entries that are to be released to the public contain testimony from a judge and a White House servant that Mary Todd Lincoln, wife of President Abraham Lincoln, padded the White House expense account while she was first lady ("News Fronts," 1994, p. 490).

Safeguard Client and Source Privacy

Another serious challenge for information professionals is the question of how much personal and private information on individuals should be obtained for clients from a credit company, governmental databases, and other sources. Increasingly, database products are being introduced—and sold—that provide specific information about individuals. For instance, does a person tend to be litigious? One company thinks it has an answer. An advertisement for a new database for use by physicians claims that this type of information can help them avoid malpractice suits. In another much publicized situation, there is now a database available identifying persons with bad driving records, information that could be used by car rental agencies or others to screen potential risky clients. As discussed in previous chapters, it appears that an increasing number of databases containing significant amounts of personal data will be for sale in the future. Businesses of all kinds are recognizing that personal data can be useful for a variety of end purposes, including targeted fund-raising and marketing and advertising campaigns.

Government sources are also collecting and distributing large amounts of private data about individuals, often without fully complying with the provisions of the Privacy Act. The 1990 study by the U.S. Government General Accounting Office, "Computers and Privacy: How the Government Obtains, Verifies, Uses, and Protects Personal Data," surveyed 189 federal agencies and found that there are more than 2,000 predominantly computerized systems of personal data maintained by these agencies. The survey also revealed that contrary to the provisions of the 1990 Privacy Act that some "cross-matching"—running one database against another—was still going on. The survey amply illustrates how personal data is widely exchanged and cross-matched to produce "profiles" of individuals.

All of these systems are being developed despite a generally acknowledged social value we place on guarding our privacy. Alan Westin (1968), a privacy expert, defines privacy as "the right to control information about one's self" (p. 2). Most writers and privacy analysts believe that current legal or social safeguards are adequate to protect an individual's data from "leaking" from numerous governmental and credit databases into other specialized products intended for targeted marketing or screening purposes.

If systems filled with personal data are allowed to proliferate, then ease of obtaining personal data effectively reduces the privacy safety zone of the individual. In many cases, the individual's right to privacy and personal liberty may oppose the right of the public or another individual to know and find out certain information. Large personal information data banks permit the selling, aggregating, and reshaping of personal information in many new forms unanticipated by the giver who originally provided the information. Commercial practices continually challenge the definition of what is to be considered private information. Legal and regulatory structures that might contain this trend are not yet in place.

In the future, information professionals may find that they are asked by clients to conduct searches of personal data as more of these sources become commercially available. Part of an IP's ethical responsibility is to use personal data carefully and to understand the sources of data and their limitations. Information professionals may find themselves weighing the decision whether to help someone through the discovery of personal data as opposed to hurting someone through the invasion of their privacy.

Information professionals may also find themselves confronted with an image problem as a result of a false public perception of the services they offer. Two recently released books intended for popular audiences point to a growing "information underground," the habitués of which are known as "information professionals" (Larson, 1992; Rothfeder, 1992). These people advertise that they are able to tap into the information underground of personal data in the service of their client and act as data sellers. As Rothfeder (1992) describes them,

> They're highly active customers of the credit bureaus, motor vehicle agencies, and real estate data banks, for instance—and also buy data from illicit suppliers, such as bank and medical networks. Straddling the two makes the underground an exciting, deliciously dangerous place to work. As a result, generally the companies in it are run by lifelong thrill seekers such as former private investigators, law enforcement veterans, and retired intelligence operatives. (p. 68)[1]

Although no one is suggesting that legitimate information professionals are likely to operate in the manner described in Rothfeder's book, it is undeniable that there is a new group of information sleuths emerging who are tapping into and, often, invading the privacy of citizens. Information professionals and the organizations they work for should be prepared for the eventuality of receiving requests of this nature and formulate an approach that meets good ethical and business standards. For example, an information broker was recently approached by a fund-raising specialist who wanted the broker to obtain personal credit and buying information about certain community individuals with annual incomes of more than $350,000. The information professional informed the fund-raiser that such personal information was not yet readily available from commercial database sources and pointed out that the services she was able to offer were confined to publicly available sources, none of which would provide the type of detailed data requested by this client. (Note, for example, that neither the Association for Computing Machinery [ACM] nor the Data Processing Management Association [DPMA] codes, presented in the Appendix of this volume, address this issue.)

Protect Records

Information professionals who work with the public have a responsibility to ensure that the records they generate and keep on business transactions with their clients are safeguarded. Most states, for example, have enacted legislation that protects the confidentiality of library and video store patron records from access, other than in cases in which a court order is obtained. The sheer proliferation of many different types of records in business organizations—including payroll, benefits, order and transaction files, customer profile files, and others—argues for heightened awareness of the need to protect these records from unauthorized access and use. Some strategies for protection include (a) periodically auditing the types of records being kept and eliminating those that are unnecessary, (b) establishing retention schedules for materials that are stored and disposing of them according to a schedule, and (c) establishing procedures that specify who may have access to records and the conditions under which they may have access. These issues are also discussed in the chapters on organizational and societal ethics.

Safeguard Intellectual Property

Information professionals must exercise a fiduciary responsibility with respect to information property. They are trustees of information and software and hence must recognize that information is property and must be safeguarded appropriately. This fiduciary relationship extends to taking precautions to block unauthorized access to proprietary databases as well as to exercising vigilance against fire, theft, or virus attacks that can compromise data and data systems owned by information professionals or their clients.

The problems of copyright violations, software piracy, and unauthorized use of artwork argue that IPs adopt ethically responsible positions to prevent these occurrences. The question of who owns information is becoming a problem of "wicked" proportions with intertwined legal and ethical issues based on questions such as, Who is the author? Who is the publisher? Who pays for information? Copyright law has rested on the dual principles of recognizing the right of the creator to be compensated for the production of an intellectual product and the somewhat contradictory principle of "fair use," which acknowledges the "right" of individuals to copy a portion of a work for personal use so long as the copied item is intended for personal use and does not result in gain to the user. Among the issues an IP must resolve on a continuing basis are these: (a) What constitutes intellectual property? (b) Who owns it? The organization or the individual IP, say, in the case of experience or expertise? (c) What right does the organization or the IP have to use the intellectual property? For example, is a corporation's ownership of an IP's expertise for a full 24 hours or only during working hours?

Provide Quality Information

Although, traditionally, it is not considered in a discussion on information and information practices, there is a growing interest in the responsibility of the creator of information products to disclose information about the quality and even the source of the information contained in a report or product. One recent case concerns information about consumers. As this book is being written, the U.S. Congress is considering a new bill, the Consumer Reporting Reform Act of 1994, which addresses the issue of inaccurate information contained in credit bureau files (Harney, 1994). The bill, if passed, will place restrictions on lenders and the way in which they use credit information for solicitation. It prohibits the use of consumer credit report information for target marketing without the consumer's permission, and it guarantees the right of consumers to have their names removed from future marketing lists. These provisions, in effect, call for a "truth in marketing and product labeling" approach to information revision.

An IP must also be aware that an information transaction can be perceived by the client and others as causing potential harm or creating unfair economic advantage. Many information professionals use a statement of limited liability or a disclaimer stating that their ability to verify the accuracy of a source and thereby alerting the client that possible errors may be present despite the caution exercised by the information professional in selecting and using a specific source and in processing the data.

Avoid Selection Bias

In the course of their work, IPs routinely make a variety of selection decisions at various stages of the information life cycle that ultimately affect the nature and extent to which materials are preserved, presented, or made known to others. The activities of selecting, clarifying, abstracting, and indexing can be value-laden, because they often carry the bias of a prevailing point of view. This can become one of the most difficult problems facing an IP, one that has not received extensive treatment in the literature. Selection bias is akin to censorship. But it is usually unintentional, unreported, difficult to detect by either clients or IPs, and may even be practiced by professionals who are unaware that they are doing it. Selection bias is difficult to detect because it is often socially determined and validated. It may in fact be the result of a form of social epistemology or ideology at work. Publications and funding decisions in science, for example, are sometimes decided on the basis of the proponent's adherence to a particular set of theories or ideas. These ideological assumptions can even affect one's ability to get access to basic data. This phenomenon was observed by Ian Mitroff (1974) in *The Subjective Side of Science*. Mitroff describes how, following the Apollo space missions, certain lunar scientists were denied access to the moon rocks because the theories they intended to test, involving hypotheses about the origin of the moon and whether moon craters resulted from volcanic activity or from extraterrestrial impact events, were unpopular with the scientists who controlled the review process.

Science is not the only arena in which selection biases have been observed. Journal editors have also come under scrutiny. Although evidence of selection bias by editors is rare, two studies indicate that the peer review process may be biased. One researcher, William Epstein (cited in Coughlin, 1988) conducted experimental research that found that the reviewers of a social work journal were more likely to accept an article if the reported results positively supported the work of social workers. If an article reported on the negative effects of social work, it was more likely to be rejected. In a controlled experiment using articles that were identical except for the direction of their conclusions, Mahoney (1977) found that journal reviewers were more likely to accept articles that reported positive results than those that contained negative results.

Another form of bias is found in classification systems. A number of librarians, for example, have called attention to the biases built into the Dewey Decimal and Library of Congress subject classifications in areas of nationalism, sexism, racism, ageism, and homophobia. In the 1980s, the San Francisco Public Library was criticized for claiming to support alternative points of view but failing to provide a subject heading for antinuclear movement in its catalog (Hauptman, 1988, p. 26).

Bias in the creation of index tools became the subject of a lawsuit concerning the indexing of the available information about a certain Sienese painter, as described earlier in the Moran and Mallory case (Swan, 1991). The plaintiffs contended that academic politics and biases in the peer review process served to suppress their findings.

Sometimes selection biases occur very early in the information life cycle, out of sight of the ultimate consumer. Recently, in a well-publicized case, *Publisher's Weekly* reported that 18 printing firms had refused to publish explicit homosexual material that was defined as "presenting safe sex information in a sex positive way" (Petersen, 1991, p. 16). The printing firms maintained that their workers, due to their conservative leanings, would refuse to print the material.

Archivists select certain records for preservation, and museum professionals select materials for display that may affect public perceptions in matters of art and culture. This was brought out vividly in an exhibit mounted by anthropology students at the University of British Columbia. The exhibit featured placards asking visitors to comment on whether they thought the museum was unduly influencing their perceptions by means of the labeling and placement of objects in a "masterpiece" gallery. The students wanted to know whether the masterpiece exhibit was creating reality rather than describing it.

Overreliance on a single source may also be unethical and perhaps illegal as well. So is failure to give appropriate credit. The *New York Times,* for example, cited a case in which an attorney had presented a long brief to his client and later billed the client for 22 hours for the work of retrieving information and turning it into a memorandum. After someone became suspicious, it was discovered that the attorney's memorandum had been lifted verbatim, but without credit, from a CD-ROM product of court decisions (see Margolick, 1993).

Information professionals should be careful to avoid building sole-source, dependent relationships with vendors, which although useful and comfortable for the information professional, may not serve client needs. This was a problem in the early days of computing when a data processing executive could turn to IBM for almost all of his or her needs. It is an even greater problem today in the ubiquitous, networked, multimedia, open-system architecture era, with so many vendors and so many different types of technology solutions. If an IP relies exclusively on a single vendor's services due to product familiarity (a kind of dependency relationship), he or she is potentially being unethical because he or she may be ignoring the welfare of the client.

An IP's power to select information sources is balanced by other professional obligations. Standards for selection are based on ideas of "objectivity" and neutrality—not being aligned with, supporting, or favoring any particular point of view. Professionals should either abstain from advocacy positions or clearly state their assumptions at the outset of their work. Neutrality and impartiality require indifference to politically based and other ideas in the context of information. Yet there are circumstances in which IPs are required to offer prescriptive or authoritative advice. In these cases, they may not be able to be completely indifferent. Nevertheless, they should strive to be as unbiased, neutral, and impartial as possible.

Manage Gatekeeping and Censorship

Information professionals not only have to guard against obscuring the available information, but they must also defend the right for certain information to be made available to all. Censorship, unlike bias selection, is well known, well understood, and extensively discussed in the educational, information science, and journalism literature. Censorship occurs when one individual or group decides *not* to include a particular piece of information in a publication, database, or collection. It is intentional. Censorship cases often involve the imposition of a particular set of standards held by the censor that may be at variance with the standards of the group or the society as a whole in the belief that certain materials or information will corrupt children, offend sensitive readers, or undermine basic values and beliefs. It is usually pursued on behalf of others. As one writer noted, "Censors do not necessarily think their own morals need protection, but they do feel compelled to save their fellows, especially minors" (American Library Association, 1990, p. 11).[2]

Information professionals sometimes find themselves in a quandary, when they feel compelled to defend the right of the general society to have access to a particular work or piece of information while, at the same time, personally finding the work repugnant. Take, for example, the case of Minneapolis Public Library Director Susan Goldberg, who found herself in this position when she defended the institution's right to purchase and own a copy of Madonna's trade book *Sex,* despite the fact that the work was personally offensive to her. The Goldberg versus Madonna case reveals a great deal about censorship in operation.

On October 21, 1993, Time Warner Books released a new book by the popular rock star, Madonna, entitled *Sex.* The book was released with considerable publicity and was reviewed seriously by major newspapers and other reviewing sources that review trade publications intended for general circulation. Shortly after publication, the Minneapolis Public Library received its shipment of two copies of *Sex.* Receipt of the book was routine because the library automatically purchases works by major contemporary stars and also automatically places orders for trade books identified as potential "high-profile" books in demand by the public. Every indication was given that Time Warner expected *Sex* to be a blockbuster and one in demand by the public. The Minneapolis Public Library bought two copies; one copy was destined for the circulating collection, and one was to be placed in the special contemporary arts collection that had previously purchased and collected every work issued by Madonna.

The library followed its standard selection policies, and, consequently, the acquisition of this particular book was routine—or should have been routine. Libraries and librarians adhere to a variety of codes and creeds that promote responsibility of the library as an institution to make information of all kinds available to their patrons and to respond to their patrons' demand for literature. The Library Bill of Rights, passed by the Council of the American Library Association, affirms that "books and other library resources should be provided for the interest, information and enlightenment of all people of the community the library serves. Materials should not be excluded because of origin, background or views of those contributing to their creation." The Bill of Rights goes on to say that "Libraries should provide materials and information presenting all points of view on current and historical issues" (American Library Association, Library Bill of Rights, adopted June 18, 1948; amended February 2, 1961; June 27, 1967; and January 23, 1980, by the American Library Association Council).

Director Goldberg soon discovered, however, that the library's "routine" selection decision was not regarded as routine but, instead, resulted in "noisy, determined opposition and even threats to the library" (Goldberg, 1993, p. 31). Her position was that the library had acted correctly in adding the book to the collection because it satisfied its collection requirements, and not because she or the library agreed with Madonna's message. "We have decided that, at least in Minneapolis, the overriding concern of intellectual freedom is paramount— even though many of us, including me, find your book transparently manipulative," wrote Goldberg in an open letter to Madonna published in the *Minneapolis Star Tribune* and reprinted in the March 15, 1993, edition of the *Library Journal*.

Many other libraries, however, did not follow Minneapolis's lead. Among its peer institutions, it essentially stood alone. Although it is not known how many U.S. public libraries purchased *Sex*, it is known that many did not. A survey of 65 libraries in New Jersey, published in the *Library Journal*, revealed that not one had purchased the book. Some libraries found what they believed to be compelling reasons for not ordering it: It was expensive at $49.95 retail. This argument seems weaker when compared with the fact that the average price of a hardback trade book is in the $30.00 range and that many reference works cost $100.00 or more. Another reason given for not purchasing the book was its flimsy binding. *Sex* came with a spiral-notebook-type binding that was easily damaged and therefore, some maintained, not suitable for a library purchase. Again, this argument becomes less compelling given that libraries routinely send flimsy or poorly bound volumes to binderies for rebinding to extend their shelf life. The most common reason that libraries gave for not purchasing the book related to the sensibilities of their patrons and certain public interest groups. From Colorado, for example, the Pikes Peak Library district director told the editor of the *Library Journal* that his library had "received several hundred anti-*Sex* calls, many of them from Focus on the Family, an evangelical group" (phone survey reported in the *Library Journal,* November 15, 1992, p. 63). There was some speculation that the decision not to acquire the book was related to a library bond issue on the November 3 ballot. Christian radio stations were telling their listeners to call the library and to vote against the bond issue if the library purchased *Sex.*

Susan Goldberg's concern for the principle of free speech, her adherence to her professional ethics and duties, and her upholding of the library's policies superseded her distaste for this work. Consequently, when confronted by a censorship challenge, she supported the purchase decision by the library and defended its right to have this book on its shelves. This is professional judgment in action.

Keep Client Confidentiality

An IP has a responsibility to provide altruistic service and to protect the welfare and interest of his or her clients. Central to this theme is the principle of the special, confidential nature of the relationship between a professional and his or her client. All ethical codes hold that the transactions that occur between a client and a professional are special, private, and confidential. Lawyers, therapists, priests, and other professional groups also uphold this principle because it is central to their relationship with their clients. Closely related to this responsibility is the need to keep secure any client information, whether it is specifically identified as secret or not.

Upholding this basic principle can cause a conflict between values in certain circumstances. Suppose, for example, a client has paid an IP to produce and provide a technical research report describing a new technology. The IP then finds that the client is planning to sell this particular technology to a foreign country for a profit, in violation of national law. Is the IP obligated to maintain confidentiality with the client, or should he or she take steps to report the client to the authorities? An ethical judgment is required. Most ethicists argue that violating client confidentiality is permissible only if it will prevent future serious harm (Woodward, 1990). The general rule is that an IP should protect client confidentiality unless there is clear and sufficient evidence that a breach of confidentiality is warranted to achieve a greater benefit or avoid creating greater harm.

There is another related professional obligation, one that is less onerous but equally compelling. Information professionals, as human beings, are subject to what author Tom Wolf (1987) once called "information compulsion"— the tendency to blurt out or share something you know especially when you can gain power or prestige by doing it. An IP's fiduciary responsibilities include preventing information compulsion as well as protecting his or her client's confidentiality.

Obtain Confidential Information

One specific effect of the ubiquitous computer has been an escalation in the awareness that to be competitive, American business must engage in active ongoing strategic and tactical information gathering, defined generally as organizational intelligence. Information professionals with business clients are accustomed to fulfilling research requests about competitors' products; nevertheless, the search for competitive information can pose ethical dilemmas for an information professional. The following case illustrates this point.

Cecilia, an information professional in a large southern city, was contacted by one of her important clients who is a vice president for a cosmetics company in that city. As Cecilia knows, the cosmetics business is dependent on new research and the development of new products in a timely manner. It is an extremely volatile business, and profits depend on the ability of a company to introduce new products ahead of competing firms. Friday morning, the vice president called Cecilia and made a rush request for information about a new lipstick formulation developed by a rival company. He had heard rumors about the product and wanted to know more about it. Cecilia went to work immediately searching the chemical and cosmetic databases, and she also made a few phone calls to try to track down additional information. Friday afternoon, she reported to her client that she was only able to find out that a rival firm, Vigor, was close to announcing a new lipstick based on the new formula; she was not able to obtain any information from her sources about the formula itself. The vice president was excited. He felt he had to know more about the lipstick formula before Wednesday of next week when the firm was to announce its first-quarter earnings. The vice president asked Cecilia to get the information as soon as she could and in any manner that it took. Cecilia knew that if she called Vigor directly and identified herself as a broker for the rival cosmetic firm, they would refuse to talk to her. She remembered, however, that she had a friendly professional relationship with a colleague at the cosmetics trade association and knew that if she called this colleague and asked a general question about the lipstick formula, without revealing her client connections, she could probably get the trade association representative to call Vigor and produce the information she desired. Cecilia ultimately decided that it would be unethical for her to call the trade association to obtain the information, a decision she later had to defend to her superiors.

Another illustration of this problem is the case in which the editor of a newsletter spotted an ad for a business that was collecting, photocopying, and selling internal corporate phone directories. When the president of this new telephone directory company was contacted, he stated there was nothing wrong with this practice but admitted that his company obtained its directories in a manner that avoided having to ask for them directly, such as obtaining them from temporary employees and "other means." Although it is not clear whether copyright laws are being violated, this information may be "proprietary," which means that it is not in the public domain and is not readily accessible by anyone publicly (*The Information Advisor Newsletter*, n.d.).

U.S. businesses routinely use various legal and ethical strategies to gather information. Legal and ethical intelligence gathering includes obtaining published reports, court records, government documents, and government reports. Companies may also read consultant's reports, market surveys, financial reports, and even competitors' brochures. In certain cases, companies may analyze a competitor's product (reverse engineering) or talk with salespersons or employees as long as these reports are obtained openly and with the consent of the employee or salesperson.

Carried to an extreme, however, competitive information gathering can turn into espionage. Espionage is the practice of spying, or of using spies to obtain secret information about business competitors, and includes spreading falsehoods, confidentiality breaches, eavesdropping, computer snooping, and other techniques used to obtain secret information. Corporate intelligence gathering is legal and usually ethical; espionage, however, is generally illegal and unethical as well, wartime being the principle exception.

Information professionals must clarify their role as an intermediary for their clients. The first case makes it clear that if Cecilia calls her colleague and asks for information without identifying the fact that her interests are related to her client's request, then she has been less than truthful and even dishonest—an ethical violation. The case involving the internal corporate telephone directories illustrates the "hidden" nature of the ethical quandary. Is it ethical for an IP to knowingly purchase such a directory service when he or she knows that the means by which this information was obtained was less than forthright? To the credit of the newsletter editor, the editor questioned the ethics of purchasing this source and advocated pursuing other research alternatives, such as calling the company directly to obtain a company or employee phone book.

Obtain Informed Consent

Givers who provide information have a right to know what use will be made of it and to give their consent to its use. Largely through the initial efforts of a group called Computer Professionals for Social Responsibility, there is growing recognition that clients and others who provide information to a producer should maintain the right to know what use will eventually be made of the information. The Lotus MarketPlace: Households case, discussed earlier, makes the important point that the parties providing credit information had no say in whether they wished information from their credit records to appear in this new product. There was no consent. Other examples include the practice of the government to cross-match databases, combining one with another. In a well-publicized example, the Selective Service Administration purchased birthday records from a nationwide pizza chain. They then cross-matched the government's records with the pizza company's birthday registrations of males 18 years old and older and used the results to detect those who may have evaded the draft registration. Catching potential draft dodgers is not the only government failure to fully inform the public about information usage. Many U.S. citizens are unaware that it has been the practice of the Postal Service to license change-of-address information to companies to update their customer databases. Or consider the case of a new product called "Courtesan" that was introduced in Philadelphia in 1993. Based on public records of lawsuits, the service is designed to help physicians find out if their prospective patients have ever filed a malpractice suit against another doctor. In the words of its advertising, this product will "screen new patients you think might be 'malpractice-prone,' so you can adopt necessary defensive cautionary measures" (Lewin, 1993, p. B9).[3] Recently, other new products have come onto the market, such as a CD-ROM product that contains unlisted telephone numbers of individuals who have paid the phone company to keep these numbers out of a directory.

The information contained and used in many of these cases is considered to be "in the public record" and therefore open to use by various parties.

The point illustrated by these cases, and that has disturbed professionals and members of the public, is that the original information givers were never informed that information they were required to file for one purpose might be cross-matched, sold, or published in a directory and used for other quite different purposes. In each case, the information givers were not informed about the ultimate use of the data, and they did not give their consent to it.

Abide by Laws, Contracts, and License Agreements

Information professionals must act in a legal, honest, and trustworthy manner with regard to clients, suppliers, and vendors. An IP, for example, is likely at some point to find himself or herself in a relationship whereby he or she will obtain hardware, software, and services from another party for a payment. To obtain these services, he or she will be obliged to sign some type of contract or agreement stating the obligations and duties of each party. This can give rise to a common quandary. Say, for example, that you have purchased a microcomputer software package to use at work. You paid for it with your own funds. The license agreement for the product states you may install and use the package on a "single machine." Because your business is a sole proprietorship, you also want to work at home. You are sure you will be the only person using the package at any given time, either at home or at work and therefore feel it is OK to install the software on both machines. Is it? Suppose members of your family want to use this software. Is this acceptable as well? This simple, homey example raises ethical as well as legal questions that are still being debated.

Some vendors of on-line information control the use of their data and services through license provisions. For an IP, this means that he or she leases or uses database resources only under the conditions set out by the database owner and must abide by license provisions. Care must be exercised to ensure that license provisions are understood and adhered to in searching, formatting, and providing reports of database materials to clients. Although the study is somewhat out of date today, Everett and Crowe (1988) surveyed database suppliers concerning the question of what obligations an IP has as an independent contractor in searching a database and providing these results to a third party. Responses to this survey indicated that different database suppliers had various levels of permissions and licensing requirements that defined permissible formatting, downloading, copying, and storing of information. To summarize the results, it appears that most suppliers permit temporary storage of search results and limit or restrict searches to be offered to the original or requesting client only; no reselling permitted.

One writer (Mintz, 1991) has compiled a list of guidelines for on-line searchers that captures many of the key issues and problems concerning an IP's relation to database and information suppliers or vendors as contrasted with their responsibilities to their clients.

The information professional has the responsibility to

- maintain awareness of the range of information sources available in a given area in order to best serve the client,
- ensure that selection of a database and system by the IP is not biased due to familiarity with the source as opposed to being based upon the client needs,
- disclose to the client the limitations of the database or system in meeting the client's needs,
- indicate to the client any concerns regarding accuracy or inclusiveness of the database or system which may affect search outcomes. (Mintz, 1991, p. 10)[4]

Be a Steward of a Client's Assets, Energy, and Attention

Finally, IPs must husband their clients' resources by providing information at the right time, to the right place, in the right form, and at the right cost. Each of these requirements places stewardship demands on IPs.

Providing Information at the Right Time. Every information need has a time parameter associated with it. Ideally, most clients want their information "just in time" for the use to which they plan to put it. Information that arrives too late is usually worthless, generally wasteful, and always frustrating to clients. Timeliness depends on the user's task and may involve a very short time frame. An air traffic controller, for example, may have less than a quarter of a second in which to redirect planes approaching an airport on a collision course. This demand for information must be satisfied almost instantly. On the other hand, certain clients' information requirements are not so sensitive to time. For instance, a historian working on a biography of Millard Fillmore might be willing to wait several months while an archivist combs the files and assembles appropriate documents.

Information professionals deal with the issue of timeliness by setting up schedules, choosing appropriate technologies, and fixing client expectations.

In general, IPs must understand the periodicity of their clients' information needs. Journalists have daily deadlines. Accountants, for example, may have to render reports daily, weekly, monthly, quarterly, annually, or on some other time-specific basis.

As part of the timeliness issue, IPs must also decide where the initiative for dissemination lies. Museums, for example, "push" information out into the environment. A museum curator arranges an exhibition and makes it available to clients at prescheduled times. With a "pull" system, however, such as most executive information systems, the impetus lies with the client. That is, clients must send inquiries and requests for information from a system.

Providing Information at the Right Place. Information professionals must ensure that information is transmitted to the geographical point needed by their clients. Historically, information professions have made assumptions about where the exchange should take place. Journalists know clients will read newspapers in their homes, and radio announcers know that many clients and users listen while traveling in their cars from place to place, so they reach out to their clients in these places. Archivists, librarians, and museum curators work in cultural institutions that are housed in significant civic structures and have come to expect their clients to visit these locations to acquire and use information. Accountants, information system analysts, computer programmers, and management scientists usually visit the client in his or her organizational setting and sometimes become consultants or employees of their clients' organizations. As changes occur in computing and telecommunications technologies, assumptions made about where it is most appropriate for the client to receive information are being challenged. Today, most information can be delivered effectively electronically. In the ubiquitous, networked, multimedia era, those providing information services may have to seek out clients wherever they are located rather than wait for clients to come to them. Consequently, the spatial and geographical assumptions that IPs have made in the past may no longer hold.

Providing Information in the Right Form. As Marshall McLuhan (1965) once observed, the form a presentation takes may have as much, or more, impact as its content, the famous "the medium is the message." Information may be communicated by means of any of the senses—sight, sound, taste, touch, or smell. Information professionals have responsibility for the design of reports and the visual display of information. Their ability to package information effectively can enhance or retard their clients' ability to use the information. It may also distort, hide, or alter the meaning clients obtain from the information. Information professionals must choose the combination of text, graphics, sounds, and other experience that will most effectively be accepted and absorbed into clients' minds, because, to paraphrase a comment by Herbert Simon (1957), a client's "attention" is one of his most precious resources. Consequently, information must be "chunked" into assimilable message units that are appropriate for the client's needs. This requires considerable knowledge of psychology and human communication behavior as well as a broad understanding of technological capabilities.

Precision and accuracy in fulfilling the client's needs are also issues in packaging information. On the one hand, an individual about to embark on a relaxing seaside vacation may be looking for a good mystery book to read and will also be satisfied with a couple of interesting fiction books; not a great deal of precision in information form is necessary. On the other hand, an investor who queries a reference librarian for data about the performance history of a specific stock requires information that is specific, precise, and accurate to address his or her concerns and to inform the investment decision.

Providing Information at the Right Cost. Information professionals have a responsibility to understand the increasingly significant impact of the changing economics of information. Collecting, processing, and disseminating information consumes resources and costs. In certain circumstances, there can be no limit to the amount of resources that can be consumed in collecting and providing information. Information professionals must be sensitive at all times to whether the benefits of collecting or processing information justify the costs of doing so. They must shepherd resources and understand their clients' and society's values well enough to determine whether the costs incurred in providing information are justified by the short- and long-run returns.

The professional responsibilities discussed here all serve to direct the day-to-day activities of information professionals. They should be present in their consciousness at any given moment of truth and should guide IPs' behavior as they acquire, process, store, disseminate, and use information. Applying these responsibilities in real cases, however, requires professional judgment.

N EXERCISING PROFESSIONAL JUDGMENT

There is one additional and essential part of a professional's covenant. Not only must a professional fulfill the profession's social responsibilities, but he or she must also perform these obligations based on professional judgment. The ability to make judgments is the hallmark of a professional. Information professionals, such as accountants, software engineers, and information brokers, must continually make judgments that are characterized as *unique, uncertain, equivocal,* and frequently laden with *value conflicts.* Although IPs draw on their theoretical knowledge and training to act in their specific professional domains—be they accounting, MISs, library or information science—a key feature of professional decision making is that, in the last analysis, one's professional judgment must supersede all other sources of guidance.

A professional must be able to render judgments in numerous and varied situations. To begin with, the task of identifying who the clients and ultimate users are and understanding this relationship is a professional's first required skill. But because every client relationship is unique, an IP must use judgment as well. Client information requirements are unique because no two information provision situations are exactly the same. They are uncertain because no single, clear, and self-consistent decision or decision product is available. That is, satisfying clients' information needs is not purely a technical or analytical task. They are equivocal because every situation is subject to two or more interpretations. Finally, information provision situations often present value conflicts because in many cases two or more diverse ends are being pursued at the same time. Indeed, some of these ends may reflect social and other external demands and may even run counter to the goals of the clients.

As a case in point, during the late 1980s software expert David Parnas argued that computer programmers should not work on the Star Wars (the Strategic Defense Initiative or SDI) project because he felt the military aims were questionable, but more important, he believed that the programming task—producing billions of instructions—was beyond the competency and knowledge base of contemporary programming methods. Similarly, other programmers have refused to work on projects they believed would violate people's rights to privacy or use information in unethical ways. The software engineer, introduced at the beginning of this chapter, was exercising professional judgment when she tried to maintain the quality of her company's software by stressing the need for additional testing.

All information professionals depend on their own judgment. The exercise of judgment occurs, for example, when an information professional must design an appropriate information procedure and process for an information system. Computer programmers take the client requirements, examine a complex set of possibilities and design a procedure and set of instructions for storing and manipulating the information in a way that fulfills the client's requirements. Journalists select events to report, or their editors do, and then they make judgments about what and how much to report. Editors often enter into these decisions by cutting stories or "positioning stories" in a page location most likely to be read.

Because the information environment is changing rapidly, with new types of technologies and capabilities emerging daily, IPs have greatly expanded choices to make in the types of formats and information sources they choose to meet the needs of their clients. Accountants make judgments when they place a value on the assets of a firm. Archivists make them when they decide whether or how to index a public figure's letters. Deciding whether to develop a costly special collection presents this kind of situation for librarians, and curators must decide whether or not to acquire and display, for example, a Native American artifact that may have religious significance for American Indians. Records managers make these kinds of decisions when they set up retention schedules, and management scientists make judgments selecting particular variables, relationships, and objective functions to be used in a model.

Empathy—the ability to identify with and understand another's situation, feelings, or motives—is a key to making good judgments about clients and their needs. Just as good physicians must be able to place themselves in their patients' situations—comprehending such things as how a patient's body reacts and feels—information professionals must be able to place themselves firmly within their clients' minds and share a client's psychological climate as much as possible. This kind of client-centered awareness, however, seems to be a relatively recent development in some fields. A recent article comparing the historic and contemporary role of librarians illustrates this point.

> The library is perceived as a repository of books and documents. . . . It was understood to be a place where recorded knowledge was collected and where the "transcript" of the culture was preserved for transmission to future generations. Within this framework of values, the . . . librarian was concerned primarily with the technical requirements of collection building and maintenance, . . . and only

secondarily directed toward users who, in turn, tended to regard librarians as caretakers of the collection. (Crowe & Anthes, 1988, p. 123)

Information professionals are required to make judgments during every phase of the information life cycle, beginning with a judgment about the use that information takers will make of the information provided. Effective mutual understanding between an IP and his or her client revolves around how much attention the professional is willing to devote to receiving and digesting information from and about the client. More important, a client's "attention" must be assumed to be his or her most valuable resource. What a person attends to greatly influences who that person is. It is reasonable to expect, therefore, that clients will be experiencing many demands for their time and attention other than those the IP wants to place on them. Not only is a client's basis for allocating attention different, but clients also have varying capacities to learn and absorb information. Each comes into an information provision relationship with his or her own beginning state of knowledge. For this reason, an IP must make judgments concerning the packaging and presentation of information in a way that best fits the client's attention, knowledge, and learning attributes. Acting ethically means an IP must also consider what presentation format is fair and correct for his or her client, based on a knowledge of the client's needs, including the client's ability to pay.

▨ EMERGING ISSUES FOR IPs

Professional Ethics in the Workplace

Technological changes, particularly the type induced by information technology, translate into organizational and social impacts. As the workplace is transformed by the application of information technology, the ability to act ethically becomes more important. The negative aspects of automating the workplace include reducing job autonomy and decision making, introducing repetition and tedium to jobs, and eliminating jobs altogether. Information system implementation can rob workers of their competency. Information systems can replace the occupational skills of workers—known as deskilling or "dis-en-minding," whereby the skills of an employee are replaced by a system or a machine without suitable compensation to the worker. Information technology can also negatively affect the health and safety of workers by creating stress or through ergonomics effects, such as repetitive motion disease (e.g., carpal tunnel syndrome) or eyestrain and back spinal-muscle problems. All of these are outcomes that potentially compromise the dignity of the individual. Information professionals as ethical managers must acknowledge that information systems can cause these specific negative effects. They have a responsibility to mitigate these effects as they are identified and to ascertain that workers and the task environment support and promote healthy job practices, workplaces, and workers.

Information professionals should also seek to use information systems and tools to improve the workplace by carrying out positive innovations. The two most important areas in which information technology can improve the workplace are through (a) eliminating unproductive and unnecessary paperwork and work practices and (b) empowering people by providing them with appropriate information tools and training.

Professional Ethics and the Challenge of Globalization

As new benefits have developed from the emergence of the national networks, these have been accompanied by problems as well. Recently, a Connecticut illustrator found that his work was being scanned, digitally altered, and distributed freely over the Internet without his knowledge (Roberts, 1993). The practice resulted in hundreds of individuals and companies making free use of copyrighted material without compensation to the creator. The illustrator sued and successfully collected damages from the on-line company who distributed his images.

This case raises several questions worthy of consideration: How likely is it that you may unknowingly use someone's intellectual property without proper authorization and agreement? How likely is it that people will accuse you of stealing from them? To avoid the painful consequences of the second question, it will be important for IPs to maintain careful records and controls over their sources of materials, such as artwork appearing on the Internet and from other electronic means. The point is that there are professional standards protecting intellectual property. When it is not clear who owns the copyright, the best rule to follow for copying material is, "Don't do it." It appears that information professionals, along with other users of the new electronic technologies, should recommit themselves to the "old," basic rules of conduct and apply the same standards as they would use in dealing with intellectual property in print form.

The use of the national networks also creates new challenges and opportunities for IPs. As more information professionals make worldwide connections through their use of the Internet and other forms of social and group computing, they must develop ethical standards for working within these systems. An author, and frequent Internet user, observes that cyberspace, which he defines as a "computer mediated place where people can meet to exchange information," offers its own organizational challenge:

> It is difficult to formalize and enforce rules in cyberspace, so cyberspace communities tend to construct and enforce rules that suit their needs as specific problems arise. Many of the rules are based on the in person social conduct rules we are all familiar with. As in the physical world, it is considered improper to badger, slander, or reveal personal information about someone without their consent. . . . Some systems have rules governing behavior, but such rules are hard to formalize and enforce. On one system, the rule is both simple and vague: "Be polite." Surprisingly, it works most of the time. (Lyris, 1992, p. 172)

Cyberspace constitutes a new and major challenge for IPs, because in cyberspace the distinction between computer users, communication experts, journalists, artists, and librarians is often blurred or obscured. In this new universe, professional efforts can all fuse together into a globally distributed flow of electrons and photons. The principles of professionalism discussed in this chapter will be needed more than ever if information professionals are to be socially responsible.

SUMMARY

Professions consist of groups of people who have a specialized expertise that they use to help other humans—their clients. Because they possess this arcane knowledge that is valuable to others, they obtain a power advantage over their clients. From this power advantage stems their ethical and social responsibilities as well as certain privileges that society bestows on them in return for the services they render. More specifically, Flexner (see Metzger, 1975) described professions as groups that (a) possess more knowledge about a field of human activity than do ordinary people, (b) draw on theories deeper than those employed by technicians, (c) apply the theories and knowledge to solve human and social problems, (d) extend and refresh their knowledge through research, (e) pass the knowledge on to novices through education, and (f) undertake all of this with an altruistic spirit.

The information age has spawned a new class of professionals, information professionals or IPs, who are actively engaged in performing the functions of information life cycles. The special knowledge they possess gives them the ability to get the right information from the right source to the right client(s) at the right time in a form most suitable for the use for which it is intended at a cost justified by its use. The social purpose they serve is to manage and execute the activities in the information life cycle so as to improve their clients' intellectual state and to effectively influence their behavior or state of mind. Included in this new class are MIS specialists, systems analysts, computer programmers, software engineers, reporters, writers, photographers, camera operators, editors, publishers, broadcasters, accountants, archivists, museum curators, librarians, information brokers, database administrators, records managers, management scientists, and operations researchers. One feature of the information age is that the tasks—and therefore the responsibilities—of all of these information occupations are merging.

The responsibilities of information professions fall into two broad categories: collective social responsibilities and individual professional responsibilities. The social responsibilities include developing and maintaining a body of knowledge, educating and training professionals, setting and monitoring standards of acceptable practice, monitoring and self-regulating professional practice and practitioners, and educating the public regarding acceptable practices and expectations for the profession. In addition, some 17 individual professional responsibilities have been identified and described.

Central to the concept of being a professional, however, is the exercise of judgment. Information professionals face situations that are unique, uncertain, equivocal, and frequently laden with value conflicts. Although IPs draw on their theoretical knowledge and training to act in their specific professional domains, a key feature of professional decision making is that, in the last analysis, one's professional judgment must supersede all other sources of guidance.

◩ NOTES

1. Reprinted by permission of Brockman, Inc.

2. Reprinted with permission of the American Library Association. From *Censorship and Selection: Issues and Answers for Schools.* Copyright © 1990.

3. Copyright © 1993 by The New York Times Company. Reprinted by permission.

4. Reprinted from *Special Libraries, 82*(1), Winter, 1991, p. 10. Copyright © by the Special Libraries Association.

Information Ethics in Organizations

◧ TOWARD THE INFORMATION-BASED ORGANIZATION

Many ethical issues reach beyond the scope of an individual and are created by the activities of organizations. Because organizations are different from individuals, these ethical issues have a special character. For this reason, an ethics of organizations is needed to complement individual and professional ethics.

Today, organizations are becoming more information intensive. For example, the widely respected management theorist, Peter Drucker (1988), forecasts that by the year 2000, large business is more likely to resemble a hospital, a university, or a symphony orchestra than today's typical manufacturing company. It "will be knowledge-based, an organization composed largely of specialists who direct and discipline their own performance through organized feedback from colleagues, customers, and headquarters. For this reason, it will be what I call an information-based organization" (p. 45). Because these information-based organizations will become more pervasive, their ethics must reflect this change. Modern organizations need an ethics more firmly rooted in information.

◧ THE AGE OF ORGANIZATION

In broad historical prospective, the age of information coincides with the age of organization. Today, most people spend most of their time working in or interacting with organizations of all sorts—schools and universities, government agencies, churches and synagogues, charities and museums, and small and large businesses. Organizations are a dominate and ubiquitous phenomenon in our modern society. Indeed, the United States economy is largely dependent on large-scale business corporations. Their social and economic influence is felt quite broadly, a fact acknowledged midway through this century by A. A. Berle (1954) in *The Twentieth Century Capitalist Revolution* when he observed that corporations have become the "collective soul" and "conscience-carrier of twentieth century American society" (pp. 174-175). Much the same can be said about big science, big universities, big government, trade unions, and many other types of organizations.

What kind of "conscience-carrier" is the modern organization? A little history provides some insights. A society characterized by organizations is a relatively recent phenomenon, a product primarily of the industrial revolution. The emergence of technology and manufacturing techniques during the 18th century required a new way of coordinating work. As a result, a new way of thinking about using these new technologies more fully began to take shape. The new idea of organization had three characteristics: a hierarchical arrangement of tasks, the subordination of some tasks to others, and the assignment of increasing authority to roles at increasingly higher levels in the hierarchy to ensure that work was directed by those who possessed the most relevant knowledge of the technology and of potential markets.

By adopting this three-pronged approach, organizations were not only able to do new things, but they also gained substantial power. Organization compensates for human shortcomings and, in Lord Beveridge's (1942) epigrammatic phrase, enables "common men [to] do uncommon things" (p. 4). As theorist Herbert Simon (1957) put it later, "It is impossible for the behavior of a single, isolated individual to reach any high degree of rationality" because individuals have limited capabilities—"bounded rationality" (p. 79). Organizations overcome these natural, human limitations.

Organizations assemble groups of people, each with limitations, and arrange them and their activities in such a way that it is possible to make rational decisions and to produce complex products and services. This is achieved by installing processes of cooperation and specialization of function according to a division of labor. As these processes are multiplied, interconnected, and further diversified, organizations accumulate social and economic power that far exceeds the capabilities of individuals taken singly.

This power is concentrated, however. Organizations tend to have a singularity of focus. Normally, they are structured to pursue just a few relatively well-specified goals, such as maximizing profit or increasing their market share. Their considerable power, accordingly, is generally marshaled to achieve just these limited goals. It is this characteristic, in fact, that most people refer to when they talk about organizations being "rational." Consequently, events that are ambiguous or that do not pose strong and immediate threats to achieving an organization's stated goals tend to be ignored. Professor H. Jeff Smith (1994) calls this "organizational drift"; and it is in the "cracks and voids" that the drift creates that many ethical lapses occur. People assigned to a particular organizational job tend to perform only that task, just as it was specified for them. They generally do not think about the consequences their actions have on others. Or if they do, they tend to subjugate them to the organizational ethos and try to rationalize them away. The organizational good tends to become the greater good (see Jackall, 1988). This is further complicated by the fact that human beings always bring their own egoistic goals to their work; and some of these goals—sometimes called "careerist goals"— include getting ahead in the organization. Consequently, people who work in organizations will tend to structure things so that they can pursue their personal goals, unless they are restrained from doing so.

John De Lorean captured the essence of these organizationally induced mental blinders in a chapter titled "How Good Men Can Make Bad Decisions" in *On a Clear Day You Can See General Motors* (White, 1979). It offers his explanation as to how General Motors (GM) could produce an automobile—the Corvair—that was so hazardous that Ralph Nader (1965) labeled it "unsafe at any speed." De Lorean describes the typical GM executive as a stalwart, law-abiding citizen, generally religious, mostly a family man, who in his personal life was a model citizen. Acting alone, he would go to great lengths to keep from harming anyone. Yet placed within the GM structure, each of these men participated in a series of fragmented decisions that, collectively, severely compromised the safety of the Corvair automobiles—endangering the lives of hundreds of thousands of people. At the same time, they engaged in business practices that served to undermine federal, state, and local government policies. De Lorean attributes most of these ethical lapses to the organizational structure of GM at the time, its incentive system, and the considerable pressure that was brought to bear on each executive to meet his corporate goals and to perform well in his job as assigned. He concludes that the issue of organizational ethics needs to be addressed alongside that of individual ethics.

Organizational ethics in an information age must recognize that there are three crucial factors of production at work in any organization: people, information, and capital—capital including technology, facilities, funds, and equipment. Ethical organizations have values and policies that guide the use of all three, but information, being the latest to assume significance in the troika of resources, is usually accorded less attention. With the advent of information-based organizations, this must change. As information assumes a more central role in an organization and becomes an essential component of its total power, the decisions that its members make about information—how it is acquired, processed, stored, disseminated, and used—play a much greater part in the way an organization exercises its power. These decisions take on greater ethical significance. If appropriate policies and restraints for handling information are not in place, an organization will likely behave unethically; if appropriate and effective policies are in place, an organization is more likely to behave ethically. This is especially true of highly information-intensive organizations, such as credit bureaus, banks, insurance companies, health care institutions, airlines, newspapers, television, universities, and government agencies.

▧ ORGANIZATIONS AS MORAL AGENTS

The organizational level considers corporations, firms, companies, government agencies, educational institutions, charitable organizations, and the like, all of which act as agents in an ethical field. Many of today's social issues revolve as much—or more—around the behavior of these organizations as they do around the behavior of individuals. In fact, most of the effect on society today of information and information technology is mediated through organizations of some type. To apply the processes of corrective vision to organizations, we need to understand what an organization is, how it operates, how it articulates with the larger social system, and how it relates to its individual members.

Let's begin with a definition. What is an organization? Technically speaking, it may be defined as follows: An organization is a group of people with a common purpose (or a common set of objectives). The group performs work to achieve the organization's common purpose, and the work is divided among the members of the group according to a functional division of labor. Each individual member of an organization contributes only a portion of the work needed for the overall achievement of the common purpose. The organization's jobs and roles are organized into a hierarchy that resembles a progressive series of higher-level positions. This is referred to as a chain of command, line of authority, or line of responsibility. In addition, work is organized horizontally according to a chain of activities through which the organization adds value to its inputs and ultimately produces products and services. In many organizations, a further distinction is made between its "line," which contains those jobs and positions that directly produce products or services, and its "staff," which contains those jobs such as accounting, personnel, information systems, quality control, and the like that provide support services to the line functions.

When we talk about an organization's "behavior," we are referring to the collective outcome of actions taken by the line and staff. Because this collective behavior is an aggregate, it is considerably more difficult to pinpoint moral responsibility with organizational behavior than it is with individual behavior. This is due to the nature of the division of labor.

As we have seen, even when a single agent acting alone commits a questionable act, it is difficult to determine crucial factors such as the voluntariness and state of knowledge on which the agent acted. Even, for example, when a lone assailant murders someone within the plain sight of several witnesses and the event is captured by television cameras, problems in assigning responsibility can still arise. Questions can be raised later as to the murderer's sanity at the time, the influence of his or her parents or others, or even the murderer's knowledge of the law in this situation.

These problems of attribution are compounded manyfold when the agent is an organization and involves either directly or indirectly many people, all of whom may have contributed to the final outcome. Indeed, as a general rule, the greater and more complex an organization's division of labor and the more elaborate its value adding chain, the more difficult it is to assign moral responsibility.

Consider the case of a credit bureau that submitted an erroneous credit report to a mortgage lender who, relying on this information, made a denial decision that substantially harmed a potential borrower. Who is responsible? Peeling back the credit bureau's value-adding chain and its organizational structure reveals some of the difficulties involved in assigning responsibility. The final information taker was the officer at the mortgage bank who made the decision. Is he to blame? He had called a service agent at the bureau for a credit report on the applicant, and the agent, in response, had faxed him the erroneous report. Is the service agent responsible? She had retrieved the file on her computer terminal, read the information from the screen, and printed it out on a printer so that it could be faxed. Is the computer programmer responsible? The computer operator? The data contained in the file was keyed in by a data entry clerk. Was she responsible? Before the data reached the data entry clerk, it was reviewed for validity by a quality control (QC) clerk. Was the QC clerk responsible? At least five other people handled the data before it reached the QC clerk. Are they responsible? Several retail establishments contributed data on the potential borrower's purchases and payments. Are they responsible?

All of these parties participated directly in the information value-adding chain. What about indirect participants? The credit bureau has a manager who is in charge of all data collection activities. Is she responsible? There is also a manager who supervises the processing of all data. Is he responsible? There is a delivery and distribution manager. Is she responsible? There is a chief information officer responsible for all computer programs, telecommunications, and operations. Is he responsible? There is a CEO. What is her responsibility? And, of course, there is the credit bureau's board of directors. Are they responsible? There are probably tens, if not hundreds, of other organizational members who somehow came in touch with the data or who operate or administer functions through which it passed. Most, if not all of them, may be implicated.

It is a rare case in which just one person in an organization is totally and exclusively responsible for its unethical or questionable behavior. (Although senior managers and others sometimes like to identify such a person and make him or her the "scapegoat.") In most cases, many different people contributed in many different small ways to the issue. It was the sum of their activities that produced the harmful effect. Most of them may have, or at least are expected to have, adequate knowledge about their narrow job as defined, but many do not know about the process as a whole. So it is often difficult to determine whether they acted voluntarily or involuntarily, knowingly or unknowingly.

For these reasons, ethical thinking about organizations concentrates on the organization's structure and its productive and decision-making processes. Given a questionable behavior, an ethical review normally starts with the board of directors and moves down through its chain of command until it reaches the workers who were directly involved in its value-adding production chain. At each step, we ask, What did this person contribute to the final outcome? Then we apply the processes of ethical thinking as described in Chapters 5 and 6. Finally, we determine what guidelines, policies, or procedures can be put in place to correct the unethical behavior.

▧ MAKING ORGANIZATIONS ETHICAL: A CHALLENGE

Developing corrective steps requires a broad understanding of the socio-economic context in which the organization operates. Generally speaking, two important social forces purportedly serve to keep organizations ethical: the law and the market. These are the first places to look for help, but according to University of Southern California Law Professor Christopher D. Stone, both are, unfortunately, inadequate to the task. In *Where the Law Ends*, Stone (1975)[1] observes that social science has produced a large body of literature that clearly demonstrates that social groups—from mobs to formal, continuing institutions—are "distinct phenomena with distinct ways of behaving." He laments the fact that few, if any, of these insights have been incorporated into the body of the law. "And this is especially unfortunate," he concludes, "since it is quite likely not (whatever the fears) the individual cutpurse, stalking the streets, who is the society's most troublesome participant, but rather huge, institutional systems—the corporation in particular" (p. xiii). Stone's analysis is directed primarily toward corporations, but most of it holds, with minor modifications, for organizations of all types.

How, then, is a corporation to be made ethical? Stone (1975) argues that neither the law nor market forces work well because they treat corporations basically as "black boxes." They try to control organizational behavior from the outside, and unfortunately, this control takes place only *after* the questionable behavior is completed and the damage done. They do not effectively reach into the black box and influence complex decision processes.

Many large corporations have become so powerful that, often, they can dictate exactly what products and services they will offer, how they will be made, and how they will be sold. Often, consumers who want or need certain products must choose from among only what is offered. Although many economists argue that if consumers believe that a product is unsafe, unethical, or unnecessary, they will take their patronage elsewhere; in practice, there are several flaws in this way of thinking. It assumes that the consumers possess considerable knowledge, including (a) that they know in fact they are or will be injured (purchasers of the Corvair, the Ford Pinto, or the Dalkon Shield initially did not know about the safety hazards involved in their use), (b) that they know where to apply pressure to get reparation in the event that they are injured, (c) that they are in a position to exert enough power to apply pressure to the offending organization and to receive amends, and (d) that "their pressure will be *translated* into warranted changes in the institution's behavior" (Stone, 1975, p. 89). These four assumptions are seldom fully realized. For example, excessive violence continues to be shown in TV programs because one or more of these conditions are not met, especially the second—knowing where and how to apply the pressure. For the most part, a large gap in knowledge and power exists between the producers of products and services and their separate, disjointed, generally weaker consumers.

Even when these four assumptions are satisfied, there is still a problem with the time needed for adjustment. Many parties can suffer a great deal during the period it normally takes between the point in time consumers in the marketplace recognize a problem and the point in time an institution's behavior is changed to rectify that problem. To cite a few examples, a credit bureau may be sending incorrect information to a bank, a health insurance company may be disbursing sensitive personal information, an automobile company may be selling unsafe cars, or a clinic prescribing overdoses of X-rays for a considerable period of time before consumers in the marketplace are fully aware of these practices and take steps to get them stopped—that is, before a moment of recognition emerges and an adequate resolution is reached. In the meantime, people are being hurt. Economist Milton Friedman (1962) sees few problems with this as long as corporations follow the dictates of the market and act within the constraints of the law. But is the law entirely adequate?

The law "can't do it" either, Stone (1975) claims. He cites three reasons. One, there is a time lag problem that can be even more severe than the one associated with the market adjustment process. The complex calendars of legislatures and the cumbersomeness of their processes mean that it often takes a very long time for the law to react.

Second, there are limitations connected with the making of law itself. By means of lobbying and many other processes, corporations—due to their power—can bring considerable pressure to bear on legislatures. Much of this, of course, is for the good. In some cases, however, corporations, in effect, use lobbying to make the very laws "that we trust to bind them" (Stone, 1975, p. 94). Furthermore, corporations have the resources to shape or manipulate public opinion. The greatest difficulty, however, lies in the nature of organizations themselves. Given the complex division of labor and value chain that characterizes most organizations, it is very difficult, as we have seen, to pinpoint responsibility and to assign cause and effect for injurious acts. Consequently, it is difficult to write laws that clearly apply to the responsible party or parties. This vagary complicates the legislative process and also makes the resulting laws more difficult to enforce.

Third, there are limitations connected with implementing the law. Laws have loopholes, and clever lawyers are likely to find them. The costs of enforcing a law can be substantial and may outweigh its benefits. Moreover, laws sometimes conflict with each other and thereby prove to be counterproductive. Some laws may even unwittingly contribute to unethical behavior. Laws assigning legal liability, for example, can impede or stop the flow of crucial information between responsible parties, as can antitrust laws. As a result, authorities who need decision-making or enforcement information or customers who need product safety information do not receive it.

These limitations of the market and the law led Stone (1975) to conclude that ethical behavior must originate within the corporation itself. Every corporation needs a conscience and a soul. It must exhibit the counterparts of guilt, shame, and virtue. These ethical control devices should be found in an organization's policies and practices and embedded firmly in its culture. But what does the record show about their effectiveness with respect to information?

◪ ETHICAL PROBLEMS WITH INFORMATION PRACTICES: SOME EMPIRICAL RESULTS

A conclusion similar to Stone's (1975) is reached by Professor H. Jeff Smith (1994) of Georgetown University in his book *Managing Privacy: Information Technology and Corporate America.* His study contains some of the very few insights available as to how organizations respond to the market forces, laws, regulations, and ethical concerns that pertain to the information they handle. Smith studied seven information-based organizations: three banks, three insurance organizations, and one credit card issuer. Although he uncovered no overt failures to comply with relevant laws, he did find that many employee perceptions, practices, and policies (or the lack thereof) permitted less than full compliance with the law or with social norms. In some cases, the firm's actual practice was significantly different from that intended by the "spirit" of the laws.

Smith's approach is instructive. After examining some 80 U.S. federal laws and a host of ethical advocacy and position papers, he identified six general policy precepts for handling information. Three are general legal presumptions: (a) The law and social norms should limit the specific items of information that an organization can collect, generally to just that decision-making and environmental information necessary for the organization to fulfill its business obligations to the persons or organizations providing the information. This is referred to as "legitimate personal information." (b) Legitimate information collected for one purpose should *not* be used subsequently for any purpose other than that for which it was originally collected. (c) Legitimate information collected by one organization should *not* be shared across organizational boundaries and provided to other organizations without prior approval. Extenuating circumstances and agreements, such as informed consent on the part of the person who is the subject of the information, can delimit the force of these policy presumptions, but even the requirement of informed consent demands that certain consistent policies and procedures be put into effect.

Added to these are three issues concerning how information as a whole is treated and used: (d) There can be problems with combining individual items into a unified comprehensive database, thereby revealing more about the individual and making other investigations easier to perform. This constitutes an "exposé by minute description" in which the "sum is greater than the parts." (e) There can be problems associated with error prevention or control over the information collected, processed, or disseminated. Audits should be conducted to detect *deliberate* errors and controls put in place to prevent them. Systems should be implemented to detect a "reasonable" number of *accidental* errors, errors not intended but that can be quite devastating. (f) There can be problems associated with information overload or reduced judgment. To cope with large volumes of data, bureaucracies automate or routinize some of their processes and adopt automatic decision rules. Human judgment is replaced by machine judgment, forcing the worker to hold in abeyance his or her own critical facilities. As a result, wrongheaded decisions may be made in cases involving inconsistencies, complications, extenuating circumstances, or subtleties. (Recall the discussion in Chapter 7 about the nature of professional judgment.) Reasonable care should be taken to avoid exposure to these potentially unethical and harmful decisions. Each of these latter three problems has the effect of compounding the difficulties created by the first three. In general, these six guidelines adequately cover most of the human decision processes that take place during the information life cycle.

How well do organizations fare in following these six guidelines? Disappointingly, by Smith's (1994) reckoning. With respect to policies specifying what information is to be collected (Precept a), neither the three banks nor the credit card company had any policy. The three insurance companies had vague implied policies but no explicit policies. Exactly the same pattern held for Precept b dealing with limitations on the uses to which personal information could be put. On the issue of sharing data across organizational boundaries (Precept c), the companies fared better. The insurance companies and the credit card company had explicit policies regulating this practice, whereas the three banks had implicit policies in place. The general picture that emerges is that companies are concerned about sharing information with organizations other than their own, but they are not very concerned with what information they collect or how they use it within their own corporate confines.

At the level of general information-processing policies, the situation looks much worse. No company surveyed had any policies controlling the combining of disparate items of data (Precept d), and no company had any policies to safeguard against incorrect judgments made by automated decision systems (Precept f). Not surprisingly—because generally accepted accounting principles (GAAP) require it for a "clean" audit—every company had an explicit policy and an audit procedure for detecting deliberate errors in financial data (Precept e), but their policies were, at best, implicit with respect to accidental errors and other types of data.

▨ FROM MANY MOMENTS OF TRUTH TO A MOMENT OF RECOGNITION: A CASE STUDY

There is a recurring pattern in the information policy-making cycle. It has three phases: (a) First, there is a period of *drift* during which things are ambiguous and some questionable or unethical behavior occurs, but people are generally unaware of it. (b) This is followed by a period of siege during which *external threats* begin to coalesce; some questionable or unethical behavior continues but is rationalized and defended while some form of damage control is conducted behind the scenes. (c) Finally, there is a *point of resolution* during which the organization develops its ethical stance, adopts policies, and takes action to correct its unethical behavior.

As drift occurs, many members encounter crucial moments of truth but resolve them locally without the aid of policy guidelines or without the involvement of senior management. Due to several organizational factors—knowledge limitations inherent in specialization and the division of labor, adherence to short-term corporate goals, individual egoistic goals, and corporate incentives—some of these seemingly small decisions turn out to have major consequences.

The collective impact of these consequences on consumers and other affected parties eventually forms an external threat to the organization. This threat generally begins as a smattering of isolated individual complaints. Then, the complainants discover one another and share grievances, form public interest groups, and, subsequently, become outspoken activists. Finally, more forceful measures are taken, such as lobbying for legislation and mounting boycotts.

At some point, this increasing external pressure—often together with some internal advocacy on the part of a few knowledgeable members—results in a full-blown moment of recognition for the organization. Senior management becomes involved, meetings are held, consultants are called in, focus groups are convened, and, ultimately, responsive policies and guidelines are established. Often, an official response is provided to the media and other parties during this period.

One of the case studies conducted by Professor Smith (1994) amply illustrates this pattern. He describes how a life insurance company and the Medical Information Bureau (MIB)—a nonprofit consortium of about 750 life insurance companies that was formed to exchange underwriting information among member companies as an alert against fraud—dealt with the issue of acquiring, processing, storing, disseminating, and using information obtained on patients who had taken HIV tests. In the mid-1980s, as AIDS became an increasingly alarming medical problem, life insurance companies realized that as more people contracted the virus, AIDS would pose a significant threat to the actuarial assumptions on which life expectancy is based. The cost of pending claims would have threatened to exceed by far the premium dollars available to pay for them. The first solution that underwriters adopted was to require applicants to take an HIV blood test and to use the results to make underwriting decisions. Usually, the test data was stored in the insurer's computer databases and shared with the rest of the industry through the MIB network.

At the time, HIV blood tests were frequently inaccurate or inconclusive. The social implications of the results, however, were so laden with value that they constituted, of course, highly sensitive data. Indeed, just the fact that someone took the test—whether the results were positive or negative—could prove to be very compromising, perhaps even stigmatizing, to the individual involved. Yet at that time, few, if any, life insurance companies had explicit policies for managing this highly charged data source. As a result, underwriters and other insurance employees faced hundreds of moments of truth during which they made decisions about collecting, storing, sharing, and using these test results without moral guidance from corporate policies or from senior management.

There were several instances in which employers asked health insurance companies for lists of their employees who had AIDS or who had indications of the disease, such as having tested positive to the HIV virus or who were taking AZT, a drug commonly prescribed for patients with AIDS. Occasionally, it seems, their requests were satisfied.

Commenting on the mood of the times, one life insurance executive likened the situation to the Keystone Cops. "I'd see rooms of [middle-level managers] who would all be arguing about different ways of testing and using the [test results]," he observed. "None of them really knew what they were talking about, though—including my own people!" (Smith, 1994, p. 59).

Another observer recalled the following:

> Looking back, I realize that the industry didn't know what it was doing *at all* during that time. Insurers saw a problem and jumped to a very quick conclusion: test it! But they didn't think about how those tests were going to impact the applicants, and I saw very few companies taking extra precautions in their [data management]. . . . I even know a couple [of companies] that were testing blood without telling the applicants, and one of those had left the decision up to a lab manager. . . . Their senior management hadn't even been involved in the review of [the testing process].
>
> It was very common during that period to see companies change their testing processes from one week to the next . . . [because] the tests were not reliable, and there were several competing [tests] that could be run, so there was some sorting out of those [technical questions]. Then, there were the decisions about how the results would actually be used in the underwriting process itself. Most companies just saw a positive and said "end of underwriting process, denied," but some others wanted to dig deeper. (pp. 58-59)

Two major external threats turned this period of drift into a moment of recognition. One was that various privacy and gay rights activists were quick to protest and encouraged the media to pick up their cause. The second was that many different state legislatures got on the bandwagon and passed their own unique laws, each with different provisions for notification, disclosure, storage, and transmission of HIV testing data. Although the overall legal direction was relatively clear, the result was a jumble of conflicting laws and activists' demands. The life insurance companies now faced a totally befuddling situation.

To move toward a satisfactory resolution, the MIB and the insurance companies appointed task forces composed of senior executives, knowledge-able employees, and representatives of various stakeholder groups. Out of these meetings came some preliminary information policies. It became clear that in all but exceptional cases, applicants should be notified as to exactly what tests would be run on their blood samples. Tighter data security and confidentiality controls were also put in place. One company appointed an "AIDS doctor" who was responsible for handling all AIDS-related cases and who kept all data in a special locked file. Reports were hand delivered to him and never entered into the company's computer system. Subsequently, specific procedures for notifying an applicant in the case of a positive test result were adopted.

Prior to these events, the MIB had some reasonably tight policies in place. Due to an agreement with the FTC, there were provisions for the inspection and corrections of their records because these records were judged to be "consumer reports" under the Fair Credit Reporting Act of 1970. Nevertheless, as a result of these events, today the MIB has even more explicit policies in force describing what information is to be collected; the uses to which it can be put; how and under what conditions it can be shared with other institutions; how deliberate and accidental errors will be audited and prevented; who gets access to computerized databases; and who gets access to hard-copy, oral, or other media for capturing and communicating information. In particular, the MIB database has been recoded so that there is no longer a specific code that designates "positive HIV test." This code was removed as a result of policies put in force in reaction to the events just described. The current procedure is to code positive HIV tests as "blood disorders," which makes them indistin-guishable, say, from leukemia and other blood diseases.

In the wake of the AIDS situation, the insurance companies now have either implicit or explicit policies covering each of these aspects of the infor-mation life cycle. As of the date of Smith's (1994) study, however, neither the insurance companies nor MIB had a policy in place for avoiding information overload or reduced judgment. Nor did they have policies for treating the invasion-of-privacy-by-minute-description or "the whole is greater than the sum of the parts" processing.

Based on this case study and several others, Smith (1994) comes to the same conclusion that Stone (1975) does. The external legal and market forces acting alone are not adequately effective to ensure that information about people is handled in an ethical manner. They do not provide enough guidance for organizational employees at their critical moments of truth, especially during the early phases of a new phenomenon; the time required to reach recognition is too long, and the final organizational resolution is, in the end, usually inadequate or incomplete. What more needs to be done?

▨ A FRAMEWORK FOR ETHICAL ORGANIZATIONAL INFORMATION POLICIES

The only viable ethical solution is for every organization to develop its own information policies and procedures for itself, before market forces or the law force it to and in anticipation of its future exposure. Each organization must institutionalize values and adopt an ethical information culture that addresses every phase of its information life cycles. The following items should be on its ethical agenda.

Managing Intellectual Property

Organizations need policies concerning who owns the data, software, and other intellectual property they use and how it is to be employed. Intellectual property, in its most general sense, is any data, information, knowledge, or program created by the human mind. It is not something found in nature. More specifically, it is created by laws and rules such as those that pertain to patents, trademarks, and copyrights. Laws and rules about property define what counts as property; create different kinds of property; differentiate between what can and cannot be owned; and specify how property may be acquired, used, and transferred. In an organizational setting, however, these rules can be hard to apply. Often, there is a fine line between conditions in which an employee is learning or applying his or her expertise and in which he or she is using, producing, or taking company property. Generally, existing organizational incentives and structures encourage an employee to use whatever information resources are attainable to get the job done. This means that either knowingly or unknowingly an organizational member may be tempted to violate someone's property rights.

Some of these violations can create perplexing problems for management. A large defense contractor, for example, has an implicit policy that it owns and takes responsibility for the software it delivers to its customers, however that software is produced. One of its employees on his own time developed some special software that he eventually incorporated into the company's final delivered product. At this point, the firm took the position that the employee deserved no extra compensation for the special routines because they were part of the company's product. Later, it was discovered that the employee, without his employer's knowledge, had used some purloined software to produce what he claimed was solely his software. Was the company now responsible for this violation? Still later, it was learned that the purloined software had come from a disk that had a virus on it and that the virus had been transported to the customer's software. The question of who owned the software now became even more heated. Needless to say, the company corrected the problems that their customer was experiencing with the virus and compensated the customer for damages. The employee's contract was renegotiated, and an investigation was undertaken to determine the extent of the firm's exposure. This investigation uncovered considerable use of unauthorized games on the company's personal computers, some of which were also contaminated with viruses. These discoveries led the defense contractor to revamp its policies with respect to intellectual property, including software, data, and the appropriate use of its technology.

Managing Privacy

Existing organizational structures and incentives tend to encourage members to accumulate any and all available information about people, places, and things that may be relevant to their performance on their jobs. In the process, a person's privacy can be compromised or other sensitive information revealed. As the AIDS case presented earlier shows, policies on privacy and personal information are needed to prevent unwarranted and potentially harmful use of information about people.

Managing Accuracy and Quality

Existing organizational structures and incentives tend to encourage the conservation of resources. As a consequence, information acquisition, processing, storage, dissemination, and usage processes are often not adequately tested, checked, or rechecked. In addition, the scientific and practical limitations of the measurement processes employed are not fully appreciated or carefully enough controlled, as the AIDS case reveals. Furthermore, many organizations have bureaucratic rules and procedures that tend to depersonalize their customers and reject efforts to correct the accuracy or quality of their data. The plight of Louis Marches serves as an illustration.

An immigrant, Louis Marches was a hardworking man who, with his wife Eileen, finally saved enough money to purchase a home in Los Angeles during the late 1950s. The couple took out a long-term loan from Crocker National Bank. Every month, Louis Marches would walk to his neighborhood branch bank, loan coupon book in hand, to make his payment of $195.53. He always checked with care to ensure that the teller had stamped "paid" in his book on the proper line just opposite the month for which the payment was due. And he continued to do this long after the bank had converted to its automated loan-processing system.

One mid-September early in the 1980s, Marches was notified by the bank that he had failed to make his current home mortgage payment. He grabbed his coupon book, marched to his local branch bank, and in broken English that showed the traces of his old-country heritage, tried to explain to the teller that this dunning notice was wrong. Pointing to the "paid" stamp next to September in his coupon book, he claimed that this was proof that he was current in his payments. The teller was unmoved. She punched Marches's loan account number into her computer terminal and read the results on the screen. The computer records didn't confirm his claim, nor subsequently, did an appeal to the head teller or to the branch manager. Their bureaucratic instructions were clear: The computer files contained the information of record, the "facts" they were to accept. The entries recorded in his coupon book could not be trusted. Confused and irritated, but unconvinced, Marches returned home.

On the first of October, however, Marches dutifully walked to the bank again to make his next monthly payment. He was told, however, that the bank would not accept his October payment because he was still in arrears for September. Again, he showed the teller his stamped coupon book. As before, she refused to acknowledge it, and he stormed out of the bank. In November, he returned again on schedule as he had for nearly 30 years only to be told that he was now 2 months in arrears and his payment would not be accepted. And so it went, month after month, until inevitably the bank foreclosed.

Eileen learned of the foreclosure from an overzealous bank debt collector who called at the house while she was in bed recuperating from a heart attack.

She collapsed promptly after hearing the news, suffering a near fatal stroke that left her right side paralyzed. Sometime during this melee, Marches, who until this time had done his own legal work, was introduced to an attorney who agreed to defend him. They sued the bank and finally won.

After months of anguish, the Marches received a settlement of $268,000. All that the bank officials who testified could say in their company's defense was, "Computers make mistakes. Banks make mistakes, too." Since the Marches case, however, the bank has developed better safeguards against making errors in its accounts and adopted more friendly procedures for handling complaints.

Managing Access and Burden: Information Justice

The issue of access focuses on information takers, whereas information givers are more concerned with the issue of burden. Most existing organizational structures and incentives tend to allocate access to the organization's data and computer facilities based on one's position in the organizational structure and not on the basis of "need to know." At the same time, they tend to foist the burden of producing this data onto other parts of the organization. To overcome these tendencies and to promote organizational justice, policies are needed to ensure that those who are entitled to data and information technologies—that is, those who have a legitimate need to know—receive them, whereas those without a legitimate need do not. Furthermore, no individual or any other organizational unit should be required unfairly to spend their resources producing and handling information for the primary benefit of others.

The AIDS case clearly demonstrates the need for information access policies. Some types of information are so vital to selected users that it should be communicated to them directly and immediately and the organization should be proactive in doing so. Notifying the applicant (and perhaps his or her physician) of test results is a case in point. On the other hand, there are other parties, including underwriters and employers, who probably shouldn't have access to this particular data.

The trend to flatter, horizontal, and "virtual" organizations is pressuring executives to develop more open information systems. Typically, much of a firm's financial, production, and marketing data is held closely by just a few executives. Only a very few trusted employees get access to it. Some innovative companies, however, such as Semco and Chaparral Steel, now routinely make most of this data available to all of their employees. As Gordon Forward, CEO of Chaparral Steel, says, "We believe that they are all trusted employees." VeriFone makes so much information available to some of its employees that about 220 of them are listed with the Securities and Exchange Commission as "inside traders."

Carrying the burden of producing information can also be an ethical issue. Some large companies, for example, require their customers and suppliers to provide them considerable amounts of data just to do business with them, often with little additional benefit being received for the effort involved. To cite one, from among many, of these asymmetric power relationships, consider the clout some retailers hold over some of their suppliers, which permits them to force their suppliers to provide considerable information to them and often on a just-in-time or quick-response basis (see Chapter 4). Federal agencies have become so demanding in this regard that Congress passed the Federal Reduction of Paperwork Act of 1980, which requires agencies to estimate the time and effort involved in completing their forms and surveys and to demonstrate to the Office of Management and Budget that social value exceeds the social costs.

Perhaps the greatest problems involving the fair allocation of burden are experienced between different units of the same organization. Executives at a large West Coast bank, for example, decided that to evaluate their lending programs more scientifically, they needed data on all loan applications turned down as well as those granted. A select group of branches were required to fill out a rather complete form describing the applicant, the terms of the request, and the reasons for rejection for every application not granted. The results were predictable. First, many of the branch operations officers complained bitterly, claiming that the request was unfair. The information might have been helpful to headquarters but was not useful to them. In fact, some believed it could be used against them. The branches were already understaffed, and their officers, realizing that they derived no direct value from preparing the form, pushed it to the end of their work queues. As a result, it was seldom completed. Some branches, in an effort to comply with the bank's rules, filled the forms out hastily, and generally, these forms were riddled with errors. Indeed, a postmortem on this misconceived attempt to get the branches to provide additional data, actually revealed a slight increase in defaults and missed payments in the selected branches, suggesting that, to avoid the burden of providing reasons for not granting a loan, the branches loosened their lending policies. The problem was finally solved by abandoning the old system altogether and replacing it with one that made data collection a by-product of the initial application process. Both parties fared better. Executives in headquarters got most of the data they wanted and the branch officers were spared the extra burden and the stress it placed on their operations.

Managing Information Gatekeeping

Finally, every organization needs to determine what information can or must flow to which people at what time, what information should not flow, who controls the valves, and how they are to be controlled. Existing organizational structures and incentives generally permit information, like water, to seek the route of least resistance and, as Harlan Cleveland (1982a, 1982b) observed, "leak" into places it shouldn't be. Policies and procedures for gatekeeping serve to dam the leaks and redirect the flow to where it is ethically needed most.

In summary, organizations have natural bureaucratic tendencies to ignore certain ethical considerations in handling information. To overcome these tendencies, organizations should have policies and procedures for controlling their information practices. These policies should encompass the entire information life cycle and address issues such as property, privacy, accuracy and quality, access, burden, and gatekeeping.

This is only the first step. A deeper question must also be answered: Can an organization's structure and decision-making processes still remain unchanged? Christopher Stone (1975) argues that in many cases it cannot. Significant restructuring may be needed if the deficiencies of the law and of the marketplace as ethical controlling mechanisms are to be overcome. But just what form might this restructuring take? Drawing on some of Stone's recommendations, the next section fleshes out a possibility. It also serves as a template to consider other approaches to restructuring.

◪ CHANGING CORPORATE DECISION MAKING

Because the law and the market—that is, the kinds of forces Smith's (1994) cases show awaken organizations and lift them out of moral drift—are inadequate to ensure ethical behavior, effective ethical responses must emerge from within the corporation and become part of its daily life and culture. This calls for changes in corporate decision making at all levels, beginning with the board of directors (or the board of trustees, overseers, or other governing body).

The Board of Directors

The board should be fully apprised of the full range of information issues their firm faces and understand the firm's responsibilities and vulnerabilities. Especially in information-intensive organizations, the board should have a good understanding of the many information life cycles the company carries out and how they affect internal and external stakeholders. Stone (1975) believes, furthermore, that it should be mandatory that pertinent information about these processes be reported to the board on a regular basis. What might this report include? At a minimum, an audit should be conducted to determine the applicability of the following information-oriented laws to the firm:

- First Amendment of the Constitution
- Fair Information Practices of 1973
- Freedom of Information Act of 1968 as Amended (5 U.S.C. 552)
- Privacy Act of 1974 as Amended (5 U.S.C. 552a)
- Electronic Communications Privacy Act of 1986
- Computer Matching and Privacy Protection Act of 1988
- Computer Security Act of 1987
- Federal Managers Financial Integrity Act of 1982
- Fair Credit Reporting Act of 1970
- Family Educational Rights and Privacy Act of 1974
- Right to Financial Privacy Act of 1978
- Privacy Protection Act of 1980
- Cable Communications Policy Act of 1984
- Video Privacy Protection Act of 1988
- Patent Law (beginning in 1836)
- Regulations issued by the Federal Communication Commission, courts, Congress, states, legislatures, commissions, local governments
- See also the Statutes listed in the reference section

The audit should define the categories of information needed to assess the firm's performance in these areas. This would define the firm's information field. Based on this, an information system should be implemented to inform board members on a regular basis about the firm's status in its information field and, as appropriate, about changes in the field. Sanctions should be put in place so that directors would demand this kind of information and that corporate officers or the directors' staff would provide it. If the firm's exposure is great, members or perhaps a subcommittee of the board might be assigned primary responsibility for its information field. Just as the board's financial audit committee oversees the activities of the chief financial officer to ensure financial integrity, the information subcommittee would oversee the chief information officer and other appropriate executives to ensure information ethicality and integrity.

The composition of the board should also be reconsidered. Stone (1975) goes so far as to recommend that whenever an organization's exposure to information laws is significant, consideration should be given to having the general public appoint one or more directors who would in some sense be responsible for articulating the public's interest. In the event that the audit or the firm's history revealed a "demonstrated delinquency situation" or a "generic industry problem," he argues that one or more special public directors be appointed "whose expertise [is] suited to the particular area, and he [or she] would be given an appropriate, more sharply focused mandate" (pp. 174-175). In large corporations, Stone believes that inside directors should be eliminated or reduced to a minimum. This would minimize conflicts of interest and improve the board's ability to discipline corporate officers. Moreover, some of the outside directors should be financially disinterested.

Board members' job descriptions should also be changed. Their tasks should be well-defined and articulated to include their functions and responsibilities with respect to information and general information policy. One or more directors should be assigned oversight responsibility with respect to internal policies and procedures necessary to ensure legal and ethical compliance. A director's liability for wrongdoing should be clearly defined and communicated. To discharge these responsibilities, each director should be provided staff support for the purpose of analyzing proposals and monitoring results.

The CEO, CIO, and Internal Management

Whereas the board focuses on responses required to satisfy broader social demands, the firm's internal management structure should be altered to strengthen its ability to implement the necessary policies and procedures. If the problem area is central enough to the firm's activities, Stone (1975) believes that one or more high-level management positions should be established with primary responsibility for these policies and procedures. The chief information officer is the most likely candidate for assuming this role. In extreme cases, someone might be "inserted" from the outside. In any case, he or she must have sufficient clout. As Stone observes,

Of course, making a company establish an office is not enough, if all it comes to is painting a name on a door. To make the office truly effective, there must be attached to the office well-defined and meaningful powers and duties, as well as a place in the organization that guarantees the appointee's not being closeted away from critical action. (p. 189)

The considerations discussed in the previous section serve as a starting point for determining what the appropriate policies and procedures might be. This chapter's Appendix A provides a more complete checklist.

In addition, a review should be made of all the information professionals who work in the organization. Careful consideration should be given to the functions they perform and the codes of ethics they must abide by as summarized in the Appendix at the end of the book. Potential conflicts should be identified, and procedures for resolving differences when they arise should be instituted. In extreme cases, an ombudsman's role might be established. The ombudsman would be an official organizational position with wide powers enabling that person to intervene in the organization's administrative processes in the interests of the individual employees whose complaints he or she investigates.

Monitoring Systems

An ethical company needs an effective management information system to monitor and control its information-related activities. Management should be able to determine at any time whether its policies with respect to its information life cycles are being followed. It should be apprised of its current situation with respect to any material information errors that have been uncovered and what its vulnerability is to other kinds of errors. Controls on access to computer resources and data resources should be in place, and unauthorized use should be reported. Most important, however, the company should reach out into its environment and obtain information concerning its information effects on its customers, business partners, suppliers, employees, competitors, and other stakeholders.

One possibility is to require an "information impact statement" for every new company product, service, or policy. How does the proposed program alter the information field? What are its implications? Conducting these studies effectively may require "the establishment of a corporate office whose special functions spell out both *where* the holder of the office is to go to collect data (the sources), and what *categories of abstraction* he [or she] is to use (what the incumbent is to look for)" (Stone, 1975, p. 203). To avoid pleas of ignorance, responsible management should be informed on a regular basis.

Because the shredder and the "delete key" are sometimes used as devices to avoid knowing about questionable events, information storage and retention policies should be clearly defined and rigorously enforced. The original raw data should be retained for a reasonable period. Furthermore, all reports (and other intermediate products) should be signed or marked by the parties responsible for preparing them because during the process of subsequent inference making and summarizing, the original data loses some of its richness and complexity—that is, it is subjected to "uncertainty absorption." Stone (1975) believes that even raw data should bear the collector's imprimatur. This would provide a clearer audit trail for pinpointing responsibility throughout the information value-adding chain. Finally, standards of collection and computer processing should be established across firms within an industry so that investigators and others could have ready access to the information and be able to make valid comparisons. Stone sums up this way:

> The importance of a company's information processes cannot be overstated; they are as vital to the corporation as the nervous system of a human being to the body. What information the corporation seeks from its environment, where it looks for feedback (both within and without itself), where it dispatches what it learns, what it stores in memory, and what, for all intents and purposes, it "forgets" (or destroys)—all these features of its information system are fundamental determinants of the corporation's behavior. There is no reason why each of these information processes, in turn, cannot be influenced directly by the society. (p. 201)

The Decision-Making Process

Monitoring and compliance information should be fed into a redesigned decision-making process. Decisions that have effects in the information field should be made at the highest feasible level within the organization. High-level executives should not wait, as they did in each of Smith's (1994) cases, until major problems arise before they address the ethical issues surrounding their organization's information processes. Indeed, appropriate information about the ethical use of the organization's information should be made available at all levels and its maintenance of information ethics made a part of every employee's job.

The design of jobs should take this into account. "One of the factors affecting how people experience ethics at work," comments Barbara Ley Toffler (1986) in her book *Tough Choices*, "is their perception of themselves in their jobs. . . . Although no organization designs jobs to include unethical tasks or activities, sometimes the tasks or activities required by the job have the potential to create ethical dilemmas" (p. 28).

Not only should an organization prepare information impact statements and monitor its information activities, Stone (1975) argues that it should also make the results available to the public. "One of the most significant ways in which we might influence the corporate decision process in the direction of greater responsibility is to require that before the corporation can act in designated areas, it has to make certain [of its preliminary] *findings*" (p. 221) available to outside sources.

Corporate Culture

None of these proposals will be very effective unless the organization's culture is changed. This may be a substantial undertaking and require considerable effort and ingenuity because an organization's culture runs both wide and deep. The *American Heritage Dictionary* (3rd edition) defines culture as "the totality of socially transmitted behavior patterns, arts, beliefs, institutions, and all other products of human work and thought." In their classic book *Corporate Cultures,* Deal and Kennedy (1982) apply this concept of culture to organizations:

> Every business—in fact every organization—has a culture. Sometimes it is fragmented and difficult to read from the outside—some people are loyal to their bosses, others are loyal to the union, still others care only about their colleagues who work in the sales territories. . . . If you ask employees why they work, they will answer "because we need the money." On the other hand, sometimes the culture of an organization is very strong and cohesive; everyone knows the goals of the corporation, and they are working for them. Whether weak or strong, culture has a powerful influence throughout an organization; it affects practically everything—from who gets promoted and what decisions are made, to how employees dress and what sports they play. Because of this impact, we think culture also has a major effect on the success of the business. (p. 4)

To succeed and to be ethical, modern information-based organizations need an information-sensitive culture. Their members need to be keenly aware of the organization's information life cycles and how they affect its stakeholders. The organization's value system must reflect this. The attitudes, norms, customs, habits, and mores of all its members must be aligned with its overall posture with respect to information. Every organization should consider developing its own information ethic and write its own code of ethics or credo.

SUMMARY

The power of Stone's (1975) proposal lies in the corrective vision questions it raises. It is apparent from Stone's, Smith's (1994), and other studies that some organizations are experiencing difficulty in responding ethically to the new environment of the information age. A broadly accepted culture and ethos for information-based organizations has yet to emerge. Moreover, because this is also an age in which information-based organizations wield enormous social and economic power, this is a matter of considerable concern.

Many organizations do not have policies in place to ensure that they behave ethically. In fact, the very nature of most existing organizational structures and incentive systems seems to work against having such policies. Organization executives, consequently, have two choices: (a) They can change from within by adopting and enforcing appropriate ethical standards, or (b) they can be controlled from without. External controls, such as the law or the marketplace, are ultimately ineffective for solving all ethical issues. Moreover, they become major threats and saddle the organization with unnecessary burdens and hardships. To avoid this threat, executives must become involved early on and set effective policies as quickly as a clear pattern emerges. Either way, the new vision of an information-based organization should focus on policies with respect to its information life cycles and the technology it uses to carry them out. More important, all of an organization's givers, takers, and orchestrators of information must be deeply committed to an information-sensitive culture and ethos.

▨ NOTE

1. All excerpts in this chapter from Stone (1975) are reprinted with permission from *Where the Law Ends: The Social Control of Corporate Behavior* by Christopher Stone. New York: HarperCollins. Copyright © 1975 by Christopher Stone.

APPENDIX A

Information Ethics Checklist

In Chapter 4, an information system was defined as a combination of work practices, information, people, and information technologies organized to accomplish an organization's goals. Ten basic organizational functions can be identified that create an information system and define key relationships between its information givers, takers, and orchestrators. They involve two phases: planning for an organization's information life cycles (ILCs) and executing the activities in each cycle. During each phase, an organization is exposed to various ethical issues. The following checklist serves as a guide for identifying an organization's ethical vulnerability.

   I. Information Life Cycle Planning Functions

      A. Specifying ILC objectives: Are the information system's objectives and the uses that will be made of its hardware, software, and data consistent with the following?

         1. The social-ethical values of the organization

         2. The social-ethical values of its employees

         3. The social-ethical values of the society in which it operates

      B. Defining the problem and developing ILC planning premises

         1. Who are the information system's stakeholders?

         2. What are the stakeholders' major interests?

         3. Does the information system problem definition take into account the vital interests and competing claims of all affected stakeholders?

         4. Are the planning premises morally defensible?

C. Deriving conclusions from the planning premises
1. Do the conclusions follow logically from the premises?
2. Are the conclusions themselves morally defensible?

D. Determining data requirements
1. Is the data that will be acquired, processed, stored, disseminated, and used directly relevant to the problem as defined?
2. Is the needed data subject to potential uses that are *not* morally defensible? If so, what safeguards must be established?
3. Does the collection of the data infringe on the information givers' or sources' right to privacy? On other rights?
4. Are undue burdens being placed on the givers or sources to provide the information?
5. Are the givers' or sources' rights to ownership of data, software, or other intellectual property adequately protected?
6. How is the accuracy of the data ensured? Who is responsible?
7. What time dependency or expiration dates are placed on the data? How is data to be archived, updated, and disposed of?

E. Specifying the data collection method
1. Have the time, place, and conditions of data collection been announced to the givers or sources prior to collection? Are they informed of the use to which the data will be put and have necessary informed consent agreements been obtained?
2. Are the people who will collect the data oriented to the social-ethical values of the information system?
3. Who bears the cost of the burden of collection? Is it fair?
4. Is the method of collection unobtrusive? If not, are the givers and sources adequately compensated for their efforts and inconvenience? If so, are they aware that they are the subjects of data collection?
5. Does the plan provide adequate resources for data collection so that the data will be accurate, reliable, and of the highest requisite quality?

II. Information Life Cycle Execution Functions

A. Acquiring—collecting the data
1. Are the planned requirements for givers' or sources' privacy, property, informed use, informed consent, accuracy, validity, reliability, and clarity being met?
2. Is each giver or source adequately identified by a signature or mark so that a complete audit trail can be established?

B. Processing

1. Analyzing, summarizing, and comparing data

    a. Is the analysis consistent with the original objectives and planning premises?

    b. Does the analysis reflect the original data in an unbiased or balanced way?

    c. What safeguards are in place to ensure that no distortions of the data occur?

    d. Are unnecessary aggregations, matchings, or comparisons being made with the data?

    e. Is each step of the processing documented and recorded so that an audit trail is maintained?

    f. Are errors in estimation (and degrees of uncertainty absorption) adequately reported to takers, users, and other stakeholders?

2. Producing reports and conclusions

    a. Do the reports contain a balanced presentation of the results?

    b. Do all parties who have a need or right to know been given equal access to the reports?

C. Storing—retaining data and reports for future retrieval

1. What is the organization's trust relationship with its givers and sources? Are its fiduciary responsibilities being met?

2. Is the information retained long enough to satisfy all stakeholders' objectives?

3. Are the sovereignty of the stakeholders and their right to equal access preserved?

4. Are the organization's information assets (databases, files, software, etc.) secure and adequately protected from acts of God and malicious activity?

5. Are the restrictions for security, secrecy, and confidentiality enforced?

D. Dissemination—transporting data throughout the system and to takers and users

1. Is the fidelity, accuracy, and integrity of the information maintained throughout its transmission?

2. Is adequate channel capacity allocated to the top priority and highest value ethical messages?

3. Are the organization's information gatekeeping functions properly managed so that those who need the data and reports receive them in a timely manner and those who do not have a right or need to know are prohibited from receiving them?

E. Using—taking and applying the information

1. Are the decisions and actions taken on the basis of the information provided consistent with the overall social-ethical values of the organization, its employees, and the society in which it operates?

2. Are audits such as this ethical check of information conducted on a regular basis to ensure that any new ethical issues that might arise across the organization or within the information handling functions are identified and dealt with?

9

Societal Issues and Information Ethics

◩ WILL THE INFORMATION SUPERHIGHWAY CREATE A GOOD SOCIETY?

In 1993, President Clinton and Vice President Al Gore proposed that the U.S. government build an electronic "superhighway" for the country. A high-capacity, high-speed network—consisting of computers, fiber-optic cable, and sophisticated switches—is needed, they argued, to improve the nation's infrastructure. As the *New York Times* reported (Markoff, 1993), the system "could do for the flow of information—words, music, movies, medical images, manufacturing blueprints and much more—what the transcontinental railroad did for the flow of goods a century ago and the interstate highway system did in this century" (p. 15). Among the network's objectives is to improve "education, health care, scientific research and the ability of corporations to compete in the world economy" (p. 15). Many people responded favorably to the proposal in general; however, enormous differences emerged concerning questions such as, Who should build it? How should it be built? Who should manage it? How should it be controlled? Who would have access to it? Who would pay? Many different segments of society—industry, the administration, and public interest groups, to name a few—were severely divided on the answers. "I think the Government should not build and/or operate such networks," Robert E. Allen (quoted in Markoff, 1993, p. 15), chief executive officer of AT&T, said espousing one point of view as he argued in favor of the private sector's assuming the primary responsibility for the project.[1]

The proposal to design and implement a national electronic superhighway raises ethical issues well beyond the individual, professional, or organizational level. This proposal requires a response at the societal level. The United States and other advanced nations are already heavily dependent on information and information technology. The electronic superhighway will serve to increase this dependence and, in the process, change society substantially and qualitatively. How the nation's information is assembled, collected, distributed, and used will be materially affected, and this will affect many people's lives. The superhighway will have a major effect on whether or not we create a "good" society.

How should we think about these societal implications? In this chapter, four basic social values—liberty, equality, community, and control—are discussed as they apply to the role of information in a society. Each in its purest and extreme form serves as an ideal that can never be fully achieved. Consequently, trade-offs are made between them whenever an information policy is defined and implemented. Which of these values dominate at any given time is the result of social decision making and how a society forms a "polis."

▧ POLIS: THE BASIS FOR DEFINING A GOOD SOCIETY

Discovering the appropriate decision-making processes for using information and information technology in a society requires an understanding of why people form social groups in the first place and how they organize them to fulfill social relations. The forming of a polis requires the establishment of policies, norms, standards, and cultural guidelines that become part of a society's social contract and is required to govern the behavior of all of the members.

Human beings form communities so that they might collectively solve their common problems. This instinct has basic survival value and is derived, initially, from a common need for humans to cope with the forces of nature, reaching back at least as far as the early, primitive societies such as the Cro-Magnon of Lascaux. It continues to be a motivating force today, although through time additional motivations have been added. Today, human beings still find the need to come together to solve a whole host of pressing common problems, such as how to live, acquire food, build shelters, protect themselves from enemies, educate their children, add interest and entertainment to their lives, and in today's world, how to participate effectively in an information society and economy.

About five centuries before Christ, the Greeks coined the term *polis* to describe the result of this mutually inspired "coming together." Polis formed the basis of the Greeks' concept of a city. It became the ideal under which communities were organized. All of a person's requisite social relationships were to be fulfilled by his or her polis. In the Greek ideal, all relationships between a nation-state and the society; between economic enterprises and the state or society; or between individuals regarding economic, cultural, political, and religious activities were regulated within the unifying structure of the polis. In a polis, therefore, all important social relationships are intermixed and undifferentiated.

This concept of a polis raises an important question that can be expressed in several related ways: What is a good joining together of diverse people? What are the society's obligations to its members? What is a good polis? What is a good society? These are questions of governance and of social values.

Every age and every new social grouping must address anew the question of forming polis. It must find its own best way to make its own society good. This requires that the people take a fresh look at the unique societal challenges emerging at their singular time in history.

At the beginning of the industrial age, for example, widespread concerns centered on a series of major social transformations then underway, such as transforming from crafts and cottage industries to factory jobs; from rural farming to city life; from small groups to large organizations; from small, isolated markets to large marketing systems; from local distribution to regional and national distribution networks; and from moderate technology to large-scale industrial technology. These challenges were the product of industrialization and the emerging market and capitalistic system that created a new economic, technological, and social context. The American Revolution and then the French Revolution were, in part, responses to the turmoil these transformations created. (It is also interesting to note that a remarkable amount of ethical literature was written during this time.) In the end, certain basic ethical principles were established. Among them were freedom and security for each individual; equality before the law; abolition of class differences; security and inviolability of property; the separation of church and state; and the separation in the governance systems of legislative, administrative, and judicial functions.

Just as the ancient Greeks' vision of a good society would not necessarily be a good society, say, for early industrialized rural America in 1776 or a Napoleonic France in 1789, neither were these late 18th-century solutions fully applicable to the urbanized, large-scale manufacturing- and marketing-based society of the early 20th century as it emerged in industrialized, urban Detroit, Chicago, or Pittsburgh. As before, the types of technology employed, the scale of social groupings required, and the dynamics of the political economy had changed.

Today, a whole new set of information-based societal issues such as the electronic superhighway, freedom of information, and national legislation for privacy protection have surfaced. We must once again address the issue of what for us is a good society or, more specifically, what is a good information society.

N MOVING TOWARD A GOOD INFORMATION SOCIETY

Today, we are struggling with the problem of how to create a good information society. Some aspects of this future society are now emerging. Various laws concerning privacy and intellectual property and new principles, such as those for fair information practices, are shaping our views. The Freedom of Information Act of 1966, for example, has already defined a responsibility for government to be more open in its collection and dissemination of information. The national electronic superhighway will provide a means for more people to have access to more of the nation's data. All of these initiatives are changing key relations between members of our society. But are they good?

Every society must find its place among a set of competing notions of good. A network of tensions exists between these goods, formed by the debates and arguments of people who want one end or the other, and each new social policy must find its own location amid this controversy. One timeless tension focuses on the position, role, and rights assigned to individuals as members of a society. One end seeks to treat individuals as unique and give them as much freedom and autonomy as possible. The other pole seeks to treat all individuals equally. A second major and timeless tension focuses on the role of collectives in a society. One anchor strives for a sense of community in which a great variety of values, purposes, goals, and objectives are tolerated and in which interpersonal relations and collective social needs dictate social policies. On the other side, there is a strong tug to form a society as a collection of organizations, bureaucracies committed to the efficient accomplishment of just a few but important social goals. The lines between the poles of these tensions are drawn taut, and they vibrate with the introduction of each new policy or new technology until it finds a socially acceptable home. In finding a good place within this network, members of society must make trade-offs between these competing poles of goodness.

▧ BASIC ETHICAL TRADE-OFFS AT THE SOCIETAL LEVEL

At one pole, the ideal of *liberty* requires that each individual agent be free to pursue his or her own goals without regard to the activities or goals of other agents. At the other pole, the ideal of *equality* requires that all individual agents should be treated equally. There are various definitions of equality. All of them, however, provide for some potential curtailment of an agent's activities or a restriction on an agent's choice of goals to ensure that every agent operating in the field is evenly matched or has the same rights or status. Sometimes, distinctions are made between political equality—the same power to vote, legislate, or engage in the political system—and economic equality—equal levels of wealth or income.

The second basic tension is characterized by an opposition between a demand for *community,* on the one hand, and a demand for *control,* efficiency, or rational organization on the other. This is a distinction first made by the German sociologist Ferdinand Tönnies (1887/1957) who studied the new economic institutions that were emerging in Europe during the last two decades of the 19th century. These were large-scale organizations, such as corporations, cities, states, and nations, based on rules, conventions, law, and public opinion. He observed that these types of collectives were designed primarily for economic efficiency and noted how qualitatively different they were from the traditional communities in which, up to that time, most people had worked and lived. These types of organizations we generally call *bureaucracies.*

Bureaucracies—public and private, technology and sociotechnical systems, trade and trading relationships—captivated Tönnies's interest. The purpose of rational organization, he argued, is to make efficient use of society's resources. Organizations enter into contracts for the purpose of achieving just a few of society's most pressing collective goals. They are a means to an end or a limited number of social ends. (Tönnies used the German word *Gesellschaft*, to describe these rational organizations.) The ends selected are sharply differentiated and clearly defined so that they may be pursued in a manner consistent with norms of both technical and economic rationality. That is, as was discussed in Chapter 8, the purpose of bureaucracies, large organizations, and corporations is to establish control over a complex environment so that their goals can be achieved. As professor James Beniger (1986) has noted, the development of bureaucracy was a major milestone in what he calls *The Control Revolution*. Moreover, because a fundamental relationship exists between establishing control over some social or economic process and the use of information, Beniger believes that the primary motivation for producing information is to gain control over one's environment. Efficient organization, he argues, is a key factor in using information effectively for the purpose of gaining control.

Communities, on the other end of the collective continuum, are collections of people who have formed patterns of life in which their collective demands and interpersonal relationships are more important than their individual goals. They are constituted by custom, cooperation, or religion. Families, villages, small-town communities, and small informal organizations are examples. According to Tönnies (1887/1957), the creation of communities is motivated by a need to express a "natural will" and is characterized by an intense emotional spirit.

Communities are the outcome of natural interactions between the incumbents of various status roles in a society—such as mother and child, employer and employee, teacher and student—and thus are spontaneous and affective rather than planned and rational. (Tönnies referred to these by the word *Gemeinschaft*.) The collective actions of communities are internally managed and controlled and directed toward meeting the many diverse, personal, private, and intimate goals of their members. Consequently, tradition, kinships, and friendships play a central role in communities.

These two pairs of dialectical opposites—liberty versus equality on one axis and community versus control on the other—form a kind of map for describing and comparing ethical issues at the societal level (see Figure 9.1).

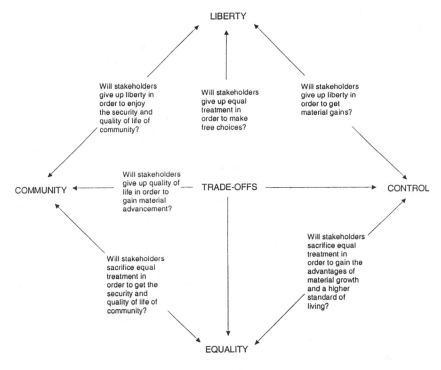

Figure 9.1. Ethical Trade-Offs at the Societal Level

SOURCE: Adapted from *The Executive's Compass: Business and the Good Society* by James O'Toole. Copyright © 1993 by Oxford University Press. Reprinted with permission of Oxford University Press and James O'Toole.

▧ THE POLES OF THE MORAL COMPASS

The map's originator, Professor James O'Toole (1993) a social anthropologist cum management theorist, refers to this orientation system as a "moral compass." It can be used to navigate through the complexities of societal-level issues and to evaluate legislation policies, programs, and technological initiatives in terms of their overall effect on a society.

The "four poles of a good society" represent strong forces of attraction. They also have the annoying property that when considered in isolation, one would generally like to have as much of each good as possible because the attraction of each pole emerges from a strong ethical argument in a great historical conversation. When considered as a whole, however, some kinds of trade-offs or compromises must be made. Thus, a new policy or initiative will tend to move a society in a new direction by giving up some of one or more goods to obtain more of the others.

Liberty

Liberty means being free. Freedom and liberty are essentially the same thing. The societal tug coming from this pole is the natural desire of all of agents to express their own free will, unencumbered and unconstrained. Thomas Hobbes (1651/1839) called this a "natural right." Immanuel Kant (1788/1956) took the idea even further: "Freedom is independence of the compulsory will of another; and insofar as it can co-exist with the freedom of all according to a universal law, it is the one sole, original inborn right belonging to every man in virtue of his humanity" (p. 193). This view, of course, derives from Kant's belief that all people should be treated as ends in themselves, not primarily as means toward someone else's ends.

The idea of liberty applies to economic agents as well. Consumers' liberty to choose the products and services they want make them "kings," for example, in Adam Smith's (1776/1986) eyes. This is the basis of Smith's view that free competition between producers and sellers, even between countries, is both ethical and economically superior. An "invisible hand" working through the market forces of supply and demand would control the effects of unrestrained self-interest as greedy producers and sellers worked, sometimes unawares, to the maximum benefit of society. This theme has been extended by the contemporary economist Milton Friedman (1962). In *Capitalism and Freedom*, he argues that competitive capitalism is "a system of economic freedom and a necessary condition for political freedom" (p. 2).

Friedman's (1962) economic arguments are part of a broader philosophical position called *libertarianism*, of which Robert Nozick is one of the greatest recent proponents. Individual liberty and freedom of thought are necessarily good, Nozick (1974) argues, and any constraints to liberty imposed by others are necessarily evil, except when absolutely needed to prevent the imposition of even greater human constraints. Private property and market mechanisms are essential for liberty, in part, because both limit the power of the state. This follows, as Nozick claims in *Anarchy, State, and Utopia*, from the libertarian principle that the *only* basic right that every individual possesses is the negative right to be free from the coercion of other human beings. People must be free to enter into contracts, use free markets to exchange goods and services, and make free use of their property. They earn this right to property, as J. S. Mill (1859/1956) had argued earlier, through the application of their labor and must be free to do what they want with their labor and with whatever products they produce by means of their labor. Government and large bureaucracies tend to interfere with these rights. Consequently, most libertarians believe that modern government is too big, and they rail at those who stress bureaucracy, efficiency, and control at the cost of liberty. Voluntary cooperation among individuals is the only satisfactory alternative to tyrannical coercion by the state. There is no example, Friedman (1962) observes, "in time or place of a society that has been marked by a large measure of political freedom . . . that has not also used something comparable to a free market to organize the bulk of economic activity" (p. 2).

Liberty and Information Ethics

What demands does the pole of liberty place on an information society? Several are clear. Here are some of the typical arguments emanating from this pole:

- All people should be free to use their intellectual and physical labor to produce whatever information-based goods and services they desire.
- By dint of one's labor the results of one's work become property that one exclusively owns. That is, the producers of intellectual property have a right to that property and to sell or dispose of it or earn income from it.
- Whoever owns information has a right to use it as he or she sees fit and to reap the rewards from its use. Information should be treated as a market commodity. Its economic value is its exchange value in the marketplace.
- Owners of computers, communications devices, and other forms of information technology and the information systems that run on them should be able to deploy this technology at their own discretion and for any legal purposes they so desire.

The force of liberty argues, in addition, that the electronic superhighway should be built and managed by the private sector as AT&T's Robert Allen has contended. Its services should be priced at market prices, and companies and people should compete for them.

Equality

The pole of equality argues, in the extreme, that there are no relevant differences between the stakeholders in an ethical field that are significant enough to be used to justify treating stakeholders unequally. Every person should be given equal, or nearly equal, shares of the social system's benefits and burdens.

Beginning with Aristotle, many philosophers had focused their attention on differences they noted between human beings—caste, class, race, gender, skills, and so on. They assumed that these differences were bestowed by nature. Jean Jacques Rousseau (1762/1947) was among the first to challenge this assumption. In *The Social Contract,* published in 1762, he took the position that all human beings are fundamentally, intrinsically the same, at least with respect to their capacity to be good and do good. The way organized society treats them accounts for their differences. Individual differences are the result of the conditions people were born into and how they were brought up and treated subsequently. "Nurture" not "nature," Rousseau argues, accounts for their differences.

Stemming from this proposal, and from a whole series of reactions to it, the concept of political equality emerged. All members have a right, proponents of this pole argue, to have a voice and participate in the governance of the polis. This right is accorded to all members regardless of race, color, or creed. Thomas Jefferson, as noted earlier, referred to this form of political equality as an unalienable right. The U.S. Constitution and Bill of Rights establish equal rights with respect to due process, civil liberties, and participation in the legislative process. This idea of political equality, although agreed to by many in the West, is still the basis for many struggles throughout the world.

The quest for economic equality has resulted in even more intense struggles. A strong tug from the pole of equality is the belief that every member of a polis has a right to a minimum standard of living. That is, there is a certain security level, a "safety net," below which no person should fall. Different societies and diverse cultures have come up with their own view as to what that minimum should be, but most agree that there should be one. This has undergirded the democratic socialist notion that, although society does not have a right to appropriate the property of the rich, it does have an obligation to guarantee the necessities of life to the poor. Otherwise, the poor are left powerless and unable to participate in—or ultimately to contribute to—the society.

Equality and Information Ethics

Similar to the argument for a minimum standard of living is the one for a minimum standard of information access for all members of the society. Consider the following editorial from the February 21, 1994, *New York Times:*

> Child number one owns a fancy computer setup that taps into electronic libraries all over the country. Child number two is computerless and poor in a rural area where the library is a single cramped room above the local gas station.
>
> The first child is already primed for the Information Superhighway. The second child is stuck on what can only be called an Information Dirt Road. If Albany continues to starve the state library system, the gap between these information haves and havenots will continue to grow, creating an information underclass that the state can ill afford. (p. B1)[2]

Getting agreement on a socially acceptable minimum and operationalizing the ideal of equality are still major challenges. Identical distribution, for example, is not absolutely necessary for a good society. As the British writer R. H. Tawney (1931) (writing in a slightly different context) observes, "Equality of environment, of access to education and the means of civilization, of security and independence, and of the social consideration [requirements] which equality . . . usually carries with it" (p. 37) is essential.

Yet in the case of providing equal access to information by means of, say, the electronic superhighway, the situation is still murky. Does this mean that each person should get exactly the same information? Most likely not. Does it mean that each person should have the same information available to him or her regardless of where he or she is located (and hence regardless of the differences of cost of delivery through the electronic superhighway system)? Also not likely, but debatable. Should the superhighway be established as a public asset and an equal budget be allocated to information provision for each person—providing equality in input but not necessarily in performance? Feasible, but also very debatable. And so it goes. The demands for equality among the members of the polis are strong and ever present. They are difficult to define and operationalize in a satisfactory way, and most important, a painful trade-off must often be made between satisfying claims for equality on one hand and claims for freedom and liberty on the other. A good society must find an optimal position on that trade-off.

Consequently, a crucial dimension of the debate surrounding establishing an electronic superhighway in the United States is how it will affect individual citizens. The pole of liberty pulls the program toward policies that feature minimal governmental intervention and maximum freedom on the part of individuals and corporations. In contrast, the pole of equality pulls the program toward policies that provide equal access to information and information-handling services. As we have seen, the attraction of these two forces is frequently in conflict, and, therefore, corrective vision at the societal level requires that alternative policies be examined from each of these perspectives and a judgment made as to where to place them on the continuum between liberty and equality.

One further observation on equality. Information technology is altering the way the quest for equality manifests itself. In the transformations that took place in the former Soviet Union and in Eastern and Central Europe, fax machines, photocopy machines, cellular phones, printing presses, and video-tapes, among other technologies, helped people debate ideas about political and economic equality among themselves and across national borders. Radio also played a key role. The British Broadcasting Corporation doubled its Russian-language programming to 18 hours a day and served as a relay for satellite broadcasts from Radio Russia so that people around the world could be apprised of events.

Newsweek (September 2, 1991) observed that the Russian leaders of the attempted coup d'état failed to understand the power of the new technology. They were "reading from an outdated manual. They sent troops to surround Moscow's main telephone exchange, occupy the radio and television center and shut down independent newspapers" (p. 39).[3] They did not attempt, although it would likely have been unsuccessful, to eliminate the personalized technologies that have become so widely distributed even in the former U.S.S.R.

Community

Native Americans tell a story about the white man and the American Indian who were digging for clams at the seashore. As each man plucked a clam from the sand, he tossed it into his bucket. At the end of the day, as they packed up to leave, the white man grabbed his pail only to discover that all of his clams had mysteriously disappeared. Somehow during the day they had jumped out and gone away. The Indian's pail, the man noticed, was still full.

"How did you do that?" he implored his companion.

"Easy," the Indian replied. "Whenever an Indian's clam sticks his head up just a little higher than the rest, all the others join together to pull him back down."

Such is the power of the tug of community. Primal peoples experience the tug of communication deeply, and it is a fundamental drive all human beings share.

A community is a collective made up of stakeholders who have divergent goals and abilities, yet their diversity is honored and appreciated by all stakeholders. This is the presumed original and natural state of all humankind, and thus the pull from this pole is primordial and strong. For primitive tribes, the creation of community was a matter of survival. Only by coming together could they eke out an existence in a harsh, uncompromising environment. As a consequence, two far-reaching social values were instilled in the process. One was an understanding that "we are all in this together." The other was a deep respect for nature—that is, to live "at one" and in harmony with nature.

In *Earthwalk,* Philip Slater (1974) makes a subtle but significant distinction between a network and a community. A network is composed of a rather homogeneous group of people who exchange information about a common topic. Networks have a centrality of purpose, but they do not necessarily claim any territory. Organizations are made up of networks. The employees of AT&T, for example, form a network, as do those of the U.S. Department of Defense. The Association for Computing Machinery also forms a network in Slater's sense. So, too, are all of the employees of a corporation who are tied together by means of a local area network through which they share accounting data and e-mail. For that matter, all of the people who subscribe, say, to the "opera" or other common interest bulletin boards also form a network.

A community, on the other hand, is composed of a rather heterogeneous group of people—young and old, rich and poor, large and small, the wise old man, the village idiot, butcher, baker, janitor, and the like—all of whom join together to satisfy their common life needs. Communities, consequently, have far more diversity than do networks. They are also much more difficult to govern. Most of us, however, spend some very important parts of our lives in communities and we rely on them to enjoy a fuller life.

Community and Information Ethics

An ongoing demand for the qualities of community is present in societal policy today. It has considerable implications for the use of information and information technology. The modern demand for community can be summed up in a single phrase: improving the quality of life. It centers on three key themes: (a) interdependence among human beings, (b) human dignity, and (c) a deep concern for nature and the natural environment.

1. A good community is one that recognizes that people are *inter*dependent, not independent. Therefore, the common responsibilities of stakeholders to each other are more important than are their individual rights. Such terms as *empathy, sympathy, charity, fraternity,* and *the brotherhood of "man"* have been used to capture the essential dimensions of the quality of relationship between members of a good community. Ultimately, achieving a good community requires some degree of altruism and acts of the "Good Samaritan."

2. Communities have a deep respect for human dignity and support it. People, as Immanuel Kant (1788/1956) argued, are treated as ends in themselves and not as means to someone else's ends. Thus, people become more important than the goods they produce, and similarly, creative activity is valued more than material consumption. What Thorstein Veblen (1914) once called an "instinct for craftsmanship" becomes essential. That is, people who are "whole" should take personal pride in their work and in the contributions it makes to their community. They should feel that they are contributing something of themselves aesthetically and emotionally to their work and their character, identity, and sense of social worth should emanate from their work. Note also that the distinction normally made in industry between work and leisure doesn't make as much sense in the context of community. With a good quality of working life, a person is renewed and refreshed by means of his or her involvement with work. In a good community, leisure and work are intermixed and mutually supportive, whereas in an industrial factory, they tend to be diametrically opposed.

3. The pole of community reminds us that we are all part of nature and must coexist with it. "The history of the earth," Rachel Carson (1962) observed, "has been a history of interaction between living things and their surroundings" (p. 5). For most of history, the earth's plants and animals were molded by the environment. Today, humankind is a major, perhaps *the* major, force shaping nature. Many contemporary environmental and ecological advocates serve to remind us of humankind's earlier relationship with nature and of how humanity learned to live with nature. A good community should not take more out of nature than is needed, they claim, and it should focus primarily on those things—now called "renewable resources"—that nature replenishes naturally within its biological rhythms. Despoiling the environment destroys nature's ability to provide clean air, water and, ultimately, sustenance for humankind. "Contaminate your bed," Chief Seattle warned President Franklin Pierce in

1854, "and you will one night suffocate in your own waste." Eastern Europe and, indeed, many of our industrial- and automobile-centered cities of the West today serve as testimonies to the wisdom of the Puget Sound chief. A key value of the pole of community consequently is this: Achieving a good community is impossible if nature will not support it.

Biologist and philosopher Garrett Hardin (1968) informs us that a crucial need today is for all human beings to recognize the limited "carrying capacity" of all natural systems. In "The Tragedy of the Commons," Hardin uses as a metaphor the shared public grazing lands, called the *commons,* that played such a vital part in most early American communities. A simple example helps make his point. Suppose a commons would accommodate only 20 grazing sheep and still replenish itself, but beginning with the 21st sheep, the land was depleted rapidly. For example, five farmers could each graze one sheep on the commons easily. But suppose that one farmer, noticing that his sheep was doing well, adds another. His lead is soon followed by the other four—bringing the total of sheep grazing on the commons to 10. This process is repeated again and the total becomes 15. It is repeated once more—bringing the total to 20. Up to this point, every farmer's output and well-being has been improving as the number of sheep he grazes in the commons has increased. This is the "comedy" phase of the story.

Suppose, however, that now the farmers try to repeat the process one more time. Problems set in with the addition of the 21st sheep and become worse and worse as each new sheep is added. The lesson of the "Tragedy of the Commons" is that self-interest, market forces, and free decision making can add joy and productivity to a system up to the point at which its carrying capacity is reached. Then, suddenly, but often predictably, joy and productivity go down dramatically, sometimes to the point at which the exploitation destroys the total productive capacity of the resource forever.

Unfortunately, examples of Hardin's (1968) story abound. Rich grasslands in the valley surrounding Tucson, Arizona, for example, made it a great cattle-raising area in the late 19th century. But the area was severely overgrazed, and today it is a desert, threaded with blistered arroyos that cut crevices into the land and carry valuable soil and water to the sea. Similarly, a few automobiles made the city and the lifestyle of Los Angeles possible. Today's millions of automobiles, however, have generated smog, pollution, and congestion and threaten to bring the city to the edge of inhabitability.

The broadcasting spectrum and the bandwidth it provides is also a commons. Ultimately, there are only so many messages that can be carried simultaneously by the airways. As with most systems, the carrying capacity of the broadcasting spectrum can be, and has been, expanded by the application of technology. More effective signal compression routines, more sensitive sending and receiving devices, and the like increase the capacity of the air and other media for carrying messages. In the end, however, some limit will be reached.

When the limits of a system's carrying capacity are reached, individuals in the system lose the freedom to choose how the channels of communication will be used. As a result, some form of allocation system must be adopted. Usually, the new allocation is based on the values, norms, and culture of the community.

This deep-seated need to return again to the foundations of the community to allocate scarce resources is one of the reasons that the pole of community ultimately has such a strong pull on a society. It is also one of the reasons a community strives from the beginning to be compatible with nature. Communities seek to avoid scarcity.

This has led communitarians, such as E. F. Schumacher, to argue that, for the most part, or in the absence of a compelling reason to do otherwise, "small is better than big, decentralized better than centralized, local than national, participation better than diktat, demassified better than standardized, and community-centered activities better than self-interested ones" (quoted in O'Toole, 1993, p. 66). This "think globally, act locally" attitude combined with several other tendencies—including a leaning toward prudence in the application of technology, an ecological perspective with consideration for the commons, and a deep concern for the human dignity of every member of an ethical field—serves to strengthen the primary pull from the pole of community.

There is a very close relationship between community and information. Next to psychological bonding, information is the most fundamental building block of a community. Members of communities create, share, and use information to survive, and this is often done, as was the case of the cave dwellers of Lascaux, with little special recognition given to the individuals who contributed to the process. Information is fundamentally "human," as Cleveland (1982a, 1982b) observes, and it is also shareable, leakable, and easily fungible. That is, it can be mixed together and interchanged readily. So information in the form of cultural guidance, education, and entertainment permeates any community.

The Clinton-Gore proposal for an electronic information superhighway is intended, in part, to fulfill some of these needs. By providing the infrastructure necessary to make computational and communications resources available to a vast cross section of the American public and by encouraging uses such as education, health care delivery, and scientific research, the superhighway program should serve to develop a more effective community. Additional programs can be envisioned, however, that would enhance the program's community building capability even further.

Some of the new uses of technology require a fresh view of the role of information in community. The modern notion that information can be abstracted and packaged and made someone's property is historically quite new. Little, if any, of the information that flows in a community and that binds it together is considered to be property in this sense. Furthermore, because information is crucial to its survival, a community wants to keep its channels of communication open and not to exceed the limits of the carrying capacity of its media. One of the objectives of the electronic superhighway is to increase the total bandwidth available to the nation and, thereby, to increase the communications carrying capacity of the nation as a whole.

One downside of the social demand for community, however, is its emphasis on social domination. So building community can work in opposition to enhancing the liberty of its stakeholders and even against reaching equality among them. The biggest threat to the pursuit of community, however, is the establishment of large-scale, bureaucratic, limited-purpose, rational organizations designed to control industrial and social processes. They are founded on a quest for efficiency by means of control and can severely limit the realization of community.

Control

Beniger (1986) uses the concept of control to describe "purposive influence toward a predetermined goal" (p. 7). It has two essential elements: (a) "*influence* of one agent over another, meaning that the former causes changes in the behavior of the latter" and (b) "*purpose,* in the sense that influence is directed toward some prior goal of the controlling agent" (p. 7). Whenever a society's activities become so complex, voluminous, fast moving, or wide-ranging that it cannot make efficient use of its resources or produce enough quality products or services, it is thrown into a crisis of control. Creating bureaucracies was the first historical solution to this problem.

As discussed in Chapter 8, bureaucracies are organizations with a clear-cut division of labor, well-defined responsibilities for each job, hierarchical authority, and specialized decision and communication functions. Their administration is marked by diffusion of authority among numerous offices and adherence to a predetermined set of inflexible rules of operation. The rules are applied impersonally to cases and clearly identified business events. Career employees are promoted up the hierarchy by objective criteria, such as merit on the job and seniority. Well-managed bureaucracies are highly efficient means to achieve limited, well-defined social goals. Thus, they are the antithesis of community and entail a movement from a government of men to an administration of things. In the production of goods, for example, raw materials are moved, formed, and processed to create products.

Bureaucracy was a European innovation, but three Americans perfected it for the modern industrial enterprise: Frederick W. Taylor, Henry Ford, and Alfred P. Sloan. In the late 1890s, Taylor became known as "the father of scientific management." The essence of his scientific management approach was to routinize the activities of individual workers by means of "time and motion" and other analytic studies of work processes, and these ideas soon spread throughout industrial America. Some people embraced them fervently; many feared them. All recognized that they were the realization of values underlying Taylor's prophecy: "In the past, the man has been first, in the future the system must be first" (Taylor, 1911/1967, p. 7).

Henry Ford perfected the concept of mass production, which reached its zenith in the building of Highland Park—the home of the Model T—and of River Rouge, claimed to be the "factory to end all factories." Ford had a fixation on control. He wanted every critical resource that flowed into and out of his plants to be under his direct control. His moving assembly line for the production of automobiles was designed to advance Taylor's idea of increased specialization. Assembling a Model T required 7,882 distinct tasks. Each was analyzed in detail and organized into a single, solid, unitary, mass production assembly line.

Ford's insights into mass production and mass consumption were extended into a full-blown theory of organization by Alfred P. Sloan. As president of General Motors (GM), Sloan helped create the multidivisional, multifunctional organizational form, and to manage its complexity, he devised new methods for measuring and coordinating GM's diverse and far-flung activities. This approach to organization resulted in an enormous increase in the efficiency of these large-scale operations and led to the earning of exceptional returns on investment as a result of what economists call "economies of scale."

Soon, other firms, such as Standard Oil, Du Pont, and Sears, Roebuck and Company, also adopted the approach. Business historian Alfred D. Chandler (1990) concludes that this type of organizational bureaucracy accounted for the immense success of the 278 largest corporations on the American scene during the first half of the 20th century. Among those impressed by these accomplishments was Vladimir Ilyich Lenin who made the idea of organizational efficiency, as pioneered by Taylor, Ford, and Sloan, a bulwark in the Bolshevik's new economic policy. This led to the construction of some of the largest (and, in terms of human misery and suffering, some of the most costly) industrial projects in the world.

Control and Information Ethics

Bureaucracy reigned as the most important method of achieving efficiency and control until World War II. The war brought the advent of the electronic computer. In the information age, computers, communications, and other information technologies work within the context of organizations to solve their problems of the crisis of control. Such applications of technology as truth phones, automatic toll tag readers, credit reporting systems, vendor just-in-time systems, and computerized airline reservation systems are designed to provide greater control over social and economic processes. As discussed in detail in the previous chapter, management information systems, command and control systems, decision support systems, and group decision support systems all share this common objective of improving the processes of control.

One of the strongest arguments in favor of the electronic superhighway is that it will help modern society solve its contemporary crisis of control. When it is completed, advocates of the Clinton-Gore proposal claim, American corporations will be able to compete more effectively in the global economy, education will be delivered more efficiently, health care will serve more people better and at less cost, and the nation will make more efficient use of its scientific resources. These benefits are all based on a societal value for efficiency and improved control, and because bureaucracy and technology make them achievable, the pursuit of these benefits becomes a very strong force pulling toward the pole of control.

▧ USING THE SOCIETAL MORAL COMPASS MAP

The moral compass is designed to stretch our thinking about ethical issues at the societal level. The four poles—liberty, equality, community, and control—

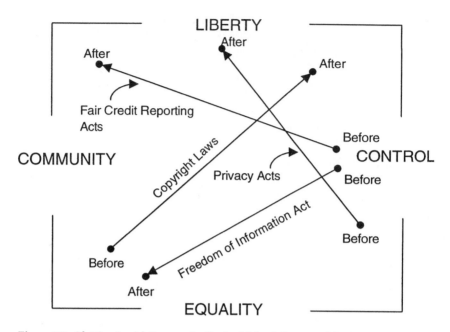

Figure 9.2. Plotting Legislation on the Societal Moral Compass Map

SOURCE: Adapted from *The Executive's Compass: Business and the Good Society* by James O'Toole. Copyright © 1993 by Oxford University Press. Reprinted with permission of Oxford University Press and James O'Toole.

are extremes. They are not found in pure unadulterated form in any social system. They do, however, represent important values that are crucial in any society. Each of the poles has a historically valid ethical claim and, accordingly, has important implications for the uses of information and information technology.

All societies must make trade-offs between these poles when they adopt new policies and programs, or when they renegotiate their social contract. The map informs these trade-off decisions and helps make them more explicit. Figure 9.1 summarizes some of the trade-offs involved. Figure 9.2 depicts a societal moral compass map for plotting social policies.

Existing national policies, for example, can be plotted on the map. For example, the post-World War II Japanese economy in general and the Ministry of International Trade and Industry's (MITI) aggressive information technology programs in particular would be plotted near the axis of control. In counterdistinction, the social democratic economy in Sweden and, for example, University of Lund Professor Pelle Ehn's (1988) project to expand the

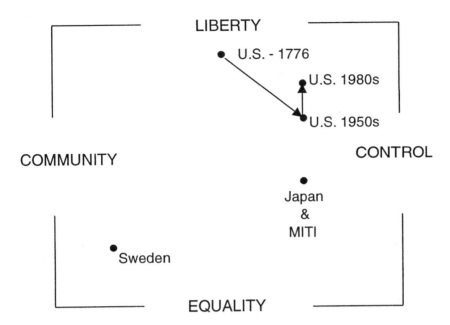

Figure 9.3. Plotting National Strategies on the Societal Moral Compass Map

SOURCE: Adapted from *The Executive's Compass: Business and the Good Society* by James O'Toole. Copyright © 1993 by Oxford University Press. Reprinted with permission of Oxford University Press and James O'Toole.

competencies and responsibilities of workers and to encourage them to participate more fully in the design of their organization's information systems are plotted somewhere near the southwest corner between community and equality (see Figure 9.3).

The U.S. economy of the late 18th century falls close to the axis of liberty. If we plot its evolution since then it has moved—due, in part, to the adoption of the philosophies of Taylor, Ford, and Sloan—toward the axis of control. Since the mid-1960s, the United States seems to have been moving back in the direction of community, and during the Reagan-Bush years toward liberty. Al Ross's program to develop a computer-based communication system for the severely physically handicapped, discussed in Chapter 5, clearly moves in the direction of equality and community.

The map is useful for promoting a dialogue for ethical reflection at the societal level. At this level, one is concerned with developing policies, programs, and social structures that promote ethical behavior in the ethical field as a whole. Most ethical issues, no matter from what level they initially arise, have societal implications.

Also, the map can be readily used to examine particular policy proposals. The method is as follows: First, plot the existing social system (or state of affairs) on the map by considering the trade-offs that have been made in favor of liberty versus equality and community versus control. Next, applying the idea of corrective vision, use the four poles to determine where on the map the new social system *should* lie if a good society is to result. Finally, identify the steps that must be taken and the policies or laws that must be adopted if the social system is to be transformed to its new location.

To illustrate the use of the societal moral compass map for examining national information policies, recall the computerized systems used for credit reporting described in Chapter 4. An individual ethical issue existed between the bank's agent who used the inaccurate information and the individual loan applicant, Ron Martin, who was the stakeholder harmed by the agent's actions. An organizational issue also existed because some of the agent's behavior was due to the structure of the bank's organization, its policies and procedures (or the lack of them), and the methods it used to enforce them. Addressing these issues also raises several crucial societal questions. Should there be a more encompassing national policy about credit reporting? What additional legislation, if any, is needed to ensure that credit reporting companies work for the overall good of society?

Plotting the Fair Credit Reporting Act

The Fair Credit Reporting Act of 1970 was passed by Congress in response to questions such as those just raised. The act accomplishes several things: It defines various legal terms surrounding credit reporting, describes permissible uses for credit reports, provides for consumer's rights in disputing credit reports, and establishes the enforcement responsibilities of the Federal Trade Commission. Arriving at these provisions entailed many trade-offs. With respect to liberty, the legislators considered the freedom of every consumer against the need for credit reporting agencies and lending organizations to have efficient, low-risk operations. In this case, liberty won out over control. As a result, the permissible uses of credit reports are limited to (a) those dictated by court orders, (b) those permitted by the written instructions of the individual consumer involved, and (c) those limited by a set of well-specified business uses, such as insurance underwriting or consumer lending. Individual liberty is further served because the law requires that any and all consumers have a right to find out the nature and substance of all their personal information contained in credit agency files (except certain medical information), the sources of that information, and a list of all parties who had received their records during the previous 6 months (during the previous 2 years in the case of access for employment purposes). If these procedures are followed as the law requires, the quality of life of every affected citizen should be improved. These improvements in community will undoubtedly be gained at the cost of some economic efficiency, especially for the credit bureaus because they must now conform to laws that limit the markets in which they can sell their information. At the same time, credit bureaus are required to provide services and establish accounting controls that will increase the cost of their operations. Consumers, in addition, are given the right to dispute any item in their reports, and the agency is required to investigate it. In the cases of continued dispute, the credit bureau is required to include a consumer's statement on the consumer report. The overall societal effect of the Fair Credit Act is plotted on Figure 9.2.

Privacy Acts

The Privacy Act of 1974 protects individual rights to privacy from government misuse of federal records that contain personal information. Government agencies are permitted to collect and maintain only data that is relevant to carrying out their mission. The agencies must specify what routine uses of the information will be made by other agencies, must gain consent of the involved individual before using the information in any unspecified way, and must account for every use of the information. Individuals are given the right to review data referring to them, request deletions and corrections, and sue to force an amendment to a record. Law enforcement, investigatory, and national security files are exempted. As shown in Figure 9.2, the Privacy Act has the overall societal effect of moving from an emphasis on governmental efficiency and control toward individual liberty.

Freedom of Information Act

The Freedom of Information Act of 1966 (FOIA) establishes a presumption that records in the possession of executive-branch agencies and departments are accessible. It guarantees the right of people to know about the business of their government and allows every citizen to obtain reasonably identifiable information from federal agencies by requiring the government to provide the fullest possible disclosure of information requested by the public. The act was amended in 1974 to further delimit the information that was exempted from it and to improve turnaround times for compliance with requests. The law also provides remedies for those persons who have been denied access to records. Both the Privacy Act and the FOIA make federal agencies accountable for their information disclosure policies and practices.

The act is based on the democratic principle that the free flow of information promotes a free society, and hence, any information acquired, processed, stored, disseminated, or used by the government should be available to the nation's citizens. The major societal effect of the FOIA is to move away from government control and efficiency toward greater equality of citizenry and a greater sense of community through the sharing of information. This effect is plotted on Figure 9.2.

Copyright Laws

Copyright laws protect information givers—designers, software developers, authors, musicians, and so on—against unauthorized duplication of their work. In socialist countries, such as Maoist China, Russia (under communism and somewhat even today), or even to some extent social democratic Sweden, intellectual property is generally considered to be a common good. Everybody can have access to it and use it. In the absence of safeguards, the ease of duplicating and sharing information, as discussed in Chapter 2, makes intellectual property readily available to many parties.

Thus, the natural and de facto intellectual property policy in many countries lies in the southwest quadrant of the societal moral compass map. To encourage givers to translate their ideas into practical, commercially available products and services, their intellectual property must be protected. The Copyright Act of 1976, the Computer Software Rental Amendment Act of 1990, and the Semiconductor Chip Protection Act of 1984 are among the recent legislative acts aimed at protecting intellectual property. All of these acts have the social effect of moving policy from an emphasis on equality and community toward a greater emphasis on liberty and control as illustrated in Figure 9.2.

The purpose of the societal moral compass map is to arrive at an informed judgment as to the balance to be struck between opposing poles in forming a good and ethical society. It is a tool, not an algorithm. It is a guide to ethical judgment that provides insight and access to historical thought, but not precise answers. Among its deficiencies is that it ignores the relative power of various parties in the ethical field and their ability to dictate outcomes. Nevertheless, it is one of the most useful tools available to consider ethical issues at the societal level.

SUMMARY

An entire society forms a polis, a community that organizes social relationships to achieve common goals. The purpose of a polis is to create a good society. As civilization has transformed from an agrarian to an industrial to an informational society, the requirements for making a good society have changed accordingly. Information issues now play a more fundamental role in our social relationships and in our ability to achieve our common goals.

Ethical issues occur on at least three levels: individual, organizational, and societal. An individual, say, who has the test results of someone who tested positive for the HIV virus has an individual ethical issue to deal with at the moment of truth at which he or she must decide whether or not to release those results or to make a decision based on them. If, in addition, the individual is acting in his or her role as a member of an organization that person and the organization are faced with an additional ethical issue: What is the ethical decision for the organization to make given its resources, goals, and obligations to society? If it is to be an ethical organization, should it have enforceable codes, credos, policies, and other guidelines to ensure that all of its members behave ethically? Should it restructure itself to ensure that ethical decisions and actions are taken? Moving up a level, these individuals and organizations are part of a larger society. Should the society as a whole have policies for treating HIV-related information?

There are two tacks to take for answering the last question. One is to examine the substance of the issue in terms of the effects on its property, privacy, accuracy, burden, access, and gatekeeping dimensions. This provides guidance as to the range of concerns to be included in the societal policy.

A second tack is to assess the overall social impacts of the proposed policy by means of the societal moral compass map. What are its effects on liberty, equality, community, and control? What are the trade-offs to be made between them?

A policy focused on liberty would stress individuals' rights to use the information they possessed in any manner they pleased. This, of course, would pit the woman who tested positive for HIV and her right to privacy against her insurance agent who gained access to the information. Whose liberty should dominate? There is also a judgment to be made about letting people act freely versus treating them equally. The pole of equality requires that all persons whose tests are HIV positive be treated the same. In its most extreme form, equality requires that either everybody receives the results or nobody does. Furthermore, a quest for equality might require that individual medical test results of all types be treated exactly the same. Pulling against the poles of liberty and equality is the demand for social efficiency and control. Which policy of disclosure will make best use of society's scarce resources? Which will best help it achieve its stated goals in the face of increased complexity, volumes, time demands, and geographic scope? Which will help society's bureaucratic organizations work more effectively? Finally, there are the ethical demands of community. Which disclosure policy serves to bind people together and improve their overall quality of life? Which fosters their interdependent needs and accords each human dignity? Which conserves nature?

The societal moral compass map serves as a tool to be used to determine ethical responsibility at the societal level. It joins the other tools of ethics described in this book as part of a tool kit for achieving individual, organizational, and societal responsibility in our information age.

◩ NOTES

1. All quotes from Markoff (1993), copyright © 1993 by The New York Times Company. Reprinted by permission.

2. Copyright © 1994 by The New York Times Company. Reprinted by permission.

3. From *Newsweek,* September 2, 1991, Newsweek, Inc. All rights reserved. Reprinted by permission.

10

Beacon Toward the Future: *Major Ethical Tensions in an Information Society*

◩ MAJOR TENSIONS IN AN INFORMATION SOCIETY

The rapidly changing landscapes of information, information technology, and their uses are having major social effects on individuals, groups, and social institutions. Even the family is not immune, because information technologies of all sorts are rapidly coming into the home. And the future portends even more such changes.

During these times of far-reaching social change, decisions about what is right or wrong, good and bad, just or unjust are more difficult to make or to explain to others because so much uncertainty and so many unknowns surround them. In times of upheaval, however, ethics and ethical thinking can help decision makers make more effective decisions—whether they be personal decisions, managerial decisions made in the course of one's work, professional decisions, or those knotty decisions that people struggle with to achieve desirable social and political ends.

Another powerful reason for applying ethics is to balance our needs to pursue our own self-interests with our duties to make the best possible decision for all parties involved. There would be little need for ethics if we could deploy our own power as we saw fit, follow our own ideas, and render our decisions solely on the basis of our own identity, expectations, and self-interests. But human life in human society does not permit this kind of totally unbounded freedom. This leads, as Hobbes (1651/1839) warned, to social chaos.

Almost all societies have sought ways to avoid the worst effects of chaos. Often, their answers are rooted in parents' obligations to their children. Consequently, from the very beginning of our lives, each of us has been exposed to some forms of behavioral controls that tell us what we "ought" and "ought not" to do. We learned this from our family or the group with which we grew from infancy to maturity. These lessons become an external force, creating within us an initial sense as to what is good or bad, right or wrong, just or unjust. We bring this incipient sense of conscience to all of our decision making.

The interplay between our conscience and our self-interests, nevertheless, creates tensions within our own minds. As individuals in society, we sometimes face conflicts between obeying the rules we have been given and pursuing those courses of action we feel are personally more useful, desirable, or just. Translated into the language of ethics, we experience a fundamental tension between the edicts of teleology—to pursue purpose—and the edicts of deontology—to obey the rules.

This basic human tension figures prominently in the social sciences, such as sociology and psychology. Freud (c. 1895/1954), for example, described it in terms of a struggle between the id and the superego. The id, as a repository of an individual's basic instincts, drives, and impulses, is driven by self-interest. This self-interested drive demands its own egoistic outcomes. One's id is pitted against one's superego, which responds to a set of rules and regulations that, according to Freud, were imposed on it by parents and by society. In Freudian psychology, the role of the ego is to manage the tension thus created between the self-interested id and the externally driven superego. As ethical agents, we must do much the same thing. Ethical agents need an ego-type mechanism to resolve the tensions they confront daily between demands put on them to obey certain rules and regulations and their desires to pursue other goals.

Individuals working in organizations must also manage tensions between following the rules and regulations laid down by higher authorities and responding to their personal conscience or to values emanating from other compelling sources. Organizations, as bureaucratic structures, are set up, in part, to mediate between the pressure individuals experience in seeking their own personal goals and the legitimate needs that organizations have for fulfilling their social purpose and achieving their goals. Organizations, therefore, have many rules, policies, and standard operating procedures, mediated through an authority structure, to guide their members' behavior. Chester I. Barnard (1938) characterizes the tension these social control mechanisms create in his seminal book, *The Functions of the Executive.* Organizational members have a "zone of indifference," he argues. They will adhere to rules or orders without consciously questioning their authority so long as the request falls within acceptable bounds. Requests falling outside of this zone, however, challenge a member's willingness to accept the organization's authority and to continue to participate positively in the organization. This conflict must be resolved if a healthy relationship is to be maintained between an organization and its members.

At the societal level, as members of a culture and various social institutions, we experience the influence of subtle and explicit norms, rules, and standards that we are also expected to obey. Yet especially in a democratic society, we also have our own personal interests and rights that we expect our social system to honor and protect. Unfortunately, social tensions inevitably arise. Our social systems do not always support our rights or desires but, rather, choose courses of action that promote such collective goals as social cohesion and stability. Greek tragedies, such as the story of Antigone (see Anouilh, 1946), illustrate how these basic conflicts arise between individual needs and societally determined rights and show that they have been around for a long time.

In summary, as we have seen, human decision makers must cope with several different sources of duties: internal rules imposed by their own human psyche; rules imposed by the groups and organizations to which they belong; and political, social, and cultural norms. As decision making moves from those decisions that affect individuals personally to those that affect the society as a whole, it falls increasingly under the influence of the needs and expectations of others. Group needs increase in importance and influence. This elevation of the decision-making domain to a higher social level is inevitable and of extreme importance in the forming of an information society. As information technology and the information itself have penetrated our individual, organizational, and societal lives more deeply, a rich set of new ethical issues has arisen. The following sections recap some of these basic tensions and discuss their ethical implications. These questions serve as a kind of early warning system to alert us to problems we will encounter as we continuously reinvent our information society.

◻ WHO OWNS INTELLECTUAL OUTPUT AND WHO IS ENTITLED TO USE IT?

In an information society, a tension is formed between (a) the demand of all people to share in the ideas, knowledge, and information produced by society—a force favoring the poles of community and equality—and (b) the rightful claim of those who produce information to reap the benefits of their efforts—a force favoring liberty and control. A person draws on his or her special intellectual abilities and works hard to produce new information—a piece of software, a piece of music, a body of data, an article, a report. What is that person's right to the results of his or her creative and mental efforts? This problem is often called the problem of intellectual property rights.

This modern information quandary focuses on the nature of information and property rights and the social benefits of having unlimited access to information. John Locke (1690/1924), the 18th-century philosopher, summarized the issue using the following line of argument. According to Locke, when humankind first appeared on earth, it held the whole world in common. But as human beings multiplied and different civilizations arose, they began to act more individually, and they began to appropriate parts of the world and carve up the commons by means of their own human labor. The first property was created in this manner. Subsequently, common law and common sense dictated that the application of intellectual and physical labor gives the producer the right to own, manage, and use that property (within restraints) and to transfer it to other parties if the producer so chooses.

The principle of property works rather well when it is applied to physical objects, but it tends to break down when it is applied to the outputs of intellectual labor. As human beings, we have the unique characteristic of being able to draw on our individual experiences and intellectual abilities to produce products such as a book, a software program, a piece of music, a body of data, an article, a report, and so on. As human beings, we create these artifacts not only for our own satisfaction but also to share with others. The principles of property and property rights have been applied to these intellectual efforts, and societal laws have been established that accord certain rights to creators of information. As a result, several important social institutions, such as copyrights, patents, and trademarks have evolved.

A quandary arises, however, because we, as human beings, also espouse a strongly held belief that a broad-based sharing of ideas, knowledge, and information benefits all in society. In some cases, many of us believe, the dissemination of information is a higher-order principle than a strict adherence to intellectual property rights. A tension arises when those who produce information rightfully claim they are entitled to reap the benefits from their production of intellectual property and therefore should be able to control the conditions under which information exchanges take place.

The seemingly bizarre case of the "dead celebrity" law helps illustrate the extent to which the tension between personal and public ownership of information exists. A few years ago, California passed legislation that prohibited parties from using an image or a photograph of a deceased personality, such as John Wayne, without explicit permission from the person's estate, because these images were considered to be personal property created by the personality. The celebrity's estate, therefore, retained rights to the images and had the right to any financial benefit obtained by displaying them. As a result, the estates of numerous luminaries are now collecting royalties for the use of drawings and photos of their deceased benefactors. This is an extreme case, but as managers, professionals, and even as individuals, we are constantly faced with problems concerning who has rights to the information, broadly defined, that people create. As a general rule, for example, when a person is employed by an organization, the organization retains rights to any information or software the employee produces while on the job.

A second aspect of the intellectual property issue arises because many intellectual works result from group contributions. The production of software codes and programs is an obvious case in point. The ethical questions that arise include the following: Given the many people who have contributed, in part, to the final outcome, to whom should the property rights be allocated?

A third issue that arises is how to delimit, if at all, the uses one is permitted to make of his or her intellectual property. Should censorship, for example, or bans, such as those imposed against James Joyce, J. D. Salinger, and other writers, be permitted? Does, for example, an employee have the "right" to use a company's abandoned software program?

In summary, the establishment of intellectual property rights in an information society bestows information givers with the right to choose those who will be the takers of the information they produce and to control the conditions under which the exchange takes place. The resulting quandary requires making three distinctions: (a) where to draw the line between the human's contribution and that provided by natural forces or possessed by society in common (i.e., public versus private property); (b) how to allocate property rights among the many people who may have contributed in part to the final outcome; and (c) how to delimit, if at all, the uses one is permitted to make of his or her property. The basic questions are, Who owns information? Who has the right to "alienate" or dispose of it? What, if any (as in the case of weapons, for example), are the socially imposed limits of its use? These questions arise at any moment of truth during which a decision is made about creating, using, or transferring information from a giver to a taker.

◩ HOW PRIVATE IS PERSONAL INFORMATION AND WHO IS ENTITLED TO IT?

Second, there is a tension in a society between (a) each member's right to know about other people, their characteristic nature and behavior, and (b) each individual member's right to be left alone. In this case, the poles of equality and control tug against the pole of individual liberty. The dignity and autonomy of an individual—one's ability to control the dissemination of information about oneself—and one's ability to use private information as he or she chooses in forming intimate relationships strongly favor personal control. Thus, when managing the acquisition, processing, storing, provision, and secondary distribution of information about individuals, the fundamental issue raised is whether individuals have a right to control information about themselves to protect their privacy, dignity, and autonomy.

Opposed to this right is the potential right of others to know about any and all other members of the society. In ancient and traditional societies, such as Eskimo society, village members possess extensive knowledge about one another because they are directly and mutually dependent on each other for their daily living and safety needs. In a complex information society, however, a society in which people are continually required to enter into relationships with a wide variety of different people and institutions, people must have a basic knowledge of the other parties with whom they intend to form relationships. To deal effectively with the complexity of these relationships, each party must gain at least enough information about the other to determine whether or not they can trust each other.

For example, a bank needs to know enough about its loan applicants to trust that they will repay the money they borrow but no more than that. To accomplish this, individuals agree to give up a certain amount of their personal information to become, as it were, "credentialed." Credit report information supplied by individuals helps satisfy this need to know. Revealing private information facilitates the making of financial transactions between strangers, once an individual has provided "credentials" that prove his or her trustworthiness. At the same time, however, these revelations make people vulnerable. The private information necessary to complete one transaction can be used for other unspecified transactions. One of the intents of privacy laws is to reduce the instance of unauthorized use of personal information.

A related issue arises when an individual challenges the amount of information that may be collected about himself or herself even though the purpose is ostensibly for the betterment of society. A recent example of this tension is illustrated by the refusal of a female juror in a court case in Texas to complete all the answers of a 100-question jury survey form that was to be used by the attorneys in voir dire proceedings to select a jury. The prospective juror was issued a contempt of court citation for refusing to comply and spent about a week in jail. The question raised here is whether or not she was obligated to give over what seemed to her to be irrelevant pieces of information about her personal reading and religious practices just because the attorneys believed this information would help them select fairer jurors. Who has the right to burden a prospective juror with extensive disclosures of personal information? Is it more important than the defendant's, the prosecutor's, or the judge's right of access to information needed to produce a fairer trial?

As long as the private, personal information exchanged is limited to agreed on (by informed consent), specific transactions, few ethical problems are involved. Problems arise, however, when an individual discovers that information collected about himself or herself for one purpose is being used for purposes other than those originally agreed on. One side says that individuals should have the right to control the distribution of information about themselves and to avoid relationships in which they do not want to participate. The other side, composed of a diverse set of players that includes some government officials and corporate executives, says that the benefits of sharing and having access to personal data far outweigh the potential for abuse. The tension arises between the desire of an individual to protect information about himself or herself and the right of the group or the institution to know certain facts about all individuals to promote social, economic, and welfare goals.

In summary, givers of information collected about themselves have a right to select the takers of that information and to specify the terms of exchange so that they can avoid relationships in which they do not want to participate. At the same time, takers and users of information have a right to acquire the personal information they need to establish trust with other parties and to enter into exchange transactions. The quandary again involves a question of where to draw the line. This moment of truth arises any time a taker attempts to acquire or use information of a personal nature about any information giver.

▧ HOW ARE ACCURACY AND QUALITY OF INFORMATION TO BE SAFEGUARDED?

A third tension exists between (a) a taker's desire—in fact sometimes a taker's need—for nearly perfect information on which to base decisions and to conduct affairs and (b) a giver's (or orchestrator's) ability or willingness to provide it. Ultimately, this is a question of capacity and of resource allocation. On the societal moral compass map (discussed in Chapter 9), this tension often takes the form of a pull for community and respect for the quality of life of the users versus the pull for control and economic efficiency in operations.

Recall the case of the professional software engineer who believed that the space shuttle's onboard flight management system was not being adequately tested. At risk were the lives of the astronauts if the system's data proved to be inaccurate. On the other hand, the vendors had limited resources to devote to the development and testing of the system. Consequently, the quality of the onboard data, and hence the quality of life of the astronauts, was dependent on the effectiveness of the resources allocated to the task. The whistle-blower, in this case, firmly believed that the information and skills being supplied by her colleagues were inadequate.

Information professionals, by dint of their knowledge and position, are accorded responsibility for stewardship and custodianship of information in its various forms. They assume a fiduciary responsibility for the information entrusted to them. The desirable conditions of sharing information and providing access to information are seriously compromised, however, if the information provided is inaccurate, of low quality, or misleading.

Misleading information is usually worse than no information at all. Consider a few examples. To yell "Fire!" in a crowded theater when no fire is present clearly can have severe or harmful consequences. Similarly, at a less extreme level, individuals who read magazines and books want to be able to distinguish fact from fiction. *JFK*, the movie based on a creative alteration of historical fact, was a representation of something that appeared to be true but in actuality was not. Banks require those who are applying for loans to provide correct information or, at least, information that is adequate for the purposes for which it is being acquired. A bank needs to be assured that application information is correct because it bases lending decisions on that information. In the same way, employers want some safeguards against applicants who falsify or inflate their education or experience.

The original sources of information are sometimes unreliable. Individuals can and do provide information that is inaccurate or even deceptive. In addition, those receiving information may have limited capability to ensure that information they receive is accurate and of high quality. For example, one of the concerns expressed about the Lotus MarketPlace: Households product, which contained considerable personal information, was that the original sources of the data—the files of credit bureaus—may contain inaccurate information.

The costs of providing and maintaining nearly error-free data, however, can be prohibitive, especially as the scope of a system continues to grow. Consequently, providers must make assessments about the level of data quality they can afford to maintain in their records, despite the fact that this resource allocation decision may not be in the best interests of all individuals affected. Additional ethical quandaries are created between those who give information for one purpose, for which high-quality information is not required, and those who use the information for other purposes without knowledge of its possible flaws. For this reason, information givers should provide some estimate about the error or uncertainty of their information.

In summary, this quandary arises at the moment of truth in which decisions are made by givers and orchestrators about the specifications and characteristics of the information they will acquire, process, store, disseminate, or provide to information takers. This includes determining the basic characteristics of the information to be provided, such as its accuracy, validity, readability, fineness of dimensionality, reliability, clearness, completeness, and timeliness. It also entails an obligation to properly inform the taker about the characteristics of the data being provided.

▨ WHO GETS ACCESS TO WHAT KINDS OF INFORMATION UNDER WHAT CONDITIONS?

In an information society, a fourth tension is created between (a) the rights of all members of the society to benefit from the information it produces and (b) the obligation of members to produce valuable information. This is the ethical problem of information justice. The poles of equality and community pull toward ensuring that all members get access to all information, whereas the poles of control and liberty pull toward reducing the social burden involved and protecting the rights of people not to produce or provide information. There are two components to this issue: information access and information burden.

As modern society has become more dependent on the production and use of information, it has become more important for members of a society to have the right to benefit from the information it produces. Society also requires certain producers to produce information. Take, for example, those great, unquenchable takers of information, government agencies, which require the public to provide many types of information. To cite but a few from among many examples, the Internal Revenue Service requires people to file tax returns, national parks ask visitors to fill out a survey, states require motor vehicle and driver's license applications for citizens to own and drive cars, and state and local governments require those seeking a fishing or hunting permit to fill out license application forms. As members of society, generally, we comply with these requests, because we recognize that collecting this information is part of the government's legitimate credentialing process. Our compliance, however, sometimes raises perplexing questions.

One question is whether or not the burden imposed on the givers of this information is appropriate or fair. Is the social cost of preparing the forms greater than the social benefits derived? The U.S. Paperwork Reduction Act is an attempt to answer this question at the national government level. It requires that most requests for information from citizens be evaluated in terms of the need for the information and the burden placed on those who must provide it. These evaluations must be approved by the Office of Management and Budget before the agency can request the information.

One of the Internal Revenue Service's (IRS) simplest forms, the 5500-EZ for pension benefit plans, notifies citizens, for example, that

> the time needed to complete and file this form will vary depending on individual circumstances. The estimated average time is:
>
> | | |
> |---|---|
> | Recordkeeping | 10 hr., 46 min. |
> | Learning about the law or the form | 1 hr., 4 min. |
> | Preparing the form | 2 hr., 13 min. |
> | Copying, assembling, and sending the form to the IRS | 16 min. |

What this notice tells us is that the U.S. government has made a determination that by requiring the implicated citizens—and, likely, there are millions—to spend an average of 14 hours and 19 minutes a year (or nearly 2 working days) carrying out the information life cycles necessary to complete this form is socially justified by the government's need to determine whether the plan is operating according to the law and that the benefits of the plan are furnished to the pension plan participant. In effect, this is the social bargain that has been struck.

Another question concerns whether or not citizens are willing to provide information that may be requested by others, such as by means of the Freedom of Information Act, and used for purposes other than those for which the information was originally collected. The IRS and the U.S. Bureau of the Census generally guarantee citizens confidentiality and anonymity, and they limit some of the secondary uses of their data. But what about other government agencies and other uses? Are citizens equally willing to help companies sell fishing or hunting supplies? Must those who give information comply when they discover that they have no control over the purposes to which the information will ultimately be put? The 1973 Code of Fair Information Practices attempts to solve some of these issues.

Another aspect of this tension involves the fact that, in many circumstances, information professionals have control over the selection of the information that will be admitted into the system. Thereby, they also determine the type of information to which users will have access. If, for example, a university library acquisitions department cancels or fails to subscribe to journals in a particular academic discipline, it will be difficult, if not impossible, for students and faculty in that field to find the articles and information they need to support their academic work. These kinds of selection decisions, as discussed in previous chapters, are required by all professionals who gather information on behalf of others, including information analysts and librarians. In cases like this, a major social trade-off should be made in which the social cost of acquiring and maintaining the information is compared with the likelihood of its being requested and the value of its use if it is requested. Selection rules and the actual selection judgments made may be materially affected by economic or marketplace conditions. For instance, a library may forego the purchase of an expensive reference book if it will be needed by only a few users and if its contents are not directly pertinent to the institution's mission. Most institutions have selection policies that guide their information professionals in making these trade-offs. Usually, these policies are based on the mission of the institution and the needs of the identified clientele to be served.

In summary, these issues of information justice arise at a moment of truth in which decisions are made within a social system as to who the information givers and takers will be, what their economic and social circumstances are, and what information will be exchanged.

◩ WHO HAS THE RIGHT TO CONTROL THE FLOW AND CONTENT OF INFORMATION?

A fifth tension exists between (a) an individual's desire to use information in a free, open, and unabashed way and (b) society's demand for acceptable behaviors permitted by its norms, mores, and taboos. Generally, information givers want to be free to express themselves in any way they see fit, and information takers want to use the information that they acquire according to their own values and interests. This is the pull of the pole of liberty. It is guaranteed, in part, by the First Amendment. Yet every society also has a strong need for community, and this requires that certain forms of expression be suppressed and that certain information not be allowed to flow. The mechanism for resolving this quandary, as discussed earlier, is called *gatekeeping.*

Gatekeeping involves compressing or blocking the channels or medium through which information flows. Unlike selection and access issues, gatekeeping decisions are related to issues of information provision and dissemination and may involve issues of taste, morality, religion, and other communal preferences. Most of us are well aware of censorship practices that suppress the circulation of artistic, literary, or educational materials containing ideas, information, and images that are distasteful to the censor. Censorship, and the right of individuals and institutions to censor, is a key quandary for a society that grants individuals the right of free expression in its constitutional and legal codes. The censor, on the other hand, considers that there are rights of individuals or groups to protect themselves from certain ideas and images. The gulf between these two positions has resulted in some highly visible clashes around book censorship, funding for public art programs, and grants for artistic endeavors. The debate revolves around the principle of freedom of speech.

In an early discussion of this issue, John Stuart Mill (1859/1956) argued that a society will be harmed to a greater degree if valuable ideas and knowledge are suppressed than if some, allegedly harmful, ideas are expressed. This is the essence of freedom of speech incorporated in the Bill of Rights, and it is vigorously defended as being absolutely necessary to maintain effective social dissent in a democratic society.

The right to freedom of speech may be abridged or limited in certain circumstances but only in the event that it is clear that the pursuit of this freedom will result in a greater harm to society. Releasing classified documents about hostage negotiations, for example, might compromise national security. Stealing and publishing corporate formulas for products might injure a company's ability to survive. Publishing the address of an individual who is being stalked by an unbalanced pursuer might place the individual in jeopardy. These are all examples of situations in which restricting access to information is desirable and practiced.

Censorship is also attempted for reasons other than to suppress obscene or pornographic materials. For example, social critics, especially those concerned about the content of many popular television shows and movies, warn that the populace's continual exposure to degrading and banal material will have long-term negative effects on the health of society. They recommend discontinuing some of these shows.

Censorship becomes controversial when an individual or a group imposes certain information on others who may not share the same norms or standards. Some groups or individuals, acting for themselves or on behalf of society at large, may desire to be protected from exposure to what they consider to be obscene or pornographic messages. Consider the case of Robert Mapplethorpe, the provocative photographer whose exhibit of photographs with explicitly homosexual themes stirred a public ruckus and raised social questions as to whether it was appropriate to use National Endowment of the Arts funds to support his showing. The controversy over the display of his homoerotic images stimulated extensive debate about the nature of artistic expression, and this stimulated much discussion about the appropriateness of using tax funds to support certain artistic activities opposed by one or more groups on moral or other grounds.

The issue of censorship is becoming more prevalent in our daily lives. *The Newsletter on Intellectual Freedom* (1992), for example, reported that in 1991, "Reports of censorship in American public schools increased fifty percent. . . . The number of incidents . . . was the greatest" (p. 1) since the group started keeping records in 1980. Nationally, 376 censorship cases were reported in 44 states during 1991.

The establishment of free-nets—free, public-access, community computer-based systems—in many cities has demonstrated how a new use of information technology can raise fresh questions about censorship. In some systems, it is possible for anyone who logs on to get access to any available information. This means that minors may get easy access to pornographic material, which has led some concerned subscribers to apply concepts from "harm to minors" laws to restrict their access. This, of course, has alarmed First Amendment supporters. Some go so far as to argue that minor-blocking policies should be banned or rescinded immediately.

A counterposition claims, however, that free-nets are more like television or movies and that, with respect to these media, public pressure is effectively brought to bear to limit the extent and nature of violence and sex they portray. Films are also "graded" so that parents and others can control access. "Let's get realistic here folks," says Lou Anschuetz of the Youngstown Free-Net. "Newspapers, TV, radio and other means of distribution are not required to provide everything that any citizen wishes to partake of. The Free-Nets are also an electronic distribution medium (unlike libraries)" (1993, p. 1). And the debate continues.

Censorship is only one form of restricting information from flowing freely. An analogy for gatekeeping is found in agricultural communities in which administrators charged with maintaining water flow for irrigation manage a series of gates that are opened or closed to permit the water to flow. In the same manner, information gatekeepers may open or close gates through which information flows. What policies should guide the opening and closing of a network of information gates? This issue is among the most subtle and challenging ethical issues of modern times. Whereas the issue of censorship is relatively well understood, frequently reported, and publicly visible, the issue of gatekeeping is not.

Exactly what information is developed and published is often the result of judgments and decisions made by numerous gatekeepers. In the printed media, the crucial gatekeeping decisions as whether or not to publish an article or a book are generally made on the basis of an editor's judgment. Moreover, vitally important information may be "fast tracked"—that is, moved very quickly from giver to taker—based on the judgment of those who publish the information. Many gatekeeping decisions may be involved in publishing some forms of information. For example, a newspaper article may begin to take shape when a witness reports on a newsworthy event. A reporter then describes the event and the impressions of the witness and writes a story. Then the story passes through a local editor, wire service controller, news bureau chief, a newspaper or broadcasting editor, and perhaps some other parties until it is presented in its final form. Each party in this chain bears some responsibility for the decisions made on the selection and shape, color and spin given to the information. They are, in effect, part of the overall gatekeeping system.

Implicit gatekeeping may take place when access to information is restricted by the unintentionally clumsy design of a data retrieval or indexing system. Users, in effect, are denied access to the information contained in these files.

Another form of gatekeeping occurs when information messages are distorted by summarizing or compression of the original message. An example of this type of activity occurred when *National Geographic* magazine decided to compress and alter a picture of two Egyptian pyramids to "fit" them onto the cover of the magazine. Was anyone harmed by this tampering? Perhaps not. But some readers complained that altering this image conveyed an untrue message and was unethical. Similar, but more serious, issues were raised when *Time* magazine altered O. J. Simpson's photograph to darken his face and make him look more sinister. These alterations potentially have harmful consequences. For one, the public is deceived or deluded. For another, the pictures could convey impressions that could result in harm to the subject or to others. If, for example, either of these picture were admitted as evidence in a court of law, the misrepresentation could have negative consequences.

In summary, this quandary arises at the moment of truth in which decisions are made about what kinds of information are permitted to flow under what conditions and what information is to be prohibited from flowing.

INFORMATION TECHNOLOGY: WORKPLACE HANDMAIDEN OR WOLF?

Finally, there is a tension involving the application of information technology itself. One position holds that technology is the workers' handmaiden, supporting and enhancing their productivity, dignity, and sense of competency. It views workers as ends in themselves and seeks to enhance their individual dignity. The contrary position views workers and the technology they use primarily as means for achieving an organization's ends. In this view, the organization's goals take precedence over those of workers. This dialectical debate is a Kantian contest between the pole of community tugging for quality of life and the pole of control pulling for more organizational efficiency.

The pole of community, in this context, stresses technological optimism. It views technology as a driving force in the concept of progress that has captured the minds of most Americans for nearly 200 years. Technology holds the solution to most social problems and serves as a handmaiden that helps liberate workers from the clutches of dreary and tiresome work. Beniger (1986), as discussed earlier, sees the benefits of information technology as deriving primarily from its ability to make other technologies work better. His intriguing thesis states that information technology has historically been applied to solve major crises in which the growing complexity of social activity outstripped society's ability to manage it. He cites, for example, the case of the growth of the railroads during the early 19th century. As the speed and range of railroad travel expanded, it quickly surpassed the capacity of the management systems to handle it. Several tragic accidents, including one spectacular head-on collision, resulted. The invention of the telegraph in 1837 provided the means to move information faster and more accurately, permitting railroad schedules to be coordinated more effectively. The combination of the telegraph and a new management control system worked to solve this crisis. This is just one instance, from among many, that demonstrates that information technology is frequently required to obtain the benefits of other technologies.

But technology may also be a curse. A new technology that is located closer than its predecessor to the control pole of the societal moral compass map is metaphorically like Little Red Riding Hood's wolf. It is dressed in grandmother's innocent-looking clothes, but it is waiting to devour unsuspecting workers. This technology will deskill their jobs, eliminate task variety and autonomy, and replace workers with computer-based expert systems. Some people foresee the possibility of an even grimmer outcome. Expert systems may well not become good enough, say, to replace 20th-century physicians, but owing to several factors—the pressure of overoptimistic public opinion, physicians' lack of self-confidence, laziness, greed, or the fear of malpractice suits—expert systems may be relied on nevertheless. In the process, valuable, perhaps exceptional, expertise will be lost. It will be replaced, at best, by modest or average results.

This darker view of the future posits the possibility that information technology will devour the jobs of many and rob meaning from the jobs of others. The key workplace effect is likely to be the deskilling of workers by substituting human knowledge and expertise with computers and computer-based expert systems. Ethically, the question must be raised whether it is appropriate to "dis-en-mind" workers of knowledge and skills, hard-won through years of education and experience. Should, for example, workers have rights to due process against having their skills made obsolete by powerful information systems, systems that may eventually displace them in the workplace?

Another effect is the loss of variety and scope in the performance of work. Case studies indicate that where information technology has "dumbed down" or reduced worker's autonomy, the workers are less satisfied and more frustrated with their work.

Finally, workers have become more aware that the interaction between their work and the information technology they use to perform their tasks may have physically damaging consequences. The growing concern about repetitive motion disorders and carpal tunnel syndrome—first identified as diseases that strike laborers such as butchers and carpenters—are now seen with increasing frequency among information workers who employ terminals and keyboards as routine tools in their jobs. Moreover, there are additional concerns about lower back pain from disk degeneration from sitting and poor posture and the unproved effects of exposure to low-level magnetic fields from cathode ray tubes/video display terminals (CRTs/VDTs).

In summary, this quandary arises at the moment of truth in which decisions are made to install and operate new technology and new information systems. As organizations have sought to re-engineer, downsize, or outsource, these decisions have been made more frequently. This is the point at which Kantian trade-offs are made between pursuing the humanistic values of individual participants in the system—treating them as ends in themselves—and pursuing the goals of others—treating individuals as means only.

SUMMARY

These decision-making tensions concerning property, privacy, accuracy, access, burden, gatekeeping, and the social and psychological effects of technology are timeless. They occur over and over again as new technologies are introduced, new kinds of information life cycles are conceived, and new information systems are designed and implemented. They affect us all in our roles as individuals, information professionals, members of organizations, and members of society.

In our current fast-paced, ubiquitous, networked, multimedia technological era, these tensions are constantly with us. Emerging as the result of the ascent of information, they are an essential condition of the Faustian bargain we have struck as we forge a new information-based society. As ethical members of an information society, we must be alert to these tensions and understand how to resolve them. If this book is successful, we will have the ethical thinking tools necessary to identify our crucial moments of truth and to respond in an effective and ethical way. We will be up to the challenge of meeting our responsibilities in the information age.

Sample Codes of Ethics

▧ Association for Computing Machinery (ACM) Code of Ethics and Professional Conduct*

Using the New ACM Code of Ethics in Decision Making

1. General Moral Imperatives.

As an ACM member I will . . .

1.1 Contribute to society and human well-being

This principle concerning the quality of life of all people affirms an obligation to protect fundamental human rights and to respect the diversity of all cultures. An essential aim of computing professionals is to minimize negative consequences of computing systems, including threats to health and safety. When

---

* Reprinted courtesy of Association for Computing Machinery. This Code and the supplemental Guidelines were developed by the Task Force for the Revision of the ACM Code of Ethics and Professional Conduct: Ronald E. Anderson, chair, Gerald Engel, Donald Gotterbarn, Grace C. Hertleim, Alex Hoffman, Bruce Jawer, Deborah G. Johnson, Doris K. Lidtke, Joyce Currie Little, Dianne Martin, Donn B. Parker, Judith A. Perrolle, and Richard S. Rosenberg. The Task Force was organized by ACM/SIGGAS and funding was provided by the ACM SIG Discretionary Fund.

designing or implementing systems, computing professionals must attempt to ensure that the products of their efforts will be used in socially responsible ways, will meet social needs, and will avoid harmful effects to health and welfare.

In addition to a safe social environment, human well-being includes a safe natural environment. Therefore, computing professionals who design and develop systems must be alert to, and make others aware of, any potential damage to the local or global environment.

1.2 Avoid harm to others

"Harm" means injury or negative consequences, such as undesirable loss of information, loss of property, property damage, or unwanted environmental impacts. This principle prohibits use of computing technology in ways that result in harm to any of the following: users, the general public, employees, employers. Harmful actions include intentional destruction or modification of files and programs leading to serious loss of resources or unnecessary expenditure of human resources such as the time and effort required to purge systems of computer viruses.

Well-intended actions, including those that accomplish assigned duties, may lead to harm unexpectedly. In such an event the responsible person or persons are obligated to undo or mitigate the negative consequences as much as possible. One way to avoid unintentional harm is to carefully consider potential impacts on all those affected by decisions made during design and implementation.

To minimize the possibility of indirectly harming others, computing professionals must minimize malfunctions by following generally accepted standards for system design and testing. Furthermore, it is often necessary to assess the social consequences of systems to project the likelihood of any serious harm to others. If system features are misrepresented to users, coworkers, or supervisors, the individual computing professional is responsible for any resulting injury.

In the work environment the computing professional has the additional obligation to report any signs of system dangers that might result in serious personal or social damage. If one's superiors do not act to curtail or mitigate such dangers, it may be necessary to "blow the whistle" to help correct the problem or reduce the risk. However, capricious or misguided reporting of violations can, itself, be harmful. Before reporting violations, all relevant aspects of the incident must be thoroughly assessed. In particular, the assessment of risk and responsibility must be credible. It is suggested that advice be sought from other computing professionals. (See principle 2.5 regarding thorough evaluations.)

1.3 Be honest and trustworthy

Honesty is an essential component of trust. Without trust an organization cannot function effectively. The honest computing professional will not make deliberately false or deceptive claims about a system or system design, but will instead provide full disclosure of all pertinent system limitations and problems.

A computer professional has a duty to be honest about his or her own qualifications, and about any circumstances that might lead to conflicts of interest.

Membership in volunteer organizations such as ACM may at times place individuals in situations where their statements or actions could be interpreted as carrying the "weight" of a larger group of professionals. An ACM member will exercise care to not misrepresent ACM or positions and policies of ACM or any ACM units.

1.4 Be fair and take action not to discriminate

The values of equality, tolerance, respect for others, and the principles of equal justice govern this imperative. Discrimination on the basis of race, sex, religion, age, disability, national origin, or other such factors is an explicit violation of ACM policy and will not be tolerated.

Inequities between different groups of people may result from the use or misuse of information and technology. In a fair society, all individuals would have equal opportunity to participate in, or benefit from, the use of computer resources regardless of race, sex, religion, age, disability, national origin, or other such similar factors. However, these ideals do not justify unauthorized use of computer resources nor do they provide an adequate basis for violation of any other ethical imperatives of this Code.

1.5 Honor property rights, including copyrights and patents

Violation of copyrights, patents, trade secrets, and the terms of license agreements is prohibited by law in most circumstances. Even when software is not so protected, such violations are contrary to professional behavior. Copies of software should be made only with proper authorization. Unauthorized duplication of materials must not be condoned.

1.6 Give proper credit for intellectual property

Computing professionals are obligated to protect the integrity of intellectual property. Specifically, one must not take credit for others' ideas or work, even in cases where the work has not been explicitly protected, for example, by copyright or patent.

1.7 Respect the privacy of others

Computing and communication technology enables the collection and exchange of personal information on a scale unprecedented in the history of civilization. Thus there is increased potential for violating the privacy of individuals and groups. It is the responsibility of professionals to maintain the privacy and integrity of data describing individuals. This includes taking precautions to ensure the accuracy of data, as well as protecting it from unauthorized access or accidental disclosure to inappropriate individuals. Furthermore, procedures must be established to allow individuals to review their records and correct inaccuracies.

This imperative implies that only the necessary amount of personal information be collected in a system, that retention and disposal periods for that information be clearly defined and enforced, and that personal information gathered for a specific purpose not be used for other purposes without consent of the individual(s). These principles apply to electronic communications, including electronic mail, and prohibit procedures that capture or monitor electronic user data, including messages, without the permission of users or *bona fide* authorization related to system operation and maintenance. User data observed during the normal duties of system operation and maintenance must be treated with strictest confidentiality, except in cases where it is evidence for violation of law, organizational regulations, or this Code. In these cases, the nature or contents of that information must be disclosed only to proper authorities.

1.8 Honor confidentiality

The principle of honesty extends to issues of confidentiality of information whenever one has made an explicit promise to honor confidentiality or, implicitly, when private information not directly related to the performance of one's duties becomes available. The ethical concern is to respect all obligations of confidentiality to employers, clients, and users unless discharged from such obligations by requirements of the law or other principles of this Code.

2. More Specific Professional Responsibilities.

As an ACM computing professional I will . . .

2.1 Strive to achieve the highest quality, effectiveness, and dignity in both the process and products of professional work

Excellence is perhaps the most important obligation of a professional. The computing professional must strive to achieve quality and to be cognizant of the serious negative consequences that may result from poor quality in a system.

2.2 Acquire and maintain professional competence

Excellence depends on individuals who take responsibility for acquiring and maintaining professional competence. A professional must participate in setting standards for appropriate levels of competence and strive to achieve those standards. Upgrading technical knowledge and competence can be achieved in several ways: doing independent study; attending seminars, conferences, or courses; and being involved in professional organizations.

2.3 Know and respect existing laws pertaining to professional work

ACM members must obey existing local, state, province, national, and international law unless there is a compelling ethical basis not to do so. Policies and procedures of the organizations in which one participates must also be obeyed. But compliance must be balanced with the recognition that sometimes existing laws and rules may be immoral or inappropriate and, therefore, must be challenged.

Violation of a law or regulation may be ethical when that law or rule has inadequate moral basis or when it conflicts with another law judged to be more important. If one decides to violate a law or rule because it is viewed as unethical, or for any other reason, one must fully accept responsibility for one's actions and for the consequences.

2.4 Accept and provide appropriate professional review

Quality professional work, especially in the computing profession, depends on professional reviewing and critiquing. Whenever appropriate, individual members should seek and utilize peer review as well as provide critical review of the work of others.

2.5 Give comprehensive and thorough evaluations of computer systems and their impacts, including analysis of possible risks

Computer professionals must strive to be perceptive, thorough, and objective when evaluating, recommending, and presenting system descriptions and alternatives. Computer professionals are in a position of special trust and therefore have a special responsibility to provide objective, credible evaluations to employers, clients, users, and the public. When providing evaluations the professional must also identify any relevant conflicts of interest, as stated in imperative 1.3.

As noted in the discussion of principle 1.2 on avoiding harm, any signs of danger from systems must be reported to those who have opportunity and/or responsibility to resolve them. See the guidelines for imperative 1.2 for more details concerning harm, including the reporting of professional violations.

2.6 Honor contracts, agreements, and assigned responsibilities

Honoring one's commitments is a matter of integrity and honesty. For the computer professional this includes ensuring that system elements perform as intended. Also, when one contracts for work with another party, one has an obligation to keep that party properly informed about progress toward computing that work.

A computing professional has a responsibility to request a change in any assignment that he or she feels cannot be completed as defined. Only after serious consideration and with full disclosure of risks and concerns to the employer or client, should one accept the assignment. The major underlying principle here is the obligation to accept personal accountability for professional work. On some occasions other ethical principles may take greater priority.

A judgment that a specific assignment should not be performed may not be accepted. Having clearly identified one's concerns and reasons for that judgment, but failing to procure a change in that assignment, one may yet be obligated, by contract or by law, to proceed as directed. The computing professional's ethical judgment should be the final guide in deciding whether or not to proceed. Regardless of the decision, one must accept the responsibility for the consequences. However, performing assignments "against one's own judgment" does not relieve the professional of responsibility for any negative consequences.

2.7 Improve public understanding of computing and its consequences

Computing professionals have a responsibility to share technical knowledge with the public by encouraging understanding of computing, including the impacts of computer systems and their limitations. This imperative implies an obligation to counter any false views related to computing.

2.8 Access computing and communication resources only when authorized to do so

Theft or destruction of tangible and electronic property is prohibited by imperative 1.2—"Avoid harm to others." Trespassing and unauthorized use of a computer or communication system is addressed by this imperative. Trespassing includes accessing communication networks and computer systems, or accounts and/or files associated with those systems, without explicit authorization to do so. Individuals and organizations have the right to restrict access to their systems so long as they do not violate the discrimination principle. (See 1.4.)

No one should enter or use another's computing system, software, or data files without permission. One must always have appropriate approval before using system resources, including .rm57 communication ports, file space, or system peripherals, and computer time.

3. Organizational Leadership Imperatives.

As an ACM Member and an organizational leader, I will . . .

3.1 Articulate social responsibilities of members of an organizational unit and encourage full acceptance of those responsibilities

Because organizations of all kinds have impacts on the public, they must accept responsibilities to society. Organizational procedures and attitudes oriented toward quality and the welfare of society will reduce harm to members of the public, thereby serving public interest and fulfilling social responsibility. Therefore, organizational leaders must encourage full participation in meeting social responsibilities as well as quality performance.

3.2 Manage personnel and resources to design and build information systems that enhance the quality of working life

Organizational leaders are responsible for ensuring that computer systems enhance, not degrade, the quality of working life. When implementing a computer system, organizations must consider the personal and professional development, physical safety, and human dignity of all workers. Appropriate human-computer ergonomic standards should be considered in system design and in the workplace.

3.3 Acknowledge and support proper and authorized uses of an organization's computing and communications resources

Because computer systems can become tools to harm as well as to benefit an organization, the leadership has the responsibility to clearly define appropriate and inappropriate uses of organizational computing resources. While the number and scope of such rules should be minimal, they should be fully enforced when established.

3.4 Ensure that users and those who will be affected by a system have their needs clearly articulated during the assessment and design of requirements. Later the system must be validated to meet requirements

Current system users, potential users, and other persons whose lives may be affected by a system must have their needs assessed and incorporated in the statement of requirements. System validation should ensure compliance with those requirements.

3.5 Articulate and support policies that protect the dignity of users and others affected by a computing system

Designing or implementing systems that deliberately or inadvertently demean individuals or groups is ethically unacceptable. Computer professionals who are in decision-making positions should verify that systems are designed and implemented to protect personal privacy and enhance personal dignity.

3.6 Create opportunities for members of the organization to learn the principles and limitations of computer systems

This complements the imperative on public understanding (2.7). Educational opportunities are essential to facilitate optimal participation of all organizational members. Opportunities must be available to all members to help them improve their knowledge and skills in computing, including courses that familiarize them with the consequences and limitations of particular types of systems. In particular, professionals must be made aware of the dangers of building systems around oversimplified models, the improbability of anticipating and designing for every possible operating condition, and other issues related to the complexity of this profession.

4. Compliance With the Code.

As an ACM member I will . . .

4.1 Uphold and promote the principles of this Code

The future of the computing profession depends on both technical and ethical excellence. Not only is it important for ACM computing professionals to adhere to the principles expressed in this Code, each member should encourage and support adherence by other members.

4.2 Treat violations of this Code as inconsistent with membership in the ACM

Adherence of professionals to a code of ethics is largely a voluntary matter. However, if a member does not follow this code by engaging in gross misconduct, membership in ACM may be terminated.

◳ Data Processing Management Association

Standards of Conduct*

These standards expand on the Code of Ethics by providing specific statements of behavior in support of each element of the Code. They are not objectives to be strived for; they are rules that no true professional will violate. It is first of all expected that an information processing professional will abide by the appropriate laws of his or her country and community. The following standards address tenets that apply to the profession.

In recognition of my obligation to management I shall:

- Keep my personal knowledge up-to-date and ensure that proper expertise is available when needed.
- Share my knowledge with others and present factual and objective information to management to the best of my ability.
- Accept full responsibility for work that I perform.
- Not misuse the authority entrusted to me.
- Not misrepresent or withhold information concerning the capabilities of equipment, software, or systems.
- Not take advantage of the lack of knowledge or inexperience on the part of others.

In recognition of my obligation to my fellow members and the profession I shall:

- Be honest in all my professional relationships.
- Take appropriate action in regard to any illegal or unethical practices that come to my attention. However, I will bring charges against any person only when I have reasonable basis for believing in the truth of the allegations and without regard to personal interest.
- Endeavor to share my special knowledge.
- Cooperate with others in achieving understanding and in identifying problems.

---

* Founded in 1951, DPMA is headquartered in Park Ridge, Illinois, and has 234 chapters worldwide. The association includes members from all strata of the computer science/information systems industry and is a leading element in today's information age. Reprinted with permission of DPMA.

- Not use or take credit for the work of others without specific acknowledgment and authorization.
- Not take advantage of the lack of knowledge or inexperience on the part of others for personal gain.

In recognition of my obligation to society I shall:

- Protect the privacy and confidentiality of all information entrusted to me.
- Use my skill and knowledge to inform the public in all areas of my expertise.
- To the best of my ability, ensure that the products of my work are used in a socially responsible way.
- Support, respect, and abide by the appropriate local, state, provincial, and federal laws.
- Never misrepresent or withhold information that is germane to a problem or situation of public concern, nor will I allow any such known information to remain unchallenged.
- Not use knowledge of a confidential or personal nature in any unauthorized manner or to achieve personal gain.

In recognition of my obligation to my employer I shall:

- Make every effort to ensure that I have the most current knowledge and that the proper expertise is available when needed.
- Avoid conflict of interest and ensure that my employer is aware of any potential conflicts.
- Present a fair, honest, and objective viewpoint.
- Protect the proper interests of my employer at all times.
- Protect the privacy and confidentiality of all information entrusted to me.
- Not misrepresent or withhold information that is germane to the situation.
- Not attempt to use the resources of my employer for personal gain or for any purpose without proper approval.
- Not exploit the weakness of a computer system for personal gain or personal satisfaction.

◻ American Library Association Statement on Professional Ethics, 1981*

Introduction

Since 1939, the American Library Association has recognized the importance of codifying and making known to the public and the profession the principles which guide librarians in action. This latest revision of the *Code of Ethics* reflects changes in the nature of the profession and in its social and institutional environment. It should be revised and augmented as necessary.

Librarians significantly influence or control the selection, organization, preservation, and dissemination of information. In a political system grounded in an informed citizenry, librarians are members of a profession explicitly committed to intellectual freedom and the freedom of access to information. We have a special obligation to ensure the free flow of information and ideas to present and future generations.

Code of Ethics

1. Librarians must provide the highest level of service through appropriate and usefully organized collections, fair and equitable circulation and service policies, and skillful, accurate, unbiased, and courteous responses to all requests for assistance.

2. Librarians must resist all efforts by groups or individuals to censor library materials.

3. Librarians must protect each user's right to privacy with respect to information sought or received, and materials consulted, borrowed, or acquired.

4. Librarians must adhere to the principles of due process and equality of opportunity in peer relationships and personnel actions.

5. Librarians must distinguish clearly in their actions and statements between their personal philosophies and attitudes and those of an institution or professional body.

6. Librarians must avoid situations in which personal interests might be served or financial benefits gained at the expense of library users, colleagues, or the employing institution.

---

* Adopted by ALA membership and ALA Council, June 30, 1981. Reprinted by permission of the American Library Association.

◤ American Society of Newspaper Editors*

ASNE STATEMENT OF PRINCIPLES

PREAMBLE

The First Amendment, protecting freedom of expression from abridgment by any law, guarantees to the people through their press a constitutional right, and thereby places on newspaper people a particular responsibility.

Thus journalism demands of its practitioners not only industry and knowledge but also the pursuit of a standard of integrity proportionate to the journalist's singular obligation.

To this end the American Society of Newspaper Editors sets forth this Statement of Principles as a standard encouraging the highest ethical and professional performance.

ARTICLE I: RESPONSIBILITY

The primary purpose of gathering and distributing news and opinion is to serve the general welfare by informing the people and enabling them to make judgments on the issues of the time. Newspapermen and women who abuse the power of their professional role for selfish motives or unworthy purposes are faithless to that public trust.

The American press was made free not just to inform or just to serve as a forum for debate but also to bring an independent scrutiny to bear on the forces of power in the society, including the conduct of official power at all levels of government.

ARTICLE II: FREEDOM OF THE PRESS

Freedom of the press belongs to the people. It must be defended against encroachment or assault from any quarter, public or private.

Journalists must be constantly alert to see that the public's business is conducted in public. They must be vigilant against all who would exploit the press for selfish purposes.

* Reprinted with permission of the American Society of Newspaper Editors. This Statement of Principles was adopted by the ASNE Board of Directors, Oct. 23, 1975; it supplants the 1922 Code of Ethics ("Canons of Journalism").

ARTICLE III: INDEPENDENCE

Journalists must avoid impropriety and the appearance of impropriety as well as any conflict of interest or the appearance of conflict. They should neither accept anything nor pursue any activity that might compromise or seem to compromise their integrity.

ARTICLE IV: TRUTH AND ACCURACY

Good faith with the reader is the foundation of good journalism. Every effort must be made to assure that the news content is accurate, free from bias and in context, and that all sides are presented fairly. Editorials, analytical articles, and commentary should be held to the same standards of accuracy with respect to facts as news reports.

Significant errors of fact, as well as errors of omission, should be corrected promptly and prominently.

ARTICLE V: IMPARTIALITY

To be impartial does not require the press to be unquestioning or to refrain from editorial expression. Sound practice, however, demands a clear distinction for the reader between news reports and opinion. Articles that contain opinion or personal interpretation should be clearly identified.

ARTICLE VI: FAIR PLAY

Journalists should respect the rights of people involved in the news, observe the common standards of decency and stand accountable to the public for the fairness and accuracy of their news reports.

Persons publicly accused should be given the earliest opportunity to respond.

Pledges of confidentiality to news sources must be honored at all costs, and therefore should not be given lightly. Unless there is clear and pressing need to maintain confidences, sources of information should be identified.

These principles are intended to preserve, protect, and strengthen the bond of trust and respect between American journalists and the American people, a bond that is essential to sustain the grant of freedom entrusted to both by the nation's founders.

◪ American Association of Engineering Societies*

Model Guide for Professional Conduct

Preamble

Engineers recognize that the practice of engineering has a direct and vital influence on the quality of life for all people. Therefore, engineers should exhibit high standards of competency, honesty, and impartiality; be fair and equitable; and accept a personal responsibility for adherence to applicable laws, the protection of the public health, and maintenance of safety in their professional actions and behavior. These principles govern professional conduct in serving the interests of the public, clients, employers, colleagues, and the profession.

The Fundamental Principle

The engineer as a professional is dedicated to improving competence, service, fairness, and the exercise of well-founded judgment in the practice of engineering for the public, employers, and clients with fundamental concern for the public health and safety in the pursuit of this practice.

Canons of Professional Conduct

Engineers offer services in the areas of their competence and experience, affording full disclosure of their qualifications.

Engineers consider the consequences of their work and societal issues pertinent to it and seek to extend public understanding of those relationships.

Engineers are honest, truthful, and fair in presenting information and in making public statements reflecting on professional matters and their professional role.

Engineers engage in professional relationships without bias because of race, religion, sex, age, national origin, or handicap.

Engineers act in professional matters for each employer or client as faithful agents or trustees, disclosing nothing of a proprietary nature concerning the

---

* Reprinted with permission of the American Association of Engineering Societies.

business affairs or technical processes of any present or former client or employer without specific consent.

Engineers disclose to affected parties known or potential conflicts of interest or other circumstances which might influence—or appear to influence—judgment or impair the fairness or quality of their performance.

Engineers are responsible for enhancing their professional competence throughout their careers and for encouraging similar actions by their colleagues.

Engineers accept responsibility for their actions; seek and acknowledge criticism of their work; offer honest criticism of the work of others; properly credit the contributions of others; and do not accept credit for work not theirs.

Engineers perceiving a consequence of their professional duties to adversely affect the present or future public health and safety shall formally advise their employers or clients and, if warranted, consider further disclosure.

Engineers act in accordance with all applicable laws and the _____* rules of conduct, and lend support to others who strive to do likewise. (* AAES Member Societies are urged to make reference here to the appropriate code of conduct to which their members will be bound.)

Public Policy Perspective and Positions:
Engineering Employment & Practice: Ethics

Engineering affects the quality of life for every person in the world. In order to carry out the duties and responsibilities of their profession, engineers must be honest, fair, impartial, and dedicated to public health and safety. Engineers are called upon to use their knowledge and abilities in an ever increasing number of traditional and nontraditional forums. To meet this growing challenge, standards of conduct are implicit in protecting both the engineer and the public.

AAES has recognized the importance of such guidelines for professional conduct and continues to promote their adoption among our member societies, the general scientific and engineering community, and within the various levels of government.

Policy Priorities

- Support the adoption of Codes of Ethics by all member societies
- Work toward guidelines, jointly developed by cognizant organizations, for scientists and engineers who serve as volunteers on government boards and panels

- Support the adoption of reasonable standards of ethical conduct for government employees
- Actively support the membership of all engineers in professional and technical societies that have adopted codes of ethics

⬛ American Institute of Certified Public Accountants*

Code of Professional Conduct

INTRODUCTION

Composition, Applicability, and Compliance

The Code of Professional Conduct of the American Institute of Certified Public Accountants consists of two sections—(1) the Principles and (2) the Rules. The Principles provide the framework for the Rules, which govern the performance of professional services by members. The Council of the American Institute of Certified Public Accountants is authorized to designate bodies to promulgate technical standards under the Rules, and the bylaws require adherence to those Rules and standards.

The Code of Professional Conduct was adopted by the membership to provide guidance and rules to all members—those in public practice, in industry, in government, and in education—in the performance of their professional responsibilities.

Compliance with the Code of Professional Conduct, as with all standards in an open society, depends primarily on members' understanding and voluntary actions, secondarily on reinforcement by peers and public opinion, and ultimately on disciplinary proceedings, when necessary, against members who fail to comply with the Rules.

Other Guidance

Interpretations of Rules of Conduct consist of interpretations which have been adopted, after exposure to state societies, state boards, practice units, and other interested parties, by the professional ethics division's executive committee to provide guidelines as to the scope and application of the Rules but are not intended to limit such scope or application. A member who departs from such guidelines shall have the burden of justifying such departure in any disciplinary hearing. *Interpretations* which existed before the adoption of the Code of Professional Conduct on January 12, 1988, will remain in effect until further action is deemed necessary by the appropriate senior technical committee.

Ethics Rulings consist of formal rulings made by the professional ethics division's executive committee after exposure to state societies, state boards, practice units, and other interested parties. These rulings summarize the application of Rules of Conduct and Interpretations to a particular set of factual circumstances. Members who depart from such rulings in similar circumstances will be requested to justify such departures. *Ethics Rulings* which existed before the adoption of the Code of Professional Conduct on January 12, 1988, will remain in effect until further action is deemed necessary by the appropriate senior technical committee.

Publication of an Interpretation or Ethics Ruling in *The Journal of Accountancy* constitutes notice to members. Hence, the effective date of the pronouncement is the last day of the month in which the pronouncement is published in *The Journal of Accountancy.* The professional ethics division will take into consideration the time that would have been reasonable for the member to comply with the pronouncement.

A member should also consult, if applicable, the ethical standards of his state CPA society, state board of accountancy, the Securities and Exchange Commission, and any other governmental agency which may regulate his client's business or use his report to evaluate the client's compliance with applicable laws and related regulations.

PRINCIPLES OF PROFESSIONAL CONDUCT

Preamble

Membership in the American Institute of Certified Public Accountants is voluntary. By accepting membership, a certified public accountant assumes an obligation of self-discipline above and beyond the requirements of laws and regulations.

These Principles of the Code of Professional Conduct of the American Institute of Certified Public Accountants express the profession's recognition of its responsibilities to the public, to clients, and to colleagues. They guide members in the performance of their professional responsibilities and express the basic tenets of ethical and professional conduct. The Principles call for an unswerving commitment to honorable behavior, even at the sacrifice of personal advantage.

Article I

Responsibilities

In carrying out their responsibilities as professionals, members should exercise sensitive professional and moral judgments in all their activities.

As professionals, certified public accountants perform an essential role in society. Consistent with that role, members of the American Institute of Certified Public Accountants have responsibilities to all those who use their professional services. Members also have a continuing responsibility to cooperate with each other to improve the art of accounting, maintain the public's confidence, and carry out the profession's special responsibilities for self-governance. The collective efforts of all members are required to maintain and enhance the traditions of the profession.

Article II

The Public Interest

Members should accept the obligation to act in a way that will serve the public interest, honor the public trust, and demonstrate commitment to professionalism.

A distinguishing mark of a profession is acceptance of its responsibility to the public. The accounting profession's public consists of clients, credit grantors, governments, employers, investors, the business and financial community, and others who rely on the objectivity and integrity of certified public accountants to maintain the orderly functioning of commerce. This reliance imposes a public interest responsibility on certified public accountants. The public interest is defined as the collective well-being of the community of people and institutions the profession serves.

In discharging their professional responsibilities, members may encounter conflicting pressures from among each of those groups. In resolving those conflicts, members should act with integrity, guided by the precept that when members fulfill their responsibility to the public, clients' and employers' interests are best served.

Those who rely on certified public accountants expect them to discharge their responsibilities with integrity, objectivity, due professional care, and a genuine interest in serving the public. They are expected to provide quality services, enter into fee arrangements, and offer a range of services, all in a manner that demonstrates a level of professionalism consistent with these Principles of the Code of Professional Conduct.

All who accept membership in the American Institute of Certified Public Accountants commit themselves to honor the public trust. In return for the faith that the public reposes in them, members should seek continually to demonstrate their dedication to professional excellence.

Article III

Integrity

To maintain and broaden public confidence, members should perform all professional responsibilities with the highest sense of integrity.

Integrity is an element of character fundamental to professional recognition. It is the quality from which the public trust derives and the benchmark against which a member must ultimately test all decisions.

Integrity requires a member to be, among other things, honest and candid within the constraints of client confidentiality. Service and the public trust should not be subordinated to personal gain and advantage. Integrity can accommodate the inadvertent error and the honest difference of opinion; it cannot accommodate deceit or subordination of principle.

Integrity is measured in terms of what is right and just. In the absence of specific rules, standards, or guidance, or in the face of conflicting opinions, a member should test decisions and deeds by asking: "Am I doing what a person of integrity would do? Have I retained my integrity?" Integrity requires a member to observe both the form and the spirit of technical and ethical standards; circumvention of those standards constitutes subordination of judgment.

Integrity also requires a member to observe the principles of objectivity and independence and of due care.

Article IV

Objectivity and Independence

A member should maintain objectivity and be free of conflicts of interest in discharging professional responsibilities. A member in public practice should be independent in fact and appearance when providing auditing and other attestation services.

Objectivity is a state of mind, a quality that lends value to a member's services. It is a distinguishing feature of the profession. The principle of objectivity imposes the obligation to be impartial, intellectually honest, and free of conflicts of interest. Independence precludes relationships that may appear to impair a member's objectivity in rendering attestation services.

Members often serve multiple interests in many different capacities and must demonstrate their objectivity in varying circumstances. Members in public practice render attest, tax, and management advisory services. Other members prepare financial statements in the employment of others, perform internal auditing services, and serve in financial and management capacities in industry, education, and government. They also educate and train those who aspire to admission into the profession. Regardless of service or capacity, members should protect the integrity of their work, maintain objectivity, and avoid any subordination of their judgment.

For a member in public practice, the maintenance of objectivity and independence requires a continuing assessment of client relationships and public responsibility. Such a member who provides auditing and other attestation services should be independent in fact and appearance. In providing all other services, a member should maintain objectivity and avoid conflicts of interest.

Although members not in public practice cannot maintain the appearance of independence, they nevertheless have the responsibility to maintain objectivity in rendering professional services. Members employed by others to prepare financial statements or to perform auditing, tax, or consulting services are charged with the same responsibility for objectivity as members in public practice and must be scrupulous in their application of generally accepted accounting principles and candid in all their dealings with members in public practice.

Article V

Due Care

A member should observe the profession's technical and ethical standards, strive continually to improve competence and the quality of services, and discharge professional responsibility to the best of the member's ability.

The quest for excellence is the essence of due care. Due care requires a member to discharge professional responsibilities with competence and diligence. It imposes the obligation to perform professional services to the best of a member's ability with concern for the best interest of those for whom the services are performed and consistent with the profession's responsibility to the public.

Competence is derived from a synthesis of education and experience. It begins with a mastery of the common body of knowledge required for designation as a certified public accountant. The maintenance of competence requires a commitment to learning and professional improvement that must continue throughout a member's professional life. It is a member's individual responsibility. In all engagements and in all responsibilities, each member should undertake to achieve a level of competence that will assure that the quality of the member's services meets the high level of professionalism required by these Principles.

Competence represents the attainment and maintenance of a level of understanding and knowledge that enables a member to render services with facility and acumen. It also establishes the limitations of a member's capabilities by dictating that consultation or referral may be required when a professional engagement exceeds the personal competence of a member or a member's firm. Each member is responsible for assessing his or her own competence—of evaluating whether education, experience, and judgment are adequate for the responsibility to be assumed.

Members should be diligent in discharging responsibilities to clients, employers, and the public. Diligence imposes the responsibility to render services promptly and carefully, to be thorough, and to observe applicable technical and ethical standards.

Due care requires a member to plan and supervise adequately any professional activity for which he or she is responsible.

Article VI

Scope and Nature of Services

A member in public practice should observe the Principles of the Code of Professional Conduct in determining the scope and nature of services to be provided.

The public interest aspect of certified public accountants' services requires that such services be consistent with acceptable professional behavior for certified public accountants. Integrity requires that service and the public trust not be subordinated to personal gain and advantage. Objectivity and independence require that members be free from conflicts of interest in discharging professional responsibilities. Due care requires that services be provided with competence and diligence.

Each of these Principles should be considered by members in determining whether or not to provide specific services in individual circumstances. In some instances, they may represent an overall constraint on the nonaudit services that might be offered to a specific client. No hard-and-fast rules can be developed to help members reach these judgments, but they must be satisfied that they are meeting the spirit of the Principles in this regard.

In order to accomplish this, members should

- Practice in firms that have in place internal quality-control procedures to ensure that services are competently delivered and adequately supervised.
- Determine, in their individual judgments, whether the scope and nature of other services provided to an audit client would create a conflict of interest in the performance of the audit function for that client.
- Assess, in their individual judgments, whether an activity is consistent with their role as professionals (for example, Is such activity a reasonable extension or variation of existing services offered by the member or others in the profession?).

RULES: APPLICABILITY AND DEFINITIONS

Applicability

The bylaws of the American Institute of Certified Public Accountants require that members adhere to the Rules of the Code of Professional Conduct. Members must be prepared to justify departures from these Rules.

Interpretation Addressing the Applicability of the AICPA Code of Profes-sional Conduct. For purposes of the applicability section of the Code, a "member" is a member or international associate of the American Institute of CPAs.

1. The Rules of Conduct that follow apply to all professional services performed except (a) where the wording of the rule indicates otherwise and (b) that a member who is practicing outside the United States will not be subject to discipline for departing from any of the rules stated herein as long as the member's conduct is in accord with the rules of the organized accounting profession in the country in which he or she is practicing. However, where a member's name is associated with financial statements under circumstances that would entitle the reader to assume that United States practices were followed, the member must comply with the requirements of rules 202 and 203.

2. A member may be held responsible for compliance with the rules by all persons associated with him or her in the practice of public accounting who are either under the member's supervision or are the member's partners or shareholders in the practice.

3. A member shall not permit others to carry out on his or her behalf, either with or without compensation, acts which, if carried out by the member, would place the member in violation of the rules.

Definitions

Client. A client is any person or entity, other than the member's employer, that engages a member or a member's firm to perform professional services or a person or entity with respect to which professional services are performed. The term "employer" for these purposes does not include those entities en-gaged in the practice of public accounting.

Council. The Council of the American Institute of Certified Public Ac-countants.

Enterprise. For purposes of the Code, the term "enterprise" is synonymous with the term "client."

Financial statements. Statements and footnotes related thereto that pur-port to show financial position which relates to a point in time or changes in financial position which relate to a period of time, and statements which use a cash or other incomplete basis of accounting. Balance sheets, statements of income, statements of retained earnings, statements of changes in financial position, and statements of changes in owners' equity are financial statements.

Incidental financial data included in management advisory services reports to support recommendations to a client and tax returns and supporting schedules do not, for this purpose, constitute financial statements; and the statement, affidavit, or signature of preparers required on tax returns neither constitutes an opinion on financial statements nor requires a disclaimer of such opinion.

Firm. A form of organization permitted by state law or regulation whose characteristics conform to resolutions of Council that is engaged in the practice of public accounting, including the individual owners thereof.

Institute. The American Institute of Certified Public Accountants.

Interpretations of rules of conduct. Pronouncements issued by the division of professional ethics to provide guidelines concerning the scope and application of the rules of conduct.

Member. A member, associate member, or international associate of the American Institute of Certified Public Accountants.

Practice of public accounting. The practice of public accounting consists of the performance for a client, by a member or a member's firm, while holding out as CPA(s), of the professional services of accounting, tax, personal financial planning, litigation support services, and those professional services for which standards are promulgated by bodies designated by Council, such as Statements of Financial Accounting Standards, Statements on Auditing Standards, Statements on Standards for Accounting and Review Services, Statement on Standards for Consulting Services, Statements of Governmental Accounting Standards, Statements on Standards for Attestation Engagements, and Statement on Standards for Accountants' Services on Prospective Financial Information.

However, a member or a member's firm, while holding out as CPA(s), is not considered to be in the practice of public accounting if the member or the member's firm does not perform, for any client, any of the professional services described in the preceding paragraph.

Professional services. Professional services include all services performed by a member while holding out as a CPA.

Holding out. In general, any action initiated by a member that informs others of his or her status as a CPA or AICPA-accredited specialist constitutes holding out as a CPA. This would include, for example, any oral or written representation to another regarding CPA status, use of the CPA designation on business cards or letterhead, the display of a certificate evidencing a member's CPA designation, or listing as a CPA in local telephone directories.

INDEPENDENCE, INTEGRITY, AND OBJECTIVITY

Rule 101   Independence

A member in public practice shall be independent in the performance of professional services as required by standards promulgated by bodies designated by Council.

Rule 102   Integrity and Objectivity

In the performance of any professional service, a member shall maintain objectivity and integrity, shall be free of conflicts of interest, and shall not knowingly misrepresent facts or subordinate his or her judgment to others.

GENERAL STANDARDS, ACCOUNTING PRINCIPLES

Rule 201   General Standards

A member shall comply with the following standards and with any interpretations thereof by bodies designated by Council.

- A. *Professional Competence.* Undertake only those professional services that the member or the member's firm can reasonably expect to be completed with professional competence.
- B. *Due Professional Care.* Exercise due professional care in the performance of professional services.
- C. *Planning and Supervision.* Adequately plan and supervise the performance of professional services.
- D. *Sufficient Relevant Data.* Obtain sufficient relevant data to afford a reasonable basis for conclusions or recommendations in relation to any professional services performed.

Rule 202   Compliance With Standards

A member who performs auditing, review, compilation, management consulting, tax, or other professional services shall comply with standards promulgated by bodies designated by Council.

Rule 203   Accounting Principles

A member shall not (1) express an opinion or state affirmatively that the financial statements or other financial data of any entity are presented in conformity with generally accepted accounting principles or (2) state that he or she is not aware of any material modifications that should be made to such statements or data in order for them to be in conformity with generally accepted accounting principles, if such statements or data contain any departure from an accounting principle promulgated by bodies designated by Council to establish such principles that has a material effect on the statements or data taken as a whole. If, however, the statements or data contain such a departure and the member can demonstrate that due to unusual circumstances the financial statements or data would otherwise have been misleading, the member can comply with the rule by describing the departure, its approximate effects, if practicable, and the reasons why compliance with the principle would result in a misleading statement.

RESPONSIBILITIES TO CLIENTS

Rule 301   Confidential Client Information

A member in public practice shall not disclose any confidential client information without the specific consent of the client.

This rule shall not be construed (1) to relieve a member of his or her professional obligations under rules 202 and 203, (2) to affect in any way the member's obligation to comply with a validly issued and enforceable subpoena or summons, or to prohibit a member's compliance with applicable laws and government regulations, (3) to prohibit review of a member's professional practice under AICPA or state CPA society or Board of Accountancy authorization, or (4) to preclude a member from initiating a complaint with, or responding to any inquiry made by, the professional ethics division or trial board of the Institute or a duly constituted investigative or disciplinary body of a state CPA society or Board of Accountancy.

Members of any of the bodies identified in (4) above shall not use to their own advantage or disclose any member's confidential client information that comes to their attention in carrying out those activities. This prohibition shall not restrict members' exchange of information in connection with the investigative or disciplinary proceedings described in (4) above or the professional practice reviews described in (3) above.

Rule 302   Contingent Fees

A member in public practice shall not

(1) Perform for a contingent fee any professional services for, or receive such a fee from a client for whom the member or the member's firm performs
   (a) an audit or review of a financial statement; or
   (b) a compilation of a financial statement when the member expects, or reasonably might expect, that a third party will use the financial statement and the member's compilation report does not disclose a lack of independence; or
   (c) an examination of prospective financial information; or
(2) Prepare an original or amended tax return or claim for a tax refund for a contingent fee for any client.

The prohibition in (1) above applies during the period in which the member or the member's firm is engaged to perform any of the services listed above and the period covered by any historical financial statements involved in any such listed services.

Except as stated in the next sentence, a contingent fee is a fee established for the performance of any service pursuant to an arrangement in which no fee will be charged unless a specified finding or result is attained, or in which the amount of the fee is otherwise dependent upon the finding or result of such service. Solely for purposes of this rule, fees are not regarded as being contingent if fixed by courts or other public authorities, or, in tax matters, if determined based on the results of judicial proceedings or the findings of governmental agencies.

A member's fees may vary depending, for example, on the complexity of services rendered.

RESPONSIBILITIES TO COLLEAGUES

Rule 401   [There are currently no rules in the 400 series.]

OTHER RESPONSIBILITIES AND PRACTICES

Rule 501   Act Discreditable

A member shall not commit an act discreditable to the profession.

Rule 502   Advertising and Other Forms of Solicitation

A member in public practice shall not seek to obtain clients by advertising or other forms of solicitation in a manner that is false, misleading, or deceptive. Solicitation by the use of coercion, over-reaching, or harassing conduct is prohibited.

Rule 503   Commissions and Referral Fees

A. *Prohibited commissions*

A member in public practice shall not for a commission recommend or refer to a client any product or service, or for a commission recommend or refer any product or service to be supplied by a client, or receive a commission, when the member or the member's firm also performs for that client

(a) an audit or review of a financial statement; or
(b) a compilation of a financial statement when the member expects, or reasonably might expect, that a third party will use the financial statement and the member's compilation report does not disclose a lack of independence; or
(c) an examination of prospective financial information.

This prohibition applies during the period in which the member is engaged to perform any of the services listed above and the period covered by any historical financial statements involved in such listed services.

B. *Disclosure of permitted commissions*

A member in public practice who is not prohibited by this rule from performing services or receiving a commission and who is paid or expects to be paid a commission shall disclose that fact to any person or entity to whom the member recommends or refers a product or service to which the commission relates.

C. *Referral fees*

Any member who accepts a referral fee for recommending or referring any service of a CPA to any person or entity or who pays a referral fee to obtain a client shall disclose such acceptance or payment to the client.

Rule 504   *[There is currently no rule 504.]*

Rule 505   *Form of Organization and Name*

A member may practice public accounting only in a form of organization permitted by state law or regulation whose characteristics conform to resolutions of Council.

A member shall not practice public accounting under a firm name that is misleading. Names of one or more past owners may be included in the firm name of a successor organization. Also, an owner surviving the death or withdrawal of all other owners may continue to practice under a name which includes the name of past owners for up to two years after becoming a sole practitioner.

A firm may not designate itself as "Members of the American Institute of Certified Public Accountants" unless all of its owners are members of the Institute.

APPENDIX A

Council Resolution Designating Bodies to Promulgate Technical Standards

[Omitted.]

APPENDIX B

Council Resolution Concerning Form of Organization and Name

RESOLVED: That, under rule 505, a member may practice public accounting in a business form other than a proprietorship or partnership only if such entity has the following characteristics:

1. *Ownership.* All owners shall be persons who hold themselves out to be certified public accountants or public accountants and who perform for clients one or more types of services performed by certified public accountants or public accountants. Owners shall at all times own their equity in their own right and shall be the beneficial owners of the equity capital ascribed to them.

2. *Transfer of Ownership.* Provision shall be made requiring any owner who ceases to be eligible to be an equity owner to dispose of all his or her interest within a reasonable period to a person qualified to be an owner or to the entity.

3. *Directors and Officers.* The principal executive officer shall be an owner and a member of the entity's governing body. Lay governing body members shall not exercise any authority whatsoever over professional matters.

4. *Conduct.* The form of organization shall not change the obligation of its owners, directors, officers, and other employees to comply with the Code of Professional Conduct established by the American Institute of Certified Public Accountants.

References

Abbott, A. (1988). *The system of professions: An essay on division of expert labor.* Chicago: University of Chicago Press.

Ackoff, R. E. (1967, December). Management misinformation systems. *Management Science,* pp. 147-156.

Ackoff, R. L. (1984). *Scientific method: Optimizing applied research decisions.* Melabar, FL: Robert Krieger.

Ackoff, R. L., & Emery, F. E. (1972). *On purposeful systems.* Chicago: Aldine.

Alter, S. (1992). *Information systems: A managerial perspective.* Reading, MA: Addison-Wesley.

American Library Association and American Association of School Administrators. (1990). *Censorship and selection: Issues and answers for schools.* Chicago: American Library Association.

Anouilh, J. (1946). *Antigone.* New York: Random House.

Anschuetz, L. (1993). *The Youngstown free-net.* Unpublished manuscript.

Ansoff, I. (1965). *Corporate strategy.* New York: McGraw-Hill.

Aquinas, T. (1952-1956). *Summa theologia.* Tarini, Rome: Marietta. (Original work published c. 1270)

Aristotle. (1911). *Nicomacheon ethics of Airstobles.* New York: E. P. Dutton.

Aristotle. (1925). *Nichomachean ethics* (W. D. Ross, Ed. & Trans.). Oxford, UK: Clarendon.

Augustine. (1881). *The city of God* (M. Dods, Trans.). Edinburgh: T&T Clark.

Barnard, C. I. (1938). *The functions of the executive.* Cambridge, MA: Harvard University Press.

Bell, D. (1973). *The coming of the post-industrial society: A venture in social forecasting.* New York: Basic Books.

Beniger, J. R. (1986). *The control revolution: Technological and economic origins of the information society*. Cambridge, MA: Harvard University Press.

Bentham, J. (1823). *An introduction to the principles of morals and legislation*. Oxford, UK: Oxford University Press. (Original work published 1789)

Berle, A. A. (1954). *The twentieth century capitalist revolution*. New York: Harcourt, Brace.

Beveridge, W. H. (1942). *Social insurance*. New York: Macmillan.

Braudel, F. (1981-1984). *Civilization and capitalism: 15th-18th century* (Vols. 1-3). New York: Harper & Row.

Canterbury v. Spence, 464 F.2d 772, at 785.87 (D.C. Cir. 1972).

Carlzon, J. (1987). *Moments of truth*. Cambridge, MA: Ballinger.

Carson, R. (1962). *Silent spring*. Boston: Houghton Mifflin.

Chandler, A. D., Jr. (1990). *Scale and scope: The dynamics of industrial capitalism*. Cambridge, MA: Belknap.

Churchman, C. W. (1982). *Thought and wisdom*. Seaside, CA: Intersystems.

Citicorp's folly? (1991, April 3). *Wall Street Journal*, p. 1.

Cleveland, H. (1982a, August). *Information as a resource*. Unpublished manuscript. (Available from the Aspen Institute, Wye Center, Box 222, Queenstown, MD 21658)

Cleveland, H. (1982b, December). Information as a resource. *The Futurist*, pp. 34-39.

Coughlin, E. K. (1988, February 18). Concerns about fraud, editorial bias promotes scrutiny of journal practices. *Chronicle of Higher Education, 35*, pp. A4-A7.

Crowe, L., & Anthes, S. H. (1988, March). The academic librarian and information technology: Ethical issues. *College and Research Libraries*, pp. 123-130.

Culnan, M. J., & Smith, H. J. (1992). *Lotus MarketPlace: Households: Managing information privacy concerns (A & B)*. Unpublished case study, Georgetown University School of Business, Washington, DC.

Davis, G. B., & Olson, M. H. (1985). *Management information systems: Conceptual foundations, structure, and development*. New York: McGraw-Hill.

Deal, T. E., & Kennedy, A. A. (1982). *Corporate cultures: The rites and rituals of corporate life*. Reading, MA: Addison-Wesley.

Dewey, J. (1960). *The quest for certainty*. New York: G. P. Putnam. (Original work published 1929)

Disturbing developments. (1990, September 17). *Library Hotline*, p. 1.

Dobson, C. (1991-1992, Winter). Code of ethics for informational professionals. *FL Services Newsletter*, p. 1.

Drucker, P. F. (1973). *Management*. New York: Harper & Row.

Drucker, P. F. (1988, January-February). The coming of the new organization. *Harvard Business Review,* pp. 48-53.

Drucker, P. F. (1989). *The new realities.* New York: Harper & Row.

Durkheim, E. (1951). *Suicide: A study in sociology.* New York: Free Press.

Ehn, P. (1988). *Work-oriented design of computer artifacts.* Stockholm: Arbetslivscentrum.

Ethics in Business. (1991). (Videotape 1161, Business Ethics Program). Chicago: Arthur Andersen.

Everett, J., & Crowe, E. (1988). *Information for sale: How to start and operate your own data service.* Blue Ridge Summit, PA: TAB Books.

Frankel, M. S. (1989). Professional codes: Why, how and with what impact? *Journal of Business Ethics, 8*(2/3), 109-116.

Freud, S. (1954). *The origins of psychoanalysis* (E. Mosbacher & J. Strachey, Trans.). New York: Basic Books. (Original work published c. 1895)

Friedman, M. (1962). *Capitalism and freedom.* Chicago: University of Chicago Press.

Friedman, M. (1970, September 13). The social responsibility of business is to increase its profits. *New York Times,* Sec. 6, p. 126.

Froehlich, T. J. (1992). Ethical consideration of information professionals. *Annual Review of Science and Technology (ARIST), 27,* 291-324.

Fromm, E. (1978). *To have or to be.* London: Jonathan Cape.

Goldberg, S. (1993, March 15). Open letter to Madonna. *Library Journal,* p. 31. (Reprinted from the *Minneapolis Star Tribune,* January 7, 1993, editorial page)

Goodnow, C. (1982, August 8). Silence of their world has been broken by a computer. *Seattle Post-Intelligencer,* p. E4.

Grisez, G., & Shaw, R. (1980). *Beyond the new morality: The responsibilities of freedom.* Notre Dame, IN: University of Notre Dame Press.

Hardin, G. (1968). The tragedy of the commons. *Science, 162,* 367-381.

Harney, K. (1994, June 26). Credit files to be more accessible. *Miami Herald,* p. 3G.

Harper, T. (1993, May 17). Truth phones. *International Herald Tribune,* p. 13.

Hauptman, R. (1988). *Ethical challenges.* Phoenix, AZ: Oryx.

Hemingway, E. (1932). *Death in the afternoon.* New York: Scribner.

Hobbes, T. (1839). Leviathian. In W. Molesworth (Ed.), *The English works of Thomas Hobbes* (p. 112). London: John Bohn. (Original work published 1651)

Hopper, M. D. (1990, May-June). Rattling SABRE—New ways to compete with information. *Harvard Business Review,* pp. 118-127.

The Information Advisor Newsletter, (n.d.). (Available from Information Advisory Services, Inc., 47 Wilmer Street, Rochester, NY, Robert Berkman, Editor)

Ives, B. (1989). *The Tom Thumb promise card.* (SMU-ELCSM-90-MIS1a). Dallas, TX: Southern Methodist University. (Available from the Edwin L. Cox School of Management, Southern Methodist University, Dallas, TX 75275)

Jackall, R. (1988). *Moral mazes: The world of corporate managers.* New York: Oxford University Press.

Jackson, S. (1980). *The lottery.* Cambridge, MA: R. Bentley. (Original work published c. 1949)

Kant, I. (1956). *Critique of practical reason.* Indianapolis, IN: Liberal Arts Press. (Original work published 1788)

Larson, E. (1992). *The naked consumer.* New York: Henry Holt.

Laudon, K. D., Traver, C. G., & Laudon, J. P. (1994). *Information technology and society.* Belmont, CA: Wadsworth.

Lewin, K. (1947). Channels of group life, social planning and action research. *Human Relations, 1,* 143-153.

Lewin, T. (1993, August 27). Philadelphia doctors to be offered data on patients who have sued. *New York Times,* p. B9.

Locke, J. (1924). *Two treatises of civil government.* London: J. M. Dent & Sons. (Original work published 1690)

Lyris, S. (1992). Crime & punishment in cyberspace. In B. E. Miller & M. Wolf (Eds.), *Thinking robots, an aware Internet, and cyberpunk librarians* (1992 Library and Information Technology Association [LITA] President's Program, pp. 167-173). Chicago: American Library Association.

Mahoney, M. J. (1977). Publication prejudices: An experimental study of confirmatory bias in the peer review system. *Cognitive Therapy and Research, 1*(2), 161-175.

Margolick, D. (1993, November 12). At the bar. *New York Times,* p. B11.

Markoff, J. (1993, January 24). Building the electronic superhighway. *New York Times,* Section 3, p. 15.

Maslow, A. H. (1971). Self-actualizing and beyond. In A. H. Maslow, *The farther reaches of human nature* (pp. 41-53). New York: Viking Press.

Mason, R. O. (1981). Basic concepts for designing management information systems. In R. O. Mason & E. B. Swanson (Eds.), *Measurement for management decision* (Reading 6, pp. 81-95). Reading, MA: Addison-Wesley.

May, W. F. (1983). *The physician's covenant.* Philadelphia: Westminster.

McLuhan, M. (1965). *Understanding media: The extension of man.* New York: McGraw-Hill.

Metzger, W. P. (1975). What is a profession? *Seminar Reports, 3*(1), 2-3. (Program of General and Continuing Education, Columbia University, New York)

Mill, J. S. (1956). *On liberty.* New York: Beck. (Original work published 1859)

Mintz, A. (1991). Ethics and the news librarian. *Special Libraries, 82*(1), 10.

Mitroff, I. (1974). *The subjective side of science: An inquiry into the psychology of the Apollo moon scientists.* Amsterdam: Elsevier.

Nader, R. (1965). *Unsafe at any speed.* New York: Grossman.

Naisbitt, J. (1982). *Megatrends.* New York: Warner.

Nasri, W. Z. (1986). Professional liability. *Journal of Library Administration, 7*(4), 141-145.

News fronts. (1994). *American Libraries, 25*(6), 490.

The Newsletter on Intellectual Freedom. (1992, November 6). (Available from the Office of Intellectual Freedom, American Library Association, Chicago)

Newton, L. (1989). *Ethics in America: Source reader.* Englewood Cliffs, NJ: Prentice Hall.

New York Times Company v. Sullivan, 376 U.S. 254 (1964).

Nietzsche, F. (1924). *The will to power.* In O. Levy (Ed.), *The complete works of Frederick Nietzsche* (Vol. 7). New York: Macmillan. (Original work published 1887)

Note on airline reservation systems. (1985, June). (Note #9-184-142, p. 26.) Boston, MA: Harvard Business School.

Nozick, R. (1974). *Anarchy, state, and utopia.* New York: Basic Books.

O'Toole, J. (1993). *The executive's compass: Business and the good society.* New York: Oxford University Press.

Petersen, M. (1991, November 1). 18 printers refuse to print explicit gay sex manual. *Publisher's Weekly,* p. 16.

Porat, M. V., & Rubin, M. R. (1977). *The information economy* (U.S. Department of Commerce, Office of Telecommunications Special Publication, 9 Vols., 77-121 [1] through 77-121 [9]). Washington, DC: Government Printing Office.

Rand, A. (1943). *The fountainhead.* Indianapolis, IN: Bobbs-Merrill.

Rand, A. (1957). *Atlas shrugged.* New York: Random House.

Rand, A. (1964). *The virtue of selfishness.* New York: New American Library.

Rawls, J. (1971). *A theory of justice.* Cambridge, MA: Belknap.

Reich, R. (1991). *The work of nations.* New York: Knopf.

Roberts, P. (1993, June). Electronic ethics. *Aldus Magazine,* pp. 15-18.

Rosenthal, E. (1994, January 27). Hardest medical choices shift to patients. *New York Times,* pp. A1, A13.

Ross, W. D. (1930). *The right and the good.* New York: Oxford University Press.

Rothfeder, J. (1992). *Privacy for sale.* New York: Simon & Schuster.

Rousseau, J. J. (1947). *The social contract.* New York: Hafner. (Original work published 1762)

Schwartz, E. I. (1992, June 8). The rush to keep mum. *Business Week,* p. 33.

Schwartz, J. (1983, June). Communication by computer. *American Way,* pp. 112-116.

Shannon, V. (1994, July 4). Ethics are essential when downloading from on-line services. *Washington Post,* Business Sec., p. 12.

Sharn, L. (1993, July 1). Systems let you pay from the fast lane. *USA Today,* p. 1.

Shiller, Z., Zellner, W., Stodghill, R., Maremont, M., & Bureau Reports. (1992, December 21). Clout! More and more, retail giants rule the marketplace. *Business Week,* p. 69.

Simon, H. A. (1957). *Administrative behavior* (2nd ed.). New York: Macmillan.

Sims, C. (1993, December 6). Reporter disciplined for reading his co-workers' electronic mail. *New York Times,* p. A3.

Singer, E., Jr. (1959). *Experience and reflection* (C. W. Churchman, Ed.). Philadelphia: University of Pennsylvania Press.

Slater, P. (1974). *Earthwalk.* Garden City, NY: Anchor.

Smith, A. (1986). *The wealth of nations.* London: Penguin. (Original work published 1776)

Smith, H. J. (1994). *Managing privacy: Information technology and corporate America.* Chapel Hill: University of North Carolina Press.

Sorokin, P. (1937-1941). *Social and cultural dynamics.* New York: American Book Company.

Steward, T. (1991, June 3). Brain power. *Fortune,* pp. 44-60.

Stone, C. D. (1975). *Where the law ends: The social control of corporate behavior.* New York: Harper & Row.

Swan, J. (1991). Ethics inside and out: The case of Guidoriccio. *Library Trends, 40*(2), 258-274.

Tawney, R. H. (1931). *Equality.* New York: Harcourt, Brace.

Taylor, F. W. (1967). *Principles of scientific management.* New York: Norton. (Original work published 1911)

Tennyson, A. Lord (1962). Locksley hall. In M. H. Abrams (Ed.), *The Norton anthology of English literature* (Vol. 2, pp. 739-745). New York: Norton. (Original work published 1842)

Tetzeli, R. (1994, July 11). Surviving the information overload. *Fortune,* pp. 60-65.

Thorndike Barnhart World Book dictionary (Vol. 2). (1987). Chicago: World Book.

Thucydides. (1954). *Thucydides: The Peloponnesian War* (R. Warner, Trans.). London: Penguin Classics.

Toffler, A. (1980). *The third wave.* New York: William Morrow.

Toffler, A. (1990). *Powershift: Knowledge, wealth, and violence at the edge of the 21st century.* New York: Bantam.

Toffler, B. L. (1986). *Tough choices: Managers talk ethics.* New York: John Wiley.

Tolstoy, L. N. (1966). *War and peace* (G. Bigian, Ed.). New York: Norton. (Original work published 1886)

Tönnies, F. (1957). *Community and society* (C. Loomis, Trans. & Ed.). New York: Harper & Row. (Original work published 1887)

U.S. House of Representatives, Committee on Government Operations. (1990). *Data protection, computers, and changing information practices: Hearing before the Government Information, Justice, and Agriculture Subcommittee of the Committee on Government Operations.* 101st Congress, 2nd Sess., May 16, 1990, 38-684.

Veblen, T. (1914). *The instinct of workmanship and the state of the industrial arts.* New York: B. W. Huebsch.

Weill, K. (1968). *The threepenny opera.* New York: Vanguard. (Original work published 1931)

Westin, A. (1968). *Privacy and freedom.* New York: Atheneum.

White, P. (1979). *On a clear day you can see General Motors: John De Lorean's look inside the automotive giant.* Grosse Point, MI: Wright.

Wolf, T. (1987). *The bonfire of the vanities.* New York: Farrar, Straus & Giroux.

Woodward, D. (1990). A framework for deciding issues in ethics. In A. Mintz (Ed.), *Information ethics concerns for librarianship and the information industry* (Proceedings of the 27th Annual Symposium of Graduates, Alumni and Faculty of Rutgers School of Communication, Information and Library Studies, pp. 4-23). Jefferson, NC: McFarland.

Wriston, W. (1988, February). Technology and sovereignty. *Foreign Affairs,* pp. 70-81.

Statutes

Cable Communications Policy Act of 1984, 15 U.S.C.A. § 21; 18 U.S.C.A. § 2511; 46 U.S.C.A. §§ 484-487; 47 U.S.C.A. § 35 *et seq.*; 50 U.S.C.A. § 1805 (1994).

Communication Act of 1934, 47 U.S.C.A., § 35, *et seq.* (1994).

Computer Fraud and Abuse Act of 1986, 18 U.S.C.A. §§ 1001 note, 1030, (1994).

Computer Matching and Privacy Protection Act of 1988, 5 U.S.C.A. § 552a (1994).

Computer Security Act of 1987, 15 U.S.C.A. § 271 *et seq.*; 40 U.S.C.A. § 759 (1994).

Computer Software Protection Act of 1980, Pub. L. No. 100-568, Stat. 2854, 2861.

Computer Software Rental Amendment Act of 1990, 17 U.S.C.A. § 101 *et seq.* (1994).

Copyright Act of 1976, 17 U.S.C.

Electronic Communications Privacy Act of 1986, 18 U.S.C.A. § 1367 *et seq.* (1994).

Electronic Funds Transfer Act of 1978, 15 U.S.C.A. § 1601 *et seq.* (1994).

Fair Credit Reporting Act of 1970, 15 U.S.C.A. § 1681 a -1681 t (1994).

Fair Information Practices of 1973. See U.S. Department of Health, Education and Welfare, Secretary's Advisory Committee on Automated Personal Data Systems. (1973). *Records, computers and the rights of citizens.* Washington, DC: Government Printing Office.

Family Educational Rights and Privacy Act of 1974, 20 U.S.C.A. §§ 1221 note, 1232g (1994).

Federal Managers Financial Integrity Act of 1982, 31 U.S.C.A. §§ 1105, 1113, 3512 (1994).

Federal Paperwork Reduction Act of 1980, 44 U.S.C. §§ 3501-3520.

Freedom of Information Act of 1966, 5 U.S.C.A. § 552 (1994).

Privacy Act of 1974, 5 U.S.C.A. § 552a (1994).

Privacy Protection Act of 1980, 42 U.S.C.A. § 2000aa *et seq.* (1994).

Right to Financial Privacy Act of 1978, 12 U.S.C.A. §§ 3401-3422 (1994).

Semiconductor Chip Protection Act of 1984, 17 U.S.C. §§ 901-914.

Video Privacy Protection Act of 1988, 18 U.S.C.A. § 2701 *et seq.* (1994).

Author Index

Subject Index

About the Authors

Richard O. Mason is Carr P. Collins Professor of Management Information Sciences at the Edwin L. Cox School of Business at Southern Methodist University where he teaches information systems and business ethics. He received his B.S. (1956) from Oregon State University in business and technology and his Ph.D. (1968) from the University of California, Berkeley, in business administration. He is a consultant for numerous corporations. He is also a member of the board of the Hopi Foundation and serves in an advisory capacity to Parkland Hospital, the City of Dallas. His current areas of research include social and ethical implications of information systems, strategy and information systems, and the history of information systems. He recently completed a 3-year term on the Graduate Management Admission Council (GMAC) Commission to examine the future role of graduate management education and was selected in 1989 to be a delegate to the U.S.S.R. to review Soviet plans for the Information of Soviet Society. In 1992, he was elected as a foreign member of the Russian Academy of Natural Sciences in the Information and Cybernetics section. His academic publications have appeared in numerous business and management journals. His books include *Framebreak* (1994, with I. I. Mitroff and C. Pearson), *Challenging Strategic Planning Assumptions* (1981, with I. I. Mitroff), *Strategic Management and Business Policy* (1982, with A. Rowe and K. Dickel), and *Managing With Style* (1987, with A. J. Rowe).

Florence M. Mason is the owner and principal of F. Mason and Associates. She formerly served as program coordinator for the Aspen Institute for Humanistic Studies and has 22 years experience in librarianship. She received her B.A. in

326

history from Skidmore College, Saratoga Springs, New York; her M.L.S. in library science from Simmons College; and her Ph.D. from the University of Southern California in library and information management. She is a consultant for libraries, government organizations, and corporations on long-range planning for information services. Her current practice includes developing management skills for middle managers and providing assistance to organizations on electronic information services. Her clients include Texas Utilities Company, the U.S. Army Corps of Engineers, the State Library of Kansas, and the Enoch Pratt Free Library in Baltimore, Maryland. As an adjunct faculty member at the University of North Texas in Denton and Emporia State University in Kansas, she teaches courses on information ethics, information services design, the economics of information, and managing emerging technologies.

Mary J. Culnan is an Associate Professor in the School of Business, Georgetown University, where she teaches courses on information systems. Her current research focuses on consumer privacy and direct marketing. She has testified before Congress on a range of privacy issues, including the Driver's Privacy Protection Act, the Fair Credit Reporting Act, telecommunications privacy, the use of mailing lists for direct-mail marketing, and private sector use of the Social Security number. She holds an A.B. in political science from the College of Wooster, an M.S. in library and information science from Florida State University, and Ph.D. in management from the Graduate School of Management at the University of California, Los Angeles.